DIVERSITY IN YOUTH LITERATURE

DIVERSITY IN YOUTH LITERATURE

Opening Doors through Reading

EDITED BY JAMIE CAMPBELL NAIDOO
AND SARAH PARK DAHLEN

An imprint of the American Library Association // Chicago // 2013

Printed in the United States of America

17 16 15 14 13   5 4 3 2 1

Extensive effort has gone into ensuring the reliability of the information in this book; however, the publisher makes no warranty, express or implied, with respect to the material contained herein.

ISBNs: 978-0-8389-1143-3 (paper); 978-0-8389-9621-8 (PDF). For more information on digital formats, visit the ALA Store at alastore.ala.org and select eEditions.

Library of Congress Cataloging-in-Publication Data
Diversity in youth literature : opening doors through reading / edited by Jamie Campbell Naidoo and Sarah Park Dahlen.
     pages cm
  Includes bibliographical references and index.
  ISBN 978-0-8389-1143-3 (alk. paper)
  1. Children's literature, American—Minority authors—History and criticism.
  2. Young adult literature, American—Minority authors—History and criticism.
  3. Minorities in literature. 4. Multiculturalism in literature. 5. Cultural pluralism in literature. 6. Multicultural education—United States. I. Naidoo, Jamie Campbell, editor of compilation. II. Dahlen, Sarah Park, 1979-, editor of compilation.
  PS153.M56D58 2012
  810.9'920693—dc23   2012020730

Cover design by Karen Sheets de Gracia. Image © Shutterstock, Inc.
Text design by Adrianna Sutton in Meridien and Futura.

♾ This paper meets the requirements of ANSI/NISO Z39.48-1992 (Permanence of Paper).

For the children of today and tomorrow—
the many, diverse, beautiful children.

Contents

Acknowledgments

WE WISH TO THANK our colleagues for their support as we worked on this book. Thank you Laura Camp (Sarah's graduate assistant) and Katie Olson (Jamie's graduate assistant) for helping put together the final document. No work stands on its own; it builds on the genius of those who have gone before. We thank all of the scholars who taught us what we know about children's and young adult literature, especially Joan Atkinson, Betsy Hearne, Christine Jenkins, and Virginia Walter. Stephanie Zvirin at ALA Editions has been gracious and patient in encouraging and overseeing our publication process.

We would especially like to thank our chapter contributors for sharing their knowledge and passion in each and every chapter, and for allowing us the honor of publishing their essays.

Finally, we'd like to thank Jeff 1 and Jeff 2 for their love and support of our work.

Editors' Introduction

Open Books, Open Doors: Cultural Diversity On and Off the Page

DIVERSITY GENERALLY HIGHLIGHTS a set of traits or characteristics a person possesses that is different in some way from the mainstream population. Race, ethnicity, gender, sexual orientation, age, ability, religious preference, immigration status, level of English-fluency, and socioeconomic status are just some of the many traits that can be highlighted under the umbrella of diversity in the United States.

When planning services, collections, and programs for children and teens from diverse populations, librarians and teachers often think in terms of race and ethnicity and celebrations of cultural pride. While this is ostensibly acceptable, it is a limited practice that fails to fully embrace the full spectrum of diversity within the United States as well as the scope of considerations for developing inclusive library and classroom practices.[1] Diverse populations of youth can include homeless children, transnationally adopted young adults, transgender teens, multiracial preschoolers, or Islamic preteens. Librarians and educators who truly want to embrace diversity within their community understand that their offerings should represent all of its cultural expressions including not only race and ethnicity but also ability, sexual orientation, immigration status, language proficiency, socioeconomic status, religious preference, gender, age, family composition, and domicile.

In 1965 children's author-illustrator Ezra Jack Keats wrote an op-ed piece in response to Nancy Larrick's seminal article, "The All-White World of Children's Books."[2] In this letter, Keats referenced an article he had written two years prior that stressed the importance of providing opportunities for children from all cultural groups to see "real" representations of themselves in book illustrations.[3] He also condemned Larrick's barb at his overweight black character in his picture book *The Snowy Day* and concluded with the following statement: "All people want is the opportunity to be *people* [emphasis in original]. Let us open the book covers, these long shut doors, to new and wonderful, true and inspiring books for all children about all children—the tall and short, fat and thin, dark and light, beautiful and homely."[4]

Almost fifty years later, the covers of children's and young adult books are still firmly locked in place for some youth and open only a sliver for others. Groups of youth and their families are still either entirely absent or marginally presented in youth literature. Volumes have been written about the importance of youth from all cultural backgrounds seeing representations in their books of their gender, ethnicity, race, ability, sexual orientation, religious affiliation, socioeconomic level, immigration status, and family composition. Similarly, volumes have been written that highlight the plight of various cultural groups in youth literature, citing cultural misrepresentations, omissions, and stereotypes.

Why another book on this topic? A quick glance at headlines in U.S. newspapers highlights the continued discrimination, bigotry, racism, heterosexism, handicapism, and ageism that still exist in our nation. Evidence of this hatred towards the "other" in society range from Juan Crow laws in Alabama that keep undocumented children out of schools and promote racial profiling, to the murder of an African American man in Mississippi by white teens, to the suicides of gay teens in New York and across the country as a result of bullying and gay bashing.[5]

Instances such as these indicate that youth in the United States (and by extension, possibly their caregivers and educators) lack cultural competence—the understanding and acceptance of cultures different from their own. We believe children and young adults can be taught cultural competence through high-quality, culturally authentic picture books, novels, and informational texts representing a diversity of cultural groups and perspectives. Of course, this presumes that such books exist about a particular culture and that the library or classroom holds copies of these books. This idea is also contingent upon librarians and educators having the cultural competence themselves to select culturally diverse books for children and young adults.

In *Diversity in Youth Literature: Opening Doors through Reading*, we have made a concerted effort to present chapters on the representations of culture groups that are often ignored in examinations of diverse youth literature. At the same time, we offer chapters that look at a more common cultural group through a new lens or perspective. All of these chapters are intended to open doors to cultural competence by providing guidelines and critical considerations for selecting and using books with "open pages" representing diverse cultural groups rather than focusing on a select, chosen few.

In chapter 1, Doll and Garrison lay the groundwork for understanding the various types of multicultural youth books ranging from culturally generic to culturally specific and provide suggestions for librarians and educators on how to select materials when no prior knowledge of a particular cultural group exists. Dresang builds upon this foundation in chapter 2, where she defines the idea of cultural competence and explains how diverse youth literature can be used with children and young adults to develop their cultural competency. Collectively these two chapters form the first section of the book and provide librarians and educators with a working knowledge of the issues surrounding the creation and use of youth literature about diverse cultures.

The second section of the book focuses on specific marginalized, oppressed, and under- or misrepresented cultural groups in youth literature. In chapter 3, Thomas provides a compelling overview of the history, current status, and purposes of African American children's literature, theorizing the ideological basis for its emergence and pointing out issues that continue to malign and misrepresent African Americans as less than fully human. Quiroa's important chapter updates previous studies of Latino children's literature in the United States and analyzes how books from the past seventeen years have changed in conjunction with the enormous growth of this extremely diverse and largest ethnic minority. In contrast, in chapter 5 Son and Sung illuminate patterns of representation of a less-studied and less-represented group: South Asian communities.

In chapter 6, Storie provides a long-overdue look at the ingenious Chamorro people of the Mariana Islands that have been virtually invisible members of the U.S. community for more than a century. She gives a cultural context for the Chamorro culture in the larger U.S. society and describes how specific books provide unique glimpses into the everyday experiences of these vastly diverse people. Chaudhri's "Growing Mixed/Up" chapter describes the rapidly changing face of mixed-race America and both the essentialist and nuanced ways in which their experiences are depicted in youth literature.

Sturm and Gaherty offer an examination of the Roma, also known as Gypsies, another underresearched cultural group in youth literature, whose mere label provokes images of stereotypes that have been present for decades. Regarding the past decade, Nielsen analyzes and categorizes children's literature depicting Muslims by way of Rudine Sims Bishop's *Shadow & Substance* schemata. Although representations of Muslims in youth literature have increased, especially over the past decade in the post-9/11 era, Nielsen astutely points out misinformation and misrepresentations that may continue to perpetuate misunderstanding. Continuing the idea of overcoming misinformation, Becnel describes the diverse composition of the homeless population in the United States and examines how librarians can use well-chosen children's and young adult books to scaffold understanding of homeless people. Becnel further emphasizes the potential for high-quality youth literature to eliminate the "us vs.

them" mentality created when youth encounter someone outside their cultural group.

In chapter 11, Dahlen provides a guideline in the spirit of "How to Analyze Children's Books for Racism and Sexism" for analyzing representations of transracial and transnational Asian adoption in youth literature. Given that the media tends to favor the sentimental "rescue narratives" as expressed by adoptive parents rather than adopted persons, and that adopted persons rarely author their own stories for child audiences, this chapter raises important questions regarding insider/outsider authorship, representation, and race.

While many studies have examined lesbian, gay, bisexual, transgender, and queer/questioning (LGBTQ) characters in youth books, Naidoo's chapter 12 highlights children's books for readers up to age eleven and examines the presence and overall representation of specific subsets of the LGBTQ populations, such as differently able and senior LGBT adults and transgender individuals. The chapter also advocates for serving LGBTQ families in classrooms and libraries. In the final chapter by Baylen, readers are afforded a glimpse into Filipino children's literature and given an example of a technique that allows educators and librarians to help youth connect to multicultural books and that aligns these books with teaching standards.

Scattered throughout the specialized chapters in section 2 are minichapters called Sliding Doors, which provide a very specific look at a unique element in a particular type of diverse youth literature. The Sliding Doors are pathways for using and considering books and materials about distinct cultural groups such as Latinos, Koreans, and differentlyable individuals.

While the book can be read from beginning to end, we hope that readers will read chapters 1 and 2 and then locate a specific chapter that delves deeper into a culture, stopping to consider the various pieces of literature described, the cultural topics explored, and the programming suggested. Readers can then move on to another specific chapter that reflects an identified need or interest relevant to their local population.

At the end of the chapters, we have selected an extensive list of classic and contemporary books and journal articles that address various aspects of cultural diversity in youth literature. Useful websites as well as specialized journals and book distributors and publishers of multicultural and multilingual children's and young adult works will be quite helpful to librarians and educators who are trying to build their dynamic collections of diverse youth literature. Supporting these resources are lists of library organizations concentrating on services, programs, and collections to distinct cultural groups, as well as selected youth literature awards for culturally diverse youth literature.

Regardless of where readers start and what resources they embrace, we encourage them to use high-quality, culturally authentic youth literature about diverse cultures to open doors to cultural competency in both youth and their adult caregivers. Books that promote cultural competence open doors between and among culturally diverse groups. If these doors are locked, books can help to open them just a sliver. If the doors are open only a crack, high-quality resources can open them even wider or blast them open completely. The time to open doors to "real people" through reading is long overdue—let the journey begin!

NOTES

1. This is evident in a recent experience at the Joint Conference of Libraries of Color (JCLC) where the presenter of a program on library services to LGBTQ families was criticized as being a "party-crasher" who was "piggy backing" on the territory of ethnically diverse populations.
2. Nancy Larrick, "The All-White World of Children's Books," *Saturday Review,* September 11, 1965, 63–65; Ezra Jack Keats, "The Person Takes Precedence," *Saturday Review,* October 2, 1965, 38.
3. Ezra Jack Keats, "Right to Be Real," *Saturday Review,* November 9, 1963, 56.
4. Keats, "The Person Takes Precedence," 38.
5. Campbell Robertson, "Alabama Win in Ruling on Its Immigration Law," *New York Times,* September 28, 2011, www.nytimes.com/2011/09/29/us/alabama-immi-gration-law-upheld.html; Holbrook Mohr, "Mississippi Teen Indicted for Capital Murder, Hate Crime," *Associated Press,* September 21, 2011, www.google.com/host-ednews/ap/article/ALeqM5gyxzhtck0v-xvGWM32CMJX6Z56ug?docId=f34b1e82 0bd94b54a4aaa211e74f9765; Susan Donaldson James, "Gay Buffalo Teen Commits Suicide on Eve of National Bullying Summit," September 21, 2011, http://abcnews.go.com/Health/gay-buffalo-teen-commits-suicide-eve-national-bullying/story?id=14571861.

PART I

Overview of Diversity in Children's and Young Adult Literature

Voices of Experience

Promoting Acceptance of Other Cultures

CAROL DOLL AND KASEY GARRISON

HOW DO LIBRARIANS AND EDUCATORS identify quality literature for young people when they do not have direct experience with or knowledge of the cultural groups being portrayed? There are many guidelines written for evaluating books about a specific cultural group, whether they portray African American, Latino, Asian American, Middle Eastern, Native American, LGBTQ, differently-abled, or another group of people. But the underlying question is broader: how do people become more open to and accepting of people who are different from themselves?

It is important to conceptualize a definition of multicultural literature to guide this discussion. Rudine Sims Bishop defines multicultural literature as works "that reflect the racial, ethnic, and social diversity that is characteristic of our pluralistic society and of the world."[1] Charles Temple et al. say "multicultural literature . . . reflects the multitude of cultural groups within the United States."[2] The scope and inclusiveness of these two definitions will be the foundation for the issues in this chapter. The framework for the discussion that follows is grounded in these six broad categories derived from the professional literature:

1. Classification schemes based on the "level" or type of diversity portrayed in the book.
2. Individuals' experiences in learning to understand and appreciate a culture that was not their own.
3. Authentic portrayals of culture with a little "c" focusing on the micro level of daily events.
4. The pluralistic nature of a single culture instead of one incident or viewpoint.
5. Evaluating the work of cultural insiders based on criteria appropriate to their own culture.

6. Whether or not "outsiders" can write about or illustrate a culture not their own.

This chapter will focus on recognizing elements, qualities, and the authenticity of materials representing cultures outside of one's own experience. The intent is to encourage and enable librarians to competently evaluate, select, and use multicultural materials for young people that humanize the cultures portrayed. It is important for librarians to remember that, as Hazel Rochman notes, "The best books . . . surprise us—whether they are set close to home or abroad. They extend that phrase 'like me' to include what we thought was strange and foreign. And they change our view of ourselves."[3]

CLASSIFICATION SCHEMES

Several authors have suggested ways to look at multicultural titles based on various portrayals of the culture. No single system addresses all of the issues, but each can add concepts and ideas to the discussion of multicultural titles. And, while there is some similarity among the various classification schemes, each adds something unique for consideration.

1. Temple et al. suggest categorizing titles on how critical the cultural elements are to the book as a whole.[4]
   A. *Culturally neutral* books include those titles where cultural elements are not significant, although multicultural characters may be included.[5] In *The Retired Kid*, by Jon Agee, a young boy goes to live with his grandparents in a retirement community. The characters in the pictures are multicultural; however, there is no other reference to other cultures in the book.
   B. *Culturally generic* titles intentionally include multicultural elements like characters or settings, but otherwise are focused on universal plots and themes relevant to any culture, such as being honest.[6] Little Bill accompanies his father to work in a big office downtown in *Just Like Dad*. While the characters and some of the events are African American, overall this is a story about father-son bonding.
   C. *Culturally specific* books deliberately portray a specific cultural group and provide "insights necessary to truly further readers' understanding of different cultures."[7] Gary Soto's writing authentically portrays the Latino community. *The Skirt*'s focus is on the role of *folklórico* dancing in Mexican cultures.
2. Bishop classifies titles based on the depiction of specific cultural elements in the text and illustrations.[8]
   A. In some titles with universal plots and themes, "the race or color of the characters is entirely a visual phenomenon."[9] The

elementary students in *Congratulations, Miss Malarkey!* worry that her upcoming wedding will mean a new teacher for them. The illustrations depict children who are culturally diverse, but there is no reference to such diversity in the text or plot.

B. Other titles may have "a clear social agenda" which may or may not be independent of culture. For example, commentary about social class is universally relevant, but may hold special meaning for marginalized groups.[10] In *The Moon Over Star*, Mae, the young African American narrator, recalls events in her family in 1969 set against the first Apollo moon landing. Questions and thoughts about the cost of putting man on the moon are interwoven throughout this story grounded in a loving family.

C. Some titles offer an accurate portrayal of the culture depicted, but are easily accessible to those outside the culture.[11] Condoleezza Rice shares her "extraordinary, ordinary family" in her memoir. Readers of any culture can identify with the loving relationship between child and parents, while African Americans can more readily identify with the Rices' experiences in Birmingham, Alabama, during the 1950s and 1960s.

D. A few titles provide authentic depictions of the culture, which may not be as readily accessible to outsiders. But such titles contribute "a distinctive voice, a distinctive world view" to literature for children and young adults.[12] Rigoberta Menchú, a Mayan from Guatemala, shares traditional folklore in *The Honey Jar*, a collection of stories for elementary students. In "Grandmother Moon and Grandfather Sun Were Bored," two spirits were created to bring happiness to the moon and sun after the stars failed to do this. The authenticity of this title is obvious, but some of the elements here speak more strongly to Mayans than to others.

Readers from the cultures represented in authentic books described in Bishop's fourth category may see themselves reflected within the pages. Graciela Italiano notes that while some readers may be confused by incidents portrayed in this type of book, members of that culture can personally relate to them.[13] Such titles can be difficult to identify and share precisely because they portray the culture so authentically.

Close examination of multicultural titles has revealed another category not identified in the professional literature. There can be titles written about interactions by members of a majority culture with members of a minority culture. When sensitively written, these titles have the potential to help other majority members learn how to reach out to members of a minority culture. In *No English*, second-grader Diane learns how to become a friend to Blanca, a new student from Argentina. Titles like this can promote understanding and empathy.

Examination of these schemes reveals that the categories tend to overlap, and the scales are more a continuum than discrete categories. However, each one of them identifies something unique that can enlighten the way multicultural literature is perceived. The rest of this chapter will further explore the issues and challenges involved in creating and evaluating authentic multicultural literature for children and young adults.

CULTURAL UNDERSTANDING

A small subset of the professional literature advocating acceptance of all cultures has been written by people describing their own personal journeys to understanding. Ann Nolan Clark spent years living and working as a teacher with various cultures, including German immigrants and Native peoples throughout the United States and South America. In her memoir, *Journey to the People*, based on her work in the American Southwest with the Tewa people, she conveys her own struggles to connect to and understand a culture foreign to her own upbringing. An enlightened set of five qualities of books "true to the pattern of the people in them" is the result.[14] These qualities include:

1. *Honesty*—The author conveys "sincerity in what is said" and truth is written as the writer believes it based on experience.[15]
2. *Accuracy*—The author must look and listen, "check and recheck," and flawlessly portray representative viewpoints inherent to that culture.[16]
3. *Reality*—The author depicts "laughter and tears, joys and sorrows, and the peace of all the humdrum hours" that are a natural part of human experiences.[17]
4. *Imagination*—The writer with imagination makes his own portraits with the words he writes. From this writing, "two pictures emerge – the one the writer makes" and the one created by the reader "in the images of his own experiences... with his own hopes and dreams."[18]
5. *Appreciation*—"Books should foster appreciation of beauty... of fear and the courage it takes to face it and bravery to combat it... of joy and sorrow and the knowledge that one could not be as great without contrast with the other."[19]

Taken together, Clark's five qualities advocate for an approach to writing that respectfully and authentically portrays the culture depicted. These considerations transcend the classification schemes discussed earlier. Multicultural literature for children and teens should include elements of all five concepts as appropriate to be considered of high quality.

Another unique perspective on a journey to acceptance is based on Rochman's life as a white child in South Africa under apartheid. She explains how she came to realize the full extent of her deprivation under this system. "When I lived under apartheid, I thought I was privileged—and compared with the physical suffering of black people I was immeasurably well-off—but my life was impoverished. I was blind and I was frightened. I was shut in. And I was denied access to the stories and music of the world."[20] Through her experiences, Rochman came to understand the value of diversity and the richness such variety in human culture brings to the world. While acknowledging the complexity of multicultural literature, she suggests the following considerations, with the caveat that there can be legitimate variation in the way authors actually address them:[21]

1. *Accuracy and authenticity* are both important and can be achieved by any writer *if* she does the research, lives the culture, and writes well.[22]
2. *Saints, role models, and stereotypes* should be identified and avoided. The result would be appealing, truthful tales about people with all of the good and bad traits they normally have, instead of reverential or didactic stories.[23]
3. *Ethnicity, universals, and a sense of place* should be balanced in order to truly and critically portray what it means to be this character in this place at this time.[24]
4. *Glossaries and names* are important to clarify key terms and allow readers to understand unfamiliar elements of the culture. Writers cannot rely on context alone because the readers' experiences may not provide the necessary background for understanding.[25]
5. *Sensationalism and sentimentality* must also be avoided in order to provide a realistic and accessible portrayal of a cultural group and their experiences.[26]

Both Clark and Rochman offer unique perspectives of being immersed in cultures unlike their own and embarking on journeys towards understanding. Authenticity is a common theme woven throughout their writing. While authenticity includes issues of accuracy and sincerity within the text and illustrations, it also delves deeper into the threads and patterns that craft the social fabric of the represented culture.

THE LITTLE "C"

Writers of authentic books for youth move beyond superficial portrayals into culture with a little "c." Too frequently authors concentrate on what

Elsie Begler calls the "5Fs: food, fashion, fiestas, folklore, and famous people."[27] Rochman identifies such titles as being a "'touristic' approach, stressing the exotic" and oversimplifying the complexity of the culture being "visited."[28] While these showy elements are undeniably part of the home culture, there is danger in merely scratching the surface by focusing only on them.

Begler advocates for titles that focus on culture with a little "c": "the social, economic, and political systems of a society—with people's values and beliefs providing a framework for all other aspects."[29] Jane E. Kelley believes that the "little 'c'" provides the foundation for truer understandings of people instead of the superficial versions often portrayed by the 5Fs.[30] For example, Kelley discusses the importance of harmony, empathy, loyalty, and patience in the Japanese culture.[31] Accurate portrayals of these values help to build genuine understanding of the culture often unacknowledged through discussions of Hiroshima or Toyota. Likewise, Italiano calls for "a view from somebody who has gone beyond the surface of the culture and can give children a sense that even in the midst of difficult life conditions, this is a good culture to be part of."[32] Such a portrayal can help all readers understand the value and humanity in cultures outside of their own.

Elizabeth Fitzgerald Howard notes that for authentic literature, "we know it is true because we feel it deep down."[33] Italiano calls this a "gut-level feeling."[34] Those books that enable readers to see beyond the 5Fs to the daily realities of other cultures help overcome preconceived assumptions. At the same time, if the reader lacks experience with the culture portrayed, that reader may not be able to fully appreciate the authenticity of the portrayal, and either struggle to understand or abandon the effort. While it is imperative that authentic books be available, sharing them with young readers can also be challenging.

The perspective of a cultural insider is a useful tool in navigating and evaluating literature incorporating culture with a little "c" that is outside the reader's cultural experiences. In these cases, reviews of specific titles or articles written by individuals who are cultural insiders can be vital to identifying authentic titles that can promote understanding of others.[35]

INSIDER PERSPECTIVES

Cultural insiders can provide critical perspectives on multicultural literature for children and young adults because of their unique and relevant experiences. They intimately understand the social norms of their group and use that knowledge to inform their creation or evaluation of books. These insider perspectives often identify authentic portrayals of the culture as a natural result of an individual's life experiences.

Although the insider perspective is a valuable tool in creating and reviewing multicultural literature for youth, authors writing from this perspective face challenges in confronting the mainstream's criteria and expectations. Cynthia Leitich Smith writes of difficulties she faces as a Native American author struggling to depict authentic Native American experiences and cultures in a way that is acceptable to her publishers.[36] She notes that "essentially, our work is being held up to a mainstream model that says what is indigenous is 'wrong.'"[37] She believes that when Native American humor is not readily understandable to those readers outside the culture, it can become marginalized. Demands for the author to change such elements decrease the authenticity of the culture's voice and reinforce superficial portrayals like those of the 5Fs.[38]

In creating his version of Uncle Remus stories, Julius Lester recounts a similar incident where the publisher objected to his language, grammar, and perceived sexism. While the voice, plotlines, and language were culturally relevant according to Lester, an insider to the African American culture represented, the editor felt that some of the book would not "communicate to white readers."[39] Lester notes that making the editor's requested changes "would have been a betrayal of all those black people from whose lives the stories had come, all those blacks whose stories these were. My responsibility was to them as their descendent."[40] While Lester succeeded in publishing the book without many of the requested changes, it is noteworthy that such requests are made.

Such incidents reinforce the need to evaluate materials about a culture based on the norms of that culture. For example, the Western perspective could call titles fantasy if they include spirits, ghosts, or some other magical qualities. However, in some cultures, the line between the spirit world and the perceived real world is less rigid. In these cases and in these cultures, the ghosts, spirits, and other such entities *are* reality. Such books should be classified as realism, not fantasy. For the Latino culture, Italiano states that this magical realism "has provided a way for us to understand our own reality, which borders constantly on the magical in the sense that our delineations between the real world and the spirit world are not as clear-cut as in other cultures."[41] Similar conditions apply to other cultures, such as some African and Native American groups.

Insiders are often able to provide an important perspective on reviewing books. Debbie Reese, a Pueblo Indian from Nambe, recounts instances where she has reviewed books with common negative stereotypes of Native Americans as "the aggressive savage," "the romantic, or noble Indian," and where non-Indian characters are dressed in special attire to "play Indian."[42] She believes that reviews from insiders can help librarians identify stereotypes in multicultural portrayals that might otherwise be overlooked. This type of information can be most accurate when it comes from an insider perspective. However, Jean Mendoza and Reese make the point that "what will be published, who will illustrate it, and how it will be marketed are all decisions that, historically and currently, rest primarily with European Americans, who own the largest publishing houses and continue to dominate the key decision-making positions."[43]

Nonetheless, those individuals who are themselves members of a cultural group, or who have had significant experiences with another culture, are the individuals best prepared to help outsiders understand the degree to which that culture is authentically portrayed in books. Often, the importance of that input can be minimized or even totally disregarded. While the insider perspective may be unpopular or even biased towards minority views, it is important to read, consider, and learn from those insiders courageous enough to share their insight with outsiders. At the same time, the pluralistic nature within any cultural group underlines the importance of multiple perspectives in understanding others.

CULTURAL PLURALISM

It is important to acknowledge that distinct differences exist within the large categories defining a cultural group. For example, Latinos are often categorized as anyone speaking Spanish or originating from Latin America, but this huge umbrella negates the cultural nuances among these people.[44] Asian Americans represent another group that is often lumped together because of their continental connection but could include diverse groups ranging from Arabs to Russians to Mongolians. Furthermore, one individual does not necessarily have the background needed to competently evaluate all titles representing their culture. Tadayuki Suzuki, an insider to the Japanese culture, expresses concern about critically reviewing books on aspects of Japanese culture with which she has no direct experience.[45]

Similarly, it is not possible for *one* book to authentically represent all elements of an inherently pluralistic culture. Nonetheless, the idea that one book can and should do it all pervades assumptions often made by those seeking quality multicultural materials to share with children and young adults.[46] Just as one person should not become the ultimate model for an entire group of people, one book cannot give a balanced view of any cultural group.[47] Junko Yokota notes that "it takes many books to create a multidimensional look at a culture."[48] Providing readers with comprehensive, pluralistic perspectives of the diversity within a cultural group helps convey the quality and integrity of that culture. One issue is whether or not outsiders to a particular culture can legitimately increase available viewpoints of that culture.

OUTSIDERS AS AUTHORS/ILLUSTRATORS

This continuous debate of authors writing outside of their own cultures has multiple critics, from writers to reviewers to scholars. Lester writes that he used to object to those who create works about cultures other than their own.[49] However, he once had a white student who possessed "a knowledge of black culture that went beyond what she could have gathered by reading alone. Her grasp of black literature and culture was not merely intellectual; it was visceral."[50] Based on that experience, Lester believes it is possible for outsiders to achieve understandings of cultures foreign to their own.

Others share this view, but feel that for outsiders to effectively capture the true nuances of another culture, they must essentially become insiders. This process includes extensive research and ultimately a quest for cultural understanding that poses challenges to any author or illustrator. Reese reinforces this idea in noting: "When authors write outside their own cultures, it is irresponsible not to consult several sources."[51] Italiano believes that "one has to have integrity in the task one has undertaken and to be, or become, familiar with the culture so that the book does not portray stereotypes of any kind."[52] Outsiders themselves have voiced concerns. For example, Diane Stanley shares her experience as an outsider writing about the Zulu culture, and speaks of an incident where Shaka foolishly believes that Macassar Oil rejuvenates people instead of merely covering up gray hair.[53] She chose not to include this specific event, stating, "I was afraid that this story made Shaka look foolish and reinforced ancient stereotypes. . . . because I was reaching out of my own experience to explore another culture, I did not feel comfortable using that story."[54] This form of self-censorship reveals another side of the issue about whether outsiders can accurately portray another culture.

Overall, there seems to be more support for talented, responsible authors who write outside their culture than insistence that only insiders can authentically portray a culture. Karen Patricia Smith states: "if the material is properly researched and genuine and authentic in intent and presentation, the contribution of the 'outsider' has the potential of being a valuable one."[55] Rochman contends that only gifted writers can do it: "Anybody can write about anything—if they are good enough. There will always be inauthentic or inaccurate books, and defining authenticity on some exclusionary basis or other won't change a thing. The only way to combat inaccuracy is with accuracy—not with pedigrees."[56]

Regardless of the cultural portrayal being native or foreign to the writer, Lester redirects the issue to "what it has always been—that [authors] write well, that we write with integrity, that we write as much of the truth as we are able to apprehend."[57] Writers have an obligation to consult sources and gain personal experience with the cultural perspective about which they are writing, whether they focus on ethnicity, social class, gender, age, or some other cultural trait.

Some authors have successfully written about cultures outside their own. Born in England, Paul Goble became a member of the Yakima and Sioux tribes.[58] His carefully researched books portray life among the Plains Indians. Suzanne Fisher Staples relies on her experiences as an international reporter in Pakistan, India, and Afghanistan to provide vivid, nuanced backgrounds for her stories set in Asia, including *Shabanu: Daughter of the Wind*.[59] However, it is that unusual person who can authentically portray a culture not their own.

EVALUATING MULTICULTURAL LITERATURE

The six main themes discussed throughout this chapter provide a framework to help inform the evaluation of multicultural literature for children and teens. Such evaluation is a critical piece in promoting understanding and acceptance of cultures different from the reader's own experiences.

1. Classification schemes can aid in determining the focus of a multicultural title and identifying how it fits into a library collection or school curriculum.
2. Cultural understanding can be achieved through experience and open-minded examination of the differing aspects that form the represented cultures, as shown by Clark and Rochman.
3. The little "c" of culture moves past Begler's 5Fs of "food, fashion, fiestas, folklore, and famous people" to reveal deeper cultural interpretations of a group guided by their political, economic, and social values and beliefs.[60]
4. Insider perspectives should be used to evaluate the cultures represented because they provide that critical and intimate view of culture with a little "c."
5. Cultural pluralism is an important consideration because of the diverse and dynamic nature of a single culture and its subcultures.
6. Outsiders as authors or illustrators can offer another perspective of a culture, but must do so with careful attention to authenticity and accuracy within the text and illustrations.

CONCLUSION

The question persists, how do people become more open to and accepting of people who are different from themselves? Quality multicultural literature is one way to broaden the experiences of children and young adults, enabling them to vicariously interact with people from a wide variety of cultures. It is important in today's pluralistic society to learn to accept and honor other cultures. Such knowledge increases one's exposure to others beyond personal experiences. As Clark indicated, "Life should not be limited to tradition or heritage. It should have new concepts, new ways, not to take the place of the old ones, only to enrich them."[61]

CHILDREN'S BOOKS

Agee, Jon. *The Retired Kid*. New York: Hyperion, 2008.

Aston, Dianna Hutts. *The Moon Over Star*. Illustrated by Jerry Pinkney. New York: Dial, 2008.

Finchler, Judy, and Kevin O'Malley. *Congratulations, Miss Malarkey!* Illustrated by Kevin O'Malley. New York: Walker, 2009.

Jules, Jacqueline. *No English*. Illustrated by Amy Huntington. Ann Arbor, MI: Mitten, 2007.

Menchú, Rigoberta, and Dante Liano. *The Honey Jar*. Illustrated by Domi. Toronto, Can.: Groundwood, 2006.

Rice, Condoleezza. *Condoleezza Rice: A Memoir of My Extraordinary, Ordinary Family and Me*. New York: Delacorte, 2010.

Soto, Gary. *The Skirt*. Illustrated by Eric Velasquez. New York: Delacorte, 1992.

Staples, Suzanne Fisher. *Shabanu: Daughter of the Wind*. New York: Knopf, 1989.

Watson, Kim. *Just Like Dad*. Illustrated by Daniel M. Kanemoto. New York: Simon Spotlight, 2001.

SUGGESTED READING

Boston, Genyne Henty, and Traci Baxley. "Living the Literature: Race, Gender Construction, and Black Female Adolescents." *Urban Education* 42, no. 6 (November 2007): 560–81.

Clark, Ann Nolan. "A Handful of Days." In *Something about the Author Autobiography Series* 16 (1993): 33–109.

Ernst, Shirley B., and Janelle B. Mathis. "Multicultural Literature: Reading, Writing, and Responding within a 'New' Literacy Context." *Journal of Children's Literature* 34, no.1 (Spring 2008): 10–12.

Kohl, Herbert. *Should We Burn Babar? Essays on Children's Literature and the Power of Stories*. New York: New, 1995.

Rochman, Hazel. "Is That Book Politically Correct? Truth and Trends in Historical Literature for Young People: An Editor Speaks." *Journal of Youth Services in Libraries* 7 (Winter 1994): 159–64.

NOTES

1. Rudine Sims Bishop, "Selecting Literature for a Multicultural Curriculum," in *Using Multiethnic Literature in the K-8 Classroom*, ed. Violet J. Harris, 1–19 (Norwood, MA: Christopher-Gordon, 1997), 3.

2. Charles Temple et al., *Children's Books in Children's Hands: An Introduction to Their Literature* (Boston: Allyn & Bacon, 1998), 4.

3. Hazel Rochman, "And Yet . . . Beyond Political Correctness," in *Evaluating Children's Books: A Critical Look*, ed. Roger Sutton and Betsy Hearne, 133–48 (Urbana: University of Illinois Graduate School of Library and Information Science, 1993), 146.

4. Temple et al., *Children's Books*, 85–86.

5. Ibid.

6. Ibid., 85.

7. Ibid., 86.

8. Bishop, "Selecting Literature," 7.

9. Ibid., 8.

10. Ibid., 10.

11. Ibid., 12–13.

12. Ibid., 14.

13. Graciela Italiano, "Reading Latin America: Issues in the Evaluation of Latino Children's Books in Spanish and English." In *Evaluating Children's Books: A Critical Look*, ed. Roger Sutton and Betsy Hearne, 119–32 (Urbana: University of Illinois Graduate School of Library and Information Science, 1993), 123.

14. Ann Nolan Clark, *Journey to the People* (New York: Viking, 1969), 90.

15. Ibid.

16. Ibid., 91.

17. Ibid., 94–95.

18. Ibid., 96.

19. Ibid., 97.

20. Hazel Rochman, *Against Borders: Promoting Books for a Multicultural World* (Chicago: American Library Association/Booklist Publications, 1993), 27.

21. Ibid., 19.

22. Ibid., 21–23.

23. Ibid., 23–24.

24. Ibid., 24–26.

25. Ibid., 26.

26. Ibid., 26–27.

27. Elsie Begler, "Global Cultures: The First Step Toward Understanding," *Social Education* 62, no. 5 (September 1998): 272.

28. Rochman, *Against Borders*, 23.

29. Begler, "Global Cultures," 272.

30. Jane E. Kelley, "Harmony, Empathy, Loyalty, and Patience in Japanese Children's Literature," *Social Studies* 99, no. 2 (March/April 2008): 62.

31. Ibid.

32. Italiano, "Reading Latin America," 131.

33. Elizabeth Fitzgerald Howard, "Authentic Multicultural Literature for Children: An Author's Perspective," in *The Multicolored Mirror: Cultural Substance in Literature for Children and Young Adults*, ed. Merri V. Lindgren, 91–99 (Fort Atkinson, WI: Highsmith, 1991), 92.

34. Italiano, "Reading Latin America," 123.

35. However, one should keep in mind that there is no guarantee that a cultural insider reviewed the title or that that cultural insider provided a balanced, impartial review. Resources such as *Multicultural Review* are typically reliable in that they seek out insiders or experts on specific topics to write their reviews.

36. Cynthia Leitich Smith, "A Different Drum: Native American Writing," *Horn Book Magazine* 78, no. 4 (July/August 2002): 411.

37. Ibid., 410.

38. Begler, "Global Cultures," 272.

39. Julius Lester, "The Storyteller's Voice: Reflections on the Rewriting of Uncle Remus," *New Advocate* 1, no. 3 (Summer 1988): 146.

40. Ibid., 145.

41. Italiano, "Reading Latin America," 126.

42. Debbie Reese, "Contesting Ideology in Children's Book Reviewing," *Studies in American Indian Literature* 12, no. 1 (Spring 2000): 39.

43. Jean Mendoza and Debbie Reese, "Examining Multicultural Picture Books for the Early Childhood Classroom: Possibilities and Pitfalls," *Early Childhood Research & Practice* 3, no. 2 (Fall 2001): 18.

44. Italiano, "Reading Latin America," 121.
45. Tadayuki Suzuki, "Analyzing Cultural Accuracy and Authenticity of Japanese and Japanese-American Children's Books," *Journal of Children's Literature* 35, no. 2 (Fall 2009): 50.
46. Mendoza and Reese, "Examining Multicultural Picture Books," 8.
47. Lisa Madsen Rubilar, "The Challenges of Writing from the Inside," *Multicultural Review* 19, no. 1 (Spring 2010): 33.
48. Junko Yokota, "Asian Americans in Literature for Children and Young Adults," *Teacher Librarian* 36, no. 3 (February 2009): 15.
49. Julius Lester, *On Writing for Children and Other People* (New York: Dial Books, 2004), 125.
50. Ibid., 126.
51. Debbie Reese, "Authenticity and Sensitivity," *School Library Journal* 45, no. 11 (November 1999): 37.
52. Italiano, "Reading Latin America," 124.
53. Diane Stanley, "Is That Book Politically Correct? Truth and Trends in Historical Literature for Young People: A Writer Speaks," *Journal of Youth Services in Libraries* 7 (Winter 1994): 174.
54. Ibid.
55. Karen Patricia Smith, "The Multicultural Ethic and Connections to Literature for Children and Young Adults," *Library Trends* 41, no. 3 (Winter 1993): 346.
56. Rochman, *Against Borders*, 23.
57. Lester, *On Writing for Children and Other People*, 131.
58. "Paul Goble." In *Contemporary Authors Online* (Detroit: Gale, 2010), *Literature Resource Center*, http://go.galegroup.com/ps/i.do?&id=GALE%7CH1000037324&v =2.1&u=viva_odu&it=r&p=LitRC&sw=w.
59. "Suzanne Fisher Staples." In *Contemporary Authors Online* (Detroit: Gale, 2010), *Literature Resource Center*, http://go.galegroup.com/ps/i.do?&id=GALE%7CH1000094 327&v=2.1&u=viva_odu&it=r&p=LitRC&sw=w.
60. Begler, "Global Cultures," 272.
61. Clark, *Journey to the People*, 75.

Opening Doors to Understanding

Developing Cultural Competence
through Youth Literature

ELIZA DRESANG

"I was born with water on the brain."[1]

So begins Sherman Alexie's first-person, autobiographical fictional story, *The Absolutely True Diary of a Part-Time Indian*, featuring Arnold Spirit, a fifteen-year-old American Indian who, like the author, grew up on the Spokane Indian Reservation in eastern Washington. Alexie continues with an account of the surgery needed to correct this condition.

> I was only six months old and I was supposed to croak during the surgery. And even if I somehow survived the mini-Hoover, I was supposed to suffer serious brain damage during the procedure and live the rest of my life as a vegetable.
>
> Well, I obviously survived the surgery. I wouldn't be writing this if I didn't, but I have all sorts of physical problems that are directly the result of my brain damage.
>
> First of all, I ended up having forty-two teeth. The typical human has thirty-two, right? But I had forty-two.
>
> Ten more than usual.
>
> Ten more than normal.
>
> Ten more than human.
>
> . . . . I went to the Indian Health Service to get some teeth pulled so I could eat normally, not like some slobbering vulture. But the Indian Health Service funded major dental work only once a year, so I had to have all ten extra teeth pulled in *one day*.
>
> And what's more, our white dentist believes that Indians only

felt half as much pain as white people did, so he only gave us half the Novocain.[2]

In a short space, Alexie has revealed the skill with which he tells his story, employing an appealing cadence and purposeful humor. Yet, he has immediately introduced in a subtle but unmistakable way the serious issues that Arnold must face as an Indian—so serious in fact that Arnold not only feels abnormal, he feels less than human.

Commenting on this novel, Marie, a graduate student in library and information science (LIS),[3] reports that "unintentionally, I ended up reading this book in one sitting, cover to cover. The character of Junior sucked me in and I became a fan. This is a perfect example of a YA book—it is relatable, discusses issues most teens go through, while still teaching me about a new culture."[4] However, she continues with a question regarding portrayal of the tough circumstances in which Junior lives: "I'm curious to know what you all think about the way American Indians were portrayed. . . . the drinking on the Reservation and the many funerals Junior experienced at such a young age. Do books like this perpetuate bad stereotypes or do they increase understanding?"[5]

Elizabeth, another LIS student, responds, "My view is that Alexie is addressing serious issues in the community in which he was raised. He does a good job showing the effects of alcoholism—heartache. There is no judgment through the perspective he shows; it is just matter of fact. . . . It is definitely a discussion starter with students."[6] And Rebecca adds, "I don't think the many deaths and alcoholic incidents were a stereotype—it is the truth."[7] Marisa, another graduate student, reflects that "the real power of this book is that it helps students understand that American Indians are alive today; they did not fade out with the buffalo and other historical stereotypes."[8] These students appear to be developing what we might think of as cultural competence through their discussion of Alexie's book. But what exactly does this mean?

DIVERSE YOUTH LITERATURE

By the late 1980s the term *multicultural literature* became commonly used to refer to diversity in literature for youth, although some narrowed their use of the term (and still do) to books by and about people of color while others encompassed a much wider range of diversity, including gender, sexual orientation, differing abilities, and any cultures that lack power or authority in a society. The publication of literature featuring diverse youth lagged far behind that of literature by and about white people. Eventually increased awareness on the part of publishers and potential authors and illustrators resulted in a small critical mass of authentic multicultural youth literature, in both the broader and more narrow sense of the term. Throughout much of the last half of the twentieth century, the two principal goals for diversity or multiculturalism in youth literature were increased publication and eradication of stereotypes to be replaced by authentic representations. Likewise, the chief goals for young readers were for them to have mirrors reflecting their own cultures as well as windows into cultures not their own. These goals, of course, still exist and have never yet been adequately met.[9]

MULTICULTURAL EDUCATION GOALS AND YOUTH LITERATURE
Paralleling and intertwining with these foundational purposes for diversity in youth literature was another strand of thinking about the goals for introducing what had come to be known as multicultural literature. James Banks is the director of the Center for Multicultural Education at the University of Washington. In his book, *Teaching Strategies for Ethnic Studies*, first published in 1975 and now in its eighth edition, he posited that children who experience multicultural education can and should engage in thoughtful action that will affect their own personal lives as well as the broader social and global world in which they live.[10] His hierarchy of multicultural teaching strategies starts at the lowest level with activities that involve (inadequate) teaching about such cultural items as food and holidays. At the top of his instructional hierarchy lies social activism. (See figure 2.1.) Although Banks speaks generally of curriculum rather than specifically of literature, his approach is applicable to literature as an essential component of children's education.[11] Likewise Kincheloe and Steinberg classify multiculturalism into five categories, the last of which is labeled critical multiculturalism. Their first four categories involve celebrating diversity, but fall short of advocating for change, equality, and equity in society. Critical multiculturalism, in contrast, requires carrying education into real-life activism.[12]

It was with the arrival of the twenty-first century that this broader view of multicultural education was applied specifically and systematically to the arena of youth literature. Cai put it succinctly:

> Multiculturalism involves diversity and inclusion, but more importantly, it also involves power structure and struggle. Its goal is not just to understand, accept, and appreciate cultural difference, but also to ultimately transform the existing social order in order to ensure greater voice and authority to the marginalized cultures and to achieve social equality and justice among all cultures so that people of different cultural backgrounds can live happily together in a democratic world.[13]

Almost a decade into the twenty-first century, the most focused and complete examination of multicultural literature for youth to date appeared in Botelho's and Rudman's *Critical Multicultural Analysis of Children's Lit-*

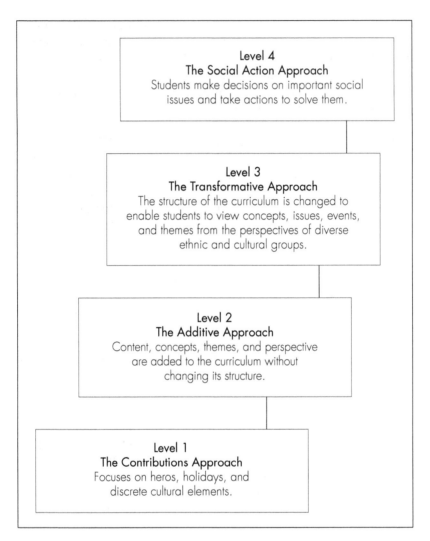

Figure 2.1: Levels of integration of ethnic content

erature: Mirrors, Windows, and Doors. The following passage describes the intent of their book:

> Critical multicultural analysis provides a philosophical shift for teaching literature, constructing curriculum, and taking up issues of diversity and social justice. It problematizes children's literature, offers a way of reading power, explores the complex web of socio-political relations, and deconstructs taken-for-granted assumptions

about language, meaning, reading, and literature. It is literary study as sociopolitical change.[14]

The authors acknowledge the importance of multicultural literature as mirrors and windows that can reflect one's life or allow one to look into another's world. But they add that open doors offer "access both into and out of one's everyday condition" and that "the door invites interaction."[15] Moreover, they see race, class, and gender as inseparable in critically examining multicultural children's literature: "Children's literature is read against its sociopolitical context. Readers ascertain what cultural themes are imbedded in the work."[16]

The writings of Banks, Kincheloe and Steinberg, and Botelho and Rudman provide the necessary background for the concept of gaining cultural competence through youth literature. This concept, as used in the context of this chapter, embraces both the notion of close sociopolitical reading and literary deconstruction as well as an end goal of inspired activism which brings that reading into the arena of social change. The next step is to examine how others have defined and modeled the cultural competence that may be partially achieved through youth literature.

CULTURAL COMPETENCE

Largely unmentioned as a concept except in relation to health services, cultural competence within the LIS field has been most deeply explored by Patricia Montiel-Overall. Her definition of cultural competence is derived from a thorough consideration of traditions within librarianship as well as those in health, social work, and education.

> Cultural competence is the ability to recognize the significance of culture in one's own life and in the lives of others; and to come to know and respect diverse cultural backgrounds and characteristics through interaction with individuals from diverse linguistic, cultural, and socioeconomic groups and to fully integrate the culture of diverse groups into services, work, and institutions in order to enhance the lives of both those being served by the library profession and those engaged in service.[17]

Montiel-Overall translates this definition into a visual model of cultural competence.[18] (See figure 2.2.)

In Montiel-Overall's model, developed from an extensive literature review, the intersection of cognitive, interpersonal, and environmental conditions is the area that embodies such competence. As can be seen in figure 2.2, the cognitive processes have to do with cultural self-awareness, sensitivity, insight, and knowledge, or translated to multicultural literature, the "mirror and window" functions. The interpersonal processes focus on

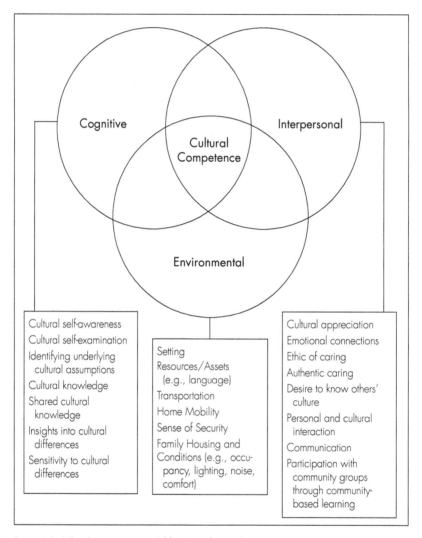

Figure 2.2: Cultural competence model for LIS professionals

the "door" aspects; when translated to multicultural literature this can be seen as cultural appreciation, an ethic of caring, and participation with others in diverse cultures. The setting (environmental processes) is how one would prepare the environment in terms of resources, security, and other tangible effects on services. According to Montiel-Overall, "the three overlapping circles indicate that the domains are not separate components of cultural competence. LIS professionals who are culturally competent have the capacity to understand the full range of possibilities within each domain."[19]

Deborah Abilock has considered the issue of cultural competence from the point of view of the school library. Her visual representation introduces the notion that students, teachers, and librarians can work to become more and more culturally competent along a scale that runs in six stages from destructiveness to the most competent, proficiency. (See figure 2.3.) Destructiveness or incapacity is described as "actively seeking to obliterate, marginalize, or disadvantage one culture, characterizing it as wrong, or foolish, or out-of-place."[20] Abilock offers some examples in a school setting of how students might be helped to move up on her scale; none, however, involve multicultural literature.[21] In her article related to school libraries, Montiel-Overall creates a continuum similar to Abilock's with four steps: cultural incapacity (representing indifference, cultural and color blindness), limited or some cultural competence, cultural competence, and cultural proficiency.[22] Also, Montiel-Overall's continuum incorporates a hierarchy of necessary actions, as Banks's does (see figure 2.1), to move from incapacity to proficiency.[23]

In order to use youth literature to examine and facilitate reaching cultural competence or the even higher, almost unobtainable level of cultural proficiency, it is essential to know the methods by which appropriate children's and young adult literature might be identified and used for this purpose.

CHOOSING DIVERSE YOUTH LITERATURE

All the time-honored criteria that are applied to choose any "good book" apply to literature with diverse issues. The concept of authenticity generates the most disputed aspect of writing, publishing, and selecting diverse literary experiences for youth. Bitter battles over this issue occurred during the 1990s, with accusations of political correctness used as a subtle form of censorship. In the ensuing decade, the vitriolic denunciations and inflexible stances have to some extent been tempered by reason and depth of understanding, but they lurk beneath the surface, threatening to erupt at any moment. Invariably my graduate students ask, "What is authentic multicultural literature?" and "How can I tell?"

I offer the following three criteria to use in assessing authenticity and an ensuing discussion of what they mean.

1. Based on substantiated fact (cultural accuracy related to sources)

A Continuum of Cultural Proficiency

Destructiveness   Incapacity   Blindness   Precompetence   Competence   Proficiency

Figure 2.3: Continuum of cultural proficiency

2. Faithful reproduction of important features of the original culture (cultural accuracy related to cultural representation)
3. True to the creator's own cultural personality, spirit, or character (cultural immersion)

A book does not necessarily have to meet all three criteria in order to be authentic multicultural literature. For example, a book can be authentic multicultural literature if it satisfies only the first two. According to the first two criteria, authentic multicultural literature must show evidence that it is grounded in the correct facts of a culture to the extent that can be determined (no. 1 above) and that authors and illustrators have adhered faithfully to the original culture in their literary interpretations of that culture's key features (no. 2 above). Well-done source notes and author notes provide one place to seek evidence of cultural accuracy.[24] Critiques or reviews by persons knowledgeable about the culture are another way to find evidence of cultural accuracy. This can be complicated by the fact that a majority of reviewers may not be knowledgeable about the culture represented.

On the other hand, I maintain that a book can also be judged culturally authentic if its author meets only the third criterion (no. 3 above). Recent perspectives on research conducted among indigenous communities demonstrate how traditionally many mainstream scholars with their academic methodologies continue to treat indigenous people as unknowledgeable others. Smith brilliantly demonstrates what indigenous peoples have to offer when they speak for themselves. Although Smith's book does not deal with literature for youth, its lessons can easily be applied to the oral traditions recounted in these communities. It reminds us that in the digital age people rightly insist on having their voices heard and regarded as authentic representations of their culture.[25]

The third scenario, when an author's or illustrator's work meets all three criteria, is the easiest to evaluate. The work of creators who represent a culture that has become their own, either through birth or extensive experience, and who have researched it to the greatest extent possible, can portray cultural subtleties.

Another issue in selection of literature is whether or not the characters and themes must be positive. Must the characters be good role models? It is, in fact, the mark of a maturing literature representing diversity that it includes characters who are both strong and weak, who make both good and bad decisions, who demonstrate both right and wrong. The propensity to want only positive portrayals comes from years of negative stereotypes. As literature about marginalized groups is written and published, the initial books tend to focus on positive themes and characters. But this is not representative of real life. Authenticity and goodness do not go hand in hand, and a well-developed body of literature must have a wide variety of portrayals.

Now we are ready to return to the question posed near the beginning of this chapter—what does it mean to gain cultural competency through youth literature?

GAINING CULTURAL COMPETENCE
THROUGH YOUTH LITERATURE

The example that follows is taken from a Multicultural Resources for Youth course, an elective for graduate students at the University of Washington (UW) Information School. A number of graduate students are teachers or otherwise work with youth. They have used the sociopolitical and cultural competency frameworks based on critical multicultural theory and cultural competency models developed for this course and report success in applying what they learned with students of various ages.

The online asynchronous university class lasts for ten weeks. Students post comments on discussion boards. Each two-week module focuses on particular issues and cultural competencies, and the readings correspond to these. The issues/cultural competencies in this module are immigration, migration, language, and terminology. The students also read the Montiel-Overall and Abilock articles mentioned above.[26] Lectures and background readings provide context for discussing the issues in relation to the literature. "We make information work!" is a component of the UW Information School's mission statement.[27] In line with this mission and the course's theoretical and philosophical base, both graduate students and those in K–12 schools are asked to reflect upon how they can use what they are learning from literature to make a difference in their personal lives and the lives of others. They often refer to the continuum of gaining competency or proficiency as well as the mirror, window, and door metaphors.

Because the students "talked" on discussion boards, I was able to examine their comments, observing what themes emerged from their conversations and how they related to their growth on the competency scale.

A number of students commented on their own level of cultural competency. The following conversation reveals students who realize through self-reflection that they have quite a way to go. Joanna noted,

I have been wondering if those of us who are part of the underserved minorities have a tendency to focus primarily on our own culture and in effect demonstrate a small degree of blindness with regards to other cultural communities.[28]

Another student responded,

Since I've been taking this class I've noticed that those of my friends from underserved minorities like to make everything about "us" VS "the white man" despite all the Caucasians we have as friends. It's true, that in the past, many of the injustices that occurred/occur are a result of this power struggle . . . but I think that feeding the "us VS. them" only reverses our progress toward cultural proficiency.[29]

To which Joanna replied,

If cultural proficiency is the lifelong commitment to cultural understanding as Abilock states,[30] it seems apparent that we need to come 'out' of ourselves and cultivate tolerance and compassion for all other races including our Caucasian counterpart. Education and awareness are a huge component of cultural competence and it is most beneficial when it travels in both directions.[31]

The thought of activism as a requirement for becoming culturally competent was clear from the beginning to some students, Mathew among them.

The readings for this course have made it evident that educators are crucial in increasing the cultural competence of their students. For teachers to be able to do this, they have to be continually educating themselves and increasing their cultural competence. In the spirit of advocacy and service, teachers need to find time to be involved with the community outside of the school. What are some other ways that you all try to effect change?[32]

Maria ties social activism to her career as a librarian:

As librarians we have a responsibility to go out into the community for assessment of collection development, services and programs. This community outreach in turns helps us to become an instrument for change by listening, providing much needed services and assisting with education and information resources.[33]

One of the required books for the course, *Esperanza Rising*, gave rise to many sociopolitical observations, some at the competent end of the scale. One of the more salient observations relates the dilemma to strike or not to strike from a student clearly moving toward cultural competency.

Pam Munoz Ryan is very skilled at creating a vivid portrait of the plight of migrant farm workers from Mexico and the tension between those fighting for more equitable pay and those fighting just to survive. I found myself wondering along with Esperanza if

I would have the courage to side with the protesters. Would any of you be able to join the fight with Marta? What can be done to effect change?[34]

Spanglish was another topic that arose, stimulated by poems from *Red Hot Salsa: Bilingual Poems and Being Young and Latino in the United States,* This discussion brought many varied comments, among them a self-reflective comment from Philip:

> I like the intertwining of English and Spanish in this poem. Coming from an immigrant Vietnamese family, I understand the mixing of two languages. Ever since I was a little child, I have always understood Vietnamese when someone speaks it to me.[35]

The discussion of the book *An Island Like You: Stories of the Barrio* inspired a sense of setting, providing an entry for one student into the experience of an unfamiliar culture.

> I really enjoyed this reading selection. The poem at the beginning clearly painted a picture of what a barrio could be like. The description of sound like "stereos blasting salsa" takes the reader into that world.[36]

A folktale, *Magic Dogs of the Volcanoes / Los Perros Mágicos de los Volcanes,* provided students with a window into the El Salvadorian culture, something they were not confident they would clearly detect in a folktale.

> How did everyone react to *Magic Dogs of the Volcanoes?* I thought this was a beautiful book—the story was compelling and interesting, the illustrations were beautiful and seemed to be authentic based on my limited knowledge of El Salvador and Latino artwork, and it was sprinkled with details about El Salvadorian culture, people, and geography.[37]

And a final comment prompted by *La Mariposa* clearly raised awareness of the language issues that migrant children face, serving as a window into their world. Erin wrote:

> I also read *La Mariposa* and was similarly surprised by the stance of the teacher. I completely agree with you that immersion and opportunities to express yourself in your native language and culture are both necessary to successfully learn a new language and acclimate to a new culture.[38]

The books and concepts from the online unit can easily be transported into a K–12 setting and used to assist students in gaining cultural competency. Likewise, public librarians can introduce multicultural literature with the idea of increasing cultural competency through book clubs and individual reader's advisory. Additional ideas for applying critical multicultural analyses of youth literature as well as suggestions for practical application can be found in the book by Botelho and Rudman.[39] A parting thought: adults who help youth move toward cultural competence also continue to grow in their own desire and quest for cultural proficiency.

CHILDREN'S AND YOUNG ADULT BOOKS

Alexie, Sherman. *The Absolutely True Diary of a Part-Time Indian*. Boston: Little, Brown, 2007.

Argueta, Manlio. *Magic Dogs of the Volcanoes / Los Perros Mágicos de los Volcanes*. Translated by Stacey Ross. Illustrated by Elly Simmons. San Francisco: Children's Book Press, 1990.

Carlson, Lori Marie. *Red Hot Salsa: Poems on Being Young and Latino in the United States*. New York: Henry Holt, 2005.

Cofer, Judith Ortez. *An Island Like You: Stories of the Barrio*. New York: Orchard, 1995.

Jimenez, Francisco. *La Mariposa*. Illustrated by Simon Silva. Boston: Houghton Mifflin, 1999.

Ryan, Pam Muñoz. *Esperanza Rising*. New York: Scholastic, 2002.

NOTES

1. Sherman Alexie, *The Absolutely True Diary of a Part-Time Indian* (Boston: Little, Brown, 2007), 1.
2. Ibid., 2.
3. Graduate students who are quoted were in an online course focused on multicultural literature taught by the author at the University of Washington Information School. Quotes are accurate, but student names are fictitious to prevent identification of individuals.
4. Personal communication with student, March 2, 2011.
5. Ibid.
6. Ibid.
7. Personal communication with student, March 5, 2011.
8. Ibid.
9. See the annual statistics on multicultural literature published by the Cooperative Children's Book Center, Madison, Wisconsin, www.education.wisc.edu/ccbc/books/pcstats.asp.
10. James A. Banks, *Teaching Strategies for Ethnic Studies*, 8th ed. (Boston: Pearson/Allyn & Bacon), 2009.
11. Ibid.
12. Joe L. Kincheloe and Shirley R. Steinberg, *Changing Multiculturalism: New Times, New Curriculum* (Buckingham, Eng.: Open University Press, 1997).
13. Mingshui Cai, *Multicultural Literature for Children and Young Adults: Reflections on Critical Issues* (Westfield, CT: Praeger, 2002), 7.
14. Maria José Botelho and Masha Kabakow Rudman, *Critical Multicultural Analysis of*

Children's Literature: *Mirrors, Windows, and Doors,* Kindle e-book edition (New York: Routledge, 2009).

15. Ibid., xiii.
16. Ibid., 5.
17. Patricia Montiel-Overall, "Cultural Competence: A Conceptual Framework for Library and Information Science Professionals," *Library Quarterly* 79, no. 2 (April 2009): 189–90.
18. Ibid., 191.
19. Ibid., 191.
20. Deborah Abilock, "Educating Students for Cross-Cultural Proficiency," *Knowledge Quest* 35, no. 2 (2006): 10.
21. Ibid.
22. Patricia Montiel-Overall and Donald Adcock, "The Need for Cultural Competence," in *School Library Services in a Multicultural Society,* ed. Patricia Montiel-Overall and Donald Adcock (Chicago: American Library Association, 2008), 6.
23. Ibid.
24. Betsy Hearne, "Cite the Source," *School Library Journal* 39 (July 1993): 22–27.
25. Linda Tuhiwai Smith, *Decolonizing Methodologies*: *Research and Indigenous Peoples* (Plymouth, Eng.: Zed Books, 1999).
26. Montiel-Overall, "Cultural Competence," 175–204; Abilock, "Educating Students," 10–12.
27. Information School, University of Washington.
28. Personal communication with student, January 28, 2011.
29. Ibid.
30. Abilock, "Educating Students," 12.
31. Personal communication with student, January 30, 2011.
32. Personal communication with student, January 28, 2011.
33. Personal communication with student, January 29, 2011.
34. Personal communication with student, January 27, 2011.
35. Personal communication with student, January 20, 2011.
36. Personal communication with student, January 26, 2011.
37. Personal communication with student, January 27, 2011.
38. Personal communication with student, January 22, 2011.
39. Botelho and Rudman. *Critical Multicultural Analysis.*

PART II

Exploring Marginalized, Oppressed, and Under/ Misrepresented Communities in Youth Literature

African American Children's Literature

Liminal Terrains and Strategies for Selfhood

EBONY ELIZABETH THOMAS

SELECTION CRITERIA FOR LIBRARIANS, school media specialists, and educators tasked with choosing children's and young adult literature by, for, and representing historically and currently minoritized groups have been established by scholars over the past three decades.[1] Yet the number of titles featuring children and teens of color significantly lags behind their population in today's American schools and society. Among these titles, texts featuring young people of African descent continue to be underrepresented on our shelves. Notable children's literature critic Rudine Sims Bishop recently observed that "African American children's literature continues to exist as a very small subset of the estimated 5000 new children's books published each year in the United States."[2] However, some authors and illustrators of books featuring African American characters have achieved recent success, winning top awards and prizes including the Newbery, the Caldecott, and the Printz awards. Recent articles in venues such as *The Horn Book* have noted an increased concern toward and attention to issues of race and representation in children's literature, and most professionals in the field recognize the necessity of including African American children's and young adult literature in their libraries and classrooms.

In this chapter, I propose that African American children's and young adult literature has arrived at a moment that literary critic Homi Bhabha theorized as liminal or "in-between" space. Bhabha contends that these spaces "provide the terrain for elaborating strategies of selfhood—singular or communal—that initiate new signs of identity, and innovative sites of collaboration, and contestation, in the act of defining the idea of society itself."[3] I propose that African American children's and young adult literature is one such space for exploring these strategies of selfhood, not just for black youth, but also for all young people everywhere. At a time when African Americans count among their numbers some of the most admired people in our nation and world, as well as some of the most maligned, African American stories ought to be read, taught, and enjoyed as an essential cipher for decoding the true meaning of the collective American story. Often, there is a tendency for librarians, educators, and others to present, narrate, and teach African American literature as a singular metanarrative. Yet in the intricate quilt of American literature, language, and life, there have always been many stories about "black folks" that vary according to any number of factors: historical period, region of the United States, religion, national origin, socioeconomic class, and citizenship status.[4] In the past, as detailed below, there were sociopolitical reasons for promoting particular kinds of stories over others, at the expense of differentiation and individuation.[5] Today, spaces are opening (albeit slowly) for authors to explore a greater diversity of possibilities for black children and youth. Whether these new spaces will expand into a renaissance or disappear altogether is a critical question the field currently faces.

My intent and purpose is not to provide an exhaustive survey of African American, African, and African diaspora children's and young adult literatures. Instead, my hope is to provide a fuller context for the creation, production, and consumption of these literatures. I begin by positioning African American children's and youth literature alongside the journey from property to fraught personhood, from forced labor to tenuous liberty, and from dehumanization to critical consciousness.[6] This survey will include a brief review of African American children's and young adult literature, with representative titles highlighted, and some gaps denoted. Finally, I conclude with implications for shifting the selection and teaching of African American stories for youth from binary black/white contexts to meaningful, expansive lenses of use to twenty-first-century libraries, schools, families, and communities.

SOME HISTORICAL CONSIDERATIONS

The origins of all children's literatures and literacies of the African diaspora can, of course, be traced back to Africa. Prior to the Atlantic slave trade and colonization, African literature was largely oral outside of Islamic areas where the Arabic language predominated. It was valued as "one of the major means by which societies educated, instructed, and socialized their younger members."[7] This literate tradition included proverbs, riddles, tales, taboos, and legends across West and Central African societies. When people of African descent were first brought to Europe and the Americas, first as exotic captives, and then later as people in bondage, new traditions began to influence their songs, wise sayings, and stories. European folklore and Christian religious traditions as well as Native American trickster tales and knowledge about the landscape and geography of the New World were incorporated into the tales of those who were enslaved and colonized—forming a new, hybridized culture.

Rich literacies and literate traditions emerged during the slavery period, despite severe penalties for most enslaved persons and some freedmen for learning how to read and write. Punishments ranged from beating to maiming and in some cases, such as forgery of free papers, being put to death. Yet even in this perilous environment, many enslaved people still risked everything to become literate, linking literacy learning and liberation for the first time in human history. We have many first-person accounts about their lives, known within the American literary canon as the slave narratives. Frederick Douglass, Olaudah Equiano, Harriet Jacobs, Henry Bibb, and many others wrote their own stories, leaving no doubt that slavery was morally and ethically evil.[8] The authors of the slave narratives typically began by writing about what it was like to be a child in bondage. Thus, in these narratives, we have the origins of textually represented African American child life. Julius Lester and Afua Cooper are but two of the many contemporary authors who have provided juvenile versions of slave narratives, both accounts from the nineteenth century intended for Abolitionist audiences as well as memories of elderly enslaved persons interviewed in the 1930s for the Federal Writers' Project.[9]

Enslaved persons who did not have access to traditional print literacies also produced, engaged in, and transmitted to their children rich literate traditions. Centuries before the invention of the telegraph, West African cultures communicated information over long distances by the use of the talking drum. When talking drums were forbidden in the United States, the enslaved persons used other means of communication. Over time, they coined a new language, African American English, a creolized and complete variety of the speech they heard from their masters.[10] They used spirituals, trickster tales, and freedom stories as metaphoric devices. It was through these stories that they protested the injustice and inhumanity of slavery, and gleaned information about escape on the Underground Railroad north. One of the most prominent African American children's authors to introduce these traditional trickster tales and freedom stories in her work was Virginia Hamilton.[11]

In 1865, chattel slavery in the United States ended at the conclusion of the Civil War. Newly liberated African Americans were eager to obtain knowledge of and proficiency in the print literacies that had been denied them. Free women, men, and children made significant political, social, and educational gains during the first decade after emancipation, also known as Reconstruction. As the prominent African American educator and founder of the Tuskegee Institute, Booker T. Washington, remembered those first years of freedom, "it was a whole race going to school."[12] Then the Compromise of 1877 removed all remaining federal troops from the Southern states that had seceded from the Union. As the North turned a blind eye, Southern redemptionists sought to set up a new caste system that brutally repressed the freedmen, denied their right to vote on the grounds of illiteracy, and suppressed their ability to get a good education or earn a living. The *Plessy v. Ferguson* decision in 1896 upheld all segregated institutions in the South, including schools. Sociologist Jim Loewen has documented thousands of incidents from the 1890s through the 1930s where black residents, homeowners, business-men, and farmers were violently forced from their homes all over the United States.[13] Until the Jazz Age and Harlem Renaissance began in the 1920s, most of the depictions of black people in mass media and society were egregiously negative.[14]

Against this backdrop, there were many pockets of resistance and counter-narrative formation. During the late nineteenth and early twentieth centuries, churches published local bulletins with stories and sketches for congregants' children. W. E. B. DuBois, cofounder of the NAACP, was also deeply concerned with the racist images of black chil-dren that prevailed, and along with writer Jessie Fauset founded *The Brownies' Book* in order to, as one seven-year-old reader put it, "begin to learn something about my own race."[15] As Bishop notes, "a magazine with a mission, *The Brownies' Book* was a prime example of literature as social action."[16] The magazine was an oasis for young African Americans in the early twentieth century amid a social backdrop of damaging cari-catures and stereotypes. It not only included literature *for* youth, but lit-erature *by* youth. One such youngster was Langston Hughes, who began his career as a nationally published teen poet in this venue.[17]

The success of *The Brownies' Book* was contemporaneous with the nadir of post-Civil War race relations in American history. Returning soldiers of color who had been treated as liberators in Europe returned home from the war to the Red Summer of 1919, filled with anti-black riots, violent expulsions, and lynchings. In some Southern towns, wearing a uniform was seen as a threat, so veterans had to hide their military insig-nia before returning to their hometown. The infamous ethnic purgings at Rosewood, Florida, and Tulsa, Oklahoma, happened during this period, as did the mental institutionalization of the entire multiracial community of Malaga Island, Maine, described in Gary D. Schmidt's Newbery Honor novel *Lizzie Bright and the Buckminster Boy*.[18] Of course, contemporary lit-erature for children at the time did not detail these events, even though many children of all races witnessed and were affected by them.

The Harlem Renaissance of the 1920s, and the three decades imme-diately following it, laid the foundation for today's African American children's and young adult literature. Sparked by the elite young poets, novelists, dramatists, and other artists envisioned by DuBois and Fauset during the early years of the NAACP, the Harlem Renaissance was the first period in American history during which African American artists and writers unapologetically appreciated and celebrated their people, culture, language, and folkways. For the first time, black people were not always victims of racism and dehumanization. They were celebrated as people with their own traditions, artistic forms, and indigenous knowledge. During this decade, former *Brownies' Book* contributor Langston Hughes rose to prominence, writing poetry for adults as well as children, and historian Carter G. Woodson established Negro History Week, which today has evolved into Black History Month.

During and after the Harlem Renaissance, writers began to position African Americans as active agents fighting for their own physical, social, and economic liberation from stifling oppression. Literary critic Katharine Capshaw Smith observed that "the major writers of the time were deeply invested in the enterprise of building a Black national identity through literary constructions of childhood."[19] Thus, much of the impetus of mid-century African American children's literature was reparative, telling celebratory tales about the victories and the achievements of African Americans in spite of collective trauma and monumental odds, promoting a bourgeois "uplift" ideology, and encouraging young people to lead the race politically and socially towards American ideals of progress and individual achievement.

AFRICAN AMERICAN METANARRATIVES:
MULTIPLE STORIES, MULTIPLE TELLERS, MULTIPLE GENRES

All human beings engage in storytelling and story creation to make sense of an oft-nonsensical world. When we humans construct and structure our inner worlds, we shape them using the logic of our lived and embodied experiences, as well as the stories that we have received from others. In the early twenty-first century, story yet remains one of the prisms that we can look into to see ourselves and to imagine what we might become. Still, even after much progress has been made towards equity in children's and young adult literature over the past half century, there are more images reflected back in those prisms for some children than others.

Stories about African Americans have long had implications for young readers from all backgrounds. It is through these stories that children and teenagers first form critical consciousness around issues of race, racial difference, diversity, and equality. As public librarians, school library media specialists, and educators, we make choices in the ways that we present, frame, and contextualize literatures about African American people, cultures, and lives. It is usually in our schools and children's libraries that young people are first introduced to these texts; however, we often leave students with the impression that there is a singular, uncontested meta-narrative, privileging only certain kinds of stories as appropriate ways of talking about African American experiences. These metanarratives have changed over time, depending upon the political climate. Children of a century ago consumed texts that presented the black American story as one of deficit, dependency, and comedy. Dianne Johnson reminds us that during this time period, "poems such as 'Ten Little Niggers' were commonly appearing in the pages of *St. Nicholas,* the preeminent American children's magazine from 1878 through 1945 . . . cartoons, misrepresentations, and stereotypes of the Negro were legion therein." Since that time, our society's sensibilities have progressed. Today's children read texts that generally present slavery as wrong, the civil rights movement as necessary, and black characters as fully human (even if not always present, or represented as authentically as others).

As the above historical section has illustrated, there have always been multiple ways of reading, talking about, and teaching what it means to be black in America. Whether black histories, life, and letters are taught as stories of triumph, pilgrimage, reaction, or deficit, or in other ways, each of our readings (and "tellings" to children) about the phenomenon of being black in America is rooted in specific philosophies and ideologies that are directly correlated to the identities, social subjectivities, and sociopolitical concerns of the individuals and groups who espouse them, both today and in the past. Since metanarratives about race are pervasive in contemporary media and culture, and there are many competing frames for analyzing this often hyper-racialized information, it has become difficult for many adults today—let alone children and young adults—to process current events, statistics, and data about black Americans and distill fact from fiction. Recently, I have argued that "the rethinking of the African American metanarrative is central to the essential work of encouraging students to move from passive consumption to thoughtful analysis of *all* of the diverse narratives in our society. Providing young readers with frames to analyze the ways in which texts are raced in explicit and implicit ways can help further their appreciation for American stories both old and new."

As we consider stories, we must also consider their tellers. A persistent debate in the field has been over who has the right to tell African American stories to young people. This is a question that has been revisited often over recent decades as greater numbers of black authors rise to prominence. In her analysis of the development of black children's picture books, Michelle H. Martin, the first African American president of the Children's Literature Association, acknowledged the importance of texts such as Ezra Jack Keats's *The Snowy Day,* which was the first book featuring an African American child to win the Caldecott Award, while highlighting the contributions of recent authors and illustrators of African descent.[20] A few years later, African American children's author Nikki Grimes asked in *The Horn Book* "if this nation can manage to put a Black man [President Barack Obama] in the Oval Office, why can't the Caldecott committee see its way clear to give the Caldecott medal to an individual artist of African descent?"[21] The numbers of books published by children's and young adult authors and illustrators of African descent fluctuate from year to year, but black voices still are a minuscule proportion of the field. The fact that most literary representations of African American children and youth come from those outside of the culture is one that invites critical consideration, and necessitates attention, if not direct action.

Another gap between African American children's and young adult literature and other offerings is found in issues of race and representation. African American writers for youth and their allies have historically (and necessarily) been concerned with recounting the past and refuting negative depictions of black children by providing authentic counter-narratives and positive images. Unfortunately, I contend that this has created an imbalance in the kinds and the types of literature featuring black characters available to all youth. While almost always present in historical stories about the antebellum South, and often featured in tales about Jim Crow and the Civil Rights Era, African American youngsters are rarely protagonists in mysteries, romances, science fiction, or fantasy stories. Although there are more middle- and upper-class black characters appearing in literature for young people, both historical and contemporary fiction in the field tends to skew towards portraying black children and families as financially impoverished, or at least struggling, especially in urban contexts.[22]

It is absolutely true that there remain a disproportionate number of black young people in poverty, and that persistent social inequities yet remain. Stories of oppression and inequality are important ones that must be told and retold. Nevertheless, those of us tasked with presenting these texts to young people would do well to consider the impressions of African American children and youth they might be left with if the majority of the black American characters they encounter are enslaved, suffering under Jim Crow, living under duress during the civil rights movement, or struggling to survive the nation's postmodern inner cities. If there are few (or zero) young African American detectives, doctors, crime fighters, superheroes, brave soldiers and knights, or princesses in our stories, what ideas about the humanity, the diversity within, and the inherent worth might young people from other cultures take away from their readings? What might black kids and teens themselves come to believe about their inherent worth? How does this affect the development of young readers' imaginations, dreams, and aspirations?

As a teacher and teacher educator, I find that my students are experiencing the same frustrations today that I dealt with ten, fifteen, and even twenty years ago when trying to search for diverse representations of African American children and teens in print. Black characters are often confined to the same roles over and over again in juvenile fiction. I posit that this is a phenomenon that leads to many black students becoming aliterate by the middle grades—when they do not see their lives, dreams, hopes, and aspirations represented in the available literature, many choose not to engage in leisure reading at all. Yet the kind of literature that mirrors their lives is not always necessarily aligned with the financial interests of publishers. A few years ago on a professional discussion list focused on children's literature, an editor at a major children's publishing house confirmed something that I have long suspected—publishers think the bulk of the reading public is just not that interested in multicultural stories (except when for political correctness's sake they have to be), and is most comfortable seeing minoritized children and youth in acceptable or expected roles. Thus, it seems that characters of color are still often positioned as multicultural "set dressing."

By extension, then, can it be said that the major purpose of characters of color, non-Judeo-Christian characters, LGBTQ characters, or other characterizations of underrepresented groups in children's and young adult literature is to serve mainstream audiences? If that is the case, it makes perfect sense that these characters often only show up in issues-oriented fiction. Some may contend that audiences just are not very interested in reading about a Hmong warrior or a Palestinian princess or a Jamaican sorcerer unless it is time for those cultures to be featured during their month/week/assembly at school. If this is not the case, then why not expand children's and young adult literature beyond binary representations of black/white, rich/poor, urban/rural, ethnic/not-ethnic, and so on? Might we finally expand our horizons to authentically represent the dreams, the visions, and the imaginations of all children? Until our literature can provide answers to these questions in the affirmative, all of us involved in selecting, choosing, and evaluating texts for the young have a responsibility to do this kind of expansive, generous, and humanizing program planning, storytelling, and teaching in our own libraries and classrooms.

CRITERIA FOR SELECTION

In her comprehensive volume, *Free within Ourselves: The Development of African American Children's Literature,* Rudine Sims Bishop provides a five-point summary of the literary tradition created about (and around) African American children and youth. These points provide succinct guidelines for those tasked with selecting texts for young people. Authentic African American children's and young adult literature

1. Celebrates the strengths of the black family as a cultural institution and vehicle for survival.
2. Bears witness to black people's determined struggle for freedom, equality, and dignity.
3. Nurtures the souls of black children by reflecting back to them, both visually and verbally, the beauty and competencies that we as adults see in them.
4. Situates itself, through its language and its content, within African American literary and cultural contexts.
5. Honors the tradition of story as a way of teaching and as a way of knowing.

LANDMARK TEXTS

The Snowy Day (Keats 1962)

First picture book featuring an African American protagonist to win the Caldecott Medal (1963).

Sounder (Armstrong 1969)

First novel with an African American protagonist to win the Newbery Medal (1970).

Martin Luther King, Jr.: Man of Peace (Patterson 1969)

First winner of the Coretta Scott King Award (established 1970).

M.C. Higgins, the Great (Hamilton 1975)

First novel by an African American author to win the Newbery Medal (1975).

Roll of Thunder, Hear My Cry (Taylor 1976)

Second novel by an African American author to win the Newbery Medal (1977).

Mufaro's Beautiful Daughters (Steptoe 1987)

Caldecott Honor Book, 1988

Bud, Not Buddy (Curtis 1999)

First novel by an African American male author to win the Newbery Medal (2000).

Monster (Myers 1999)

First novel by an African American author to win the Printz Award (2000).

The First Part Last (Johnson 2003)

First novel by an African American female author to win the Printz Award (2004).

The Lion and the Mouse (Pinkney 2009)

First picture book by an African American author/illustrator to win the Caldecott Medal (2000).

SELECTED KEY AUTHORS

Arnold Adoff

William Armstrong

Arna Bontemps

Lucille Clifton

Christopher Paul Curtis

Sharon Draper

Sharon Flake

Eloise Greenfield

Nikki Giovanni

Nikki Grimes

Virginia Hamilton	Marilyn Nelson
Langston Hughes	Andrea Davis Pinkney
Angela Johnson	Eleanora Tate
Ezra Jack Keats	Mildred D. Taylor
Julius Lester	Joyce Carol Thomas
Patricia McKissack	Rita Williams-Garcia
Walter Dean Myers	Jacqueline Woodson

SELECTED KEY ILLUSTRATORS

Moneta Barnett	Jan Spivey Gilchrist
Ashley Bryan	Fred and Patricia McKissack
Carole Byard	Christopher Myers
Bryan Collier	Kadir Nelson
Floyd Cooper	Brian Pinkney
Donald Crews	Jerry Pinkney
Nina Crews	James E. Ransome
Pat Cummings	Faith Ringgold
Leo and Diane Dillon	John Steptoe
Tom Feelings	

NOTES

1. Barbara Thrash Murphy and Barbara Rollock, *Black Authors and Illustrators of Books for Children and Young Adults* (London: Psychology, 1999); Wanda M. Brooks and Jonda C. McNair, *Embracing, Evaluating, and Examining African American Children's and Young Adult Literature* (Lanham, MD: Scarecrow, 2008).
2. Rudine Sims Bishop, *Free within Ourselves: The Development of African American Children's Literature* (Westport, CT: Greenwood, 1994), xii.
3. Homi Bhabha, *The Location of Culture* (London: Routledge, 1994), 2.
4. Ebony Elizabeth Thomas, "The Next Chapter of Our Story: Rethinking African American Metanarratives in Schooling and Society," in *Reading African American Experiences in the Obama Era: Theory, Advocacy, Activism*, ed. Ebony Elizabeth Thomas and Shanesha R. F. Brooks Tatum (New York: Peter Lang, 2011), xx.
5. Charles Johnson, "The End of the Black American Narrative," *American Scholar* 77, no. 3 (2008): 32–42.
6. Paulo Freire, *Pedagogy of the Oppressed* (New York: Continuum, 1970).
7. Asenath Bole Odaga, *Literature for Children and Young People in Kenya* (Nairobi: Kenya Literature Bureau, 1985).
8. Henry Louis Gates, "Introduction," *The Classic Slave Narratives*, ed. Henry Louis Gates (New York: Penguin, 2002).
9. Julius Lester, *To Be a Slave* (New York: Penguin, 1968); Afua Cooper, *My Name Is Henry Bibb* (Kids Can, 2009).
10. John Baugh, "A Survey of Afro-American English," in *Readings in African American Language: Aspects, Features and Perspectives*, ed. N. Norment (New York: Peter Lang, 1993); John Rickford, *African American Vernacular English: Features, Evolution, Educational Implications* (Oxford: Blackwell, 1999).
11. Virginia Hamilton, *The People Could Fly* (New York: Knopf, 1985); Virginia Hamilton, *Many Thousands Gone* (New York: Knopf, 1993); Virginia Hamilton, *Her Stories* (New York: Scholastic, 1996).

12. Adam Fairclough, *A Class of Their Own: Black Teachers in the Segregated South* (Cambridge: Harvard University Press, 2006), 27.

13. James Loewen, *Sundown Towns: A Hidden Dimension of American Racism* (New York: Simon & Schuster, 2005); James Loewen, *Lies My Teacher Told Me: Everything Your American History Textbook Got Wrong* (New York: Touchstone, 1996).

14. Marlon Riggs, director, *Ethnic Notions* (San Francisco: California Newsreel, 1987/1994), videocassette.

15. David Levering Lewis, *W.E.B. DuBois: A Biography* (New York: Macmillan, 2009), 384.

16. Bishop, *Free within Ourselves*, 23.

17. Arnold Rampersad, *The Life of Langston Hughes: 1902–1941, I, Too, Sing America* (New York: Oxford University Press, 2002), 45.

18. Gary D. Schmidt, *Lizzie Bright and the Buckminster Boy* (New York: Random House, 2006).

19. Katharine Capshaw Smith, *Children's Literature of the Harlem Renaissance* (Bloomington: Indiana University Press, 2004), xiii.

20. Michelle H. Martin, *Brown Gold: Milestones of African-American Children's Picture Books* (London: Psychology, 2004).

21. Nikki Grimes, "Speaking Out," *Horn Book Magazine* (July/August 2009).

22. Ebony Elizabeth Thomas, "Landscapes of City and Self: Place and Identity in Urban Young Adult Literature," *ALAN Review* 38, no. 2 (2011): 13–22.

Promising Portals and Safe Passages

A Review of Pre-K–12
Latino- and Latina-Themed Literature

RUTH QUIROA

THE SMALL CANON OF LATINO/LATINA-THEMED literature for grades pre-K–12 that has emerged since 1993 is generally not present in pre-service training courses, discount bookstores, or Scholastic Book Clubs and Book Fairs in numbers commensurate with the U.S. Latino/Latina population.[1] This disparity is common despite the fact that such books can provide portals into new and familiar worlds for students, librarians, and teachers alike. In order to better understand such a phenomenon, this chapter discusses factors related to publication and demographics for these books from 1993 to 2010, together with aspects of literary and cultural quality. Problematic themes in recently published texts, as well as more positive trends, are also highlighted.

THE BACKDROP: LATINOS/LATINAS IN THE UNITED STATES

Information from the 2010 U.S. Census helps provide a context for this analysis, particularly since there were nearly one million more individuals of Latino backgrounds counted than had been expected.[2] The U.S. Latino/Latina population included 50.5 million individuals, or 16.3 percent of the country's total population, and comprised the country's largest cultural group and the second largest population worldwide, with only Mexico having more "Latino" residents.[3] In fact, Latino/Latina children comprised 22 percent of all U.S. children younger than 18 in 2009, which will impact schools and libraries for years to come.[4]

PUBLISHING TRENDS

In 1970 the U.S. Commission on Civil Rights documented the racist practices of schools in the U.S. Southwest for children of Mexican descent in a
series of six reports. Report III, titled "The Excluded Student: Educational
Practices Affecting Mexican Americans in the Southwest," spoke to the
dominance of the European American language and culture in the schools,
as well as a more subtle and indirect type of cultural exclusion, namely

> the omission of Mexican American history, heritage, and folklore
> from the academic curricula. . . . The curriculum in general, and
> textbooks in particular do not inform either Anglo or Mexican
> American pupils of the substantial contributions of the Indo-His-
> panic culture to the historical development of the Southwest.[5]

During this time the Council on Interracial Books for Children also critically reviewed the cultural content of Puerto Rican and Chicano children's
trade books and other materials as reported in the council's *Bulletin*.[6] The
council found that non-native authors, who produced the majority of
Chicano-themed books, were unable to "transcend the boundaries of perspectives defined by their white American cultural biases."[7] Despite such
attention, the actual publication of these books, and particularly Mexican
American-themed texts during the 1980s, "came to a virtual standstill as a
politically conservative era took hold in the U.S."[8]

In 1980, the Cooperative Children's Book Center (CCBC) at the University of Wisconsin-Madison began producing *CCBC Choices*, an annual annotated bibliography of recommended literature for children and adolescents.
CCBC librarians selected the titles for this publication from the pre-K–12
review copies received from U.S. trade- and alternative-press publishers.
The CCBC noted that "few books by and about racial minorities and people with disabilities" were produced in 1983, although more books were
published the following year which "bore some indication of the cultural
pluralism and diversity experienced by children."[9] It was not until 1991
that "real Latino people and fictional Latino characters seem to be moving,
albeit slowly, out of their virtual invisibility within U.S. children's books."[10]

Since 1985, the CCBC has been able to consistently report statistics on
books it received with African American themes, followed in 1993 by texts
with Native American and Asian and Asian-American themes. However,
a count for Latino/Latina-themed literature was not provided until 1994,
given the limited number of such books published prior to that time.[11]
Sadly, the annual CCBC reports of Latino/Latina-themed literature for
children and young adults from 1994 to 2010 reveal a lackluster production rate, which is discouraging at best when compared with the current
growth trends for this population.[12] (See figure 4.1.) The CCBC identified a total of 1,241 Latino/Latina-themed books during this seventeen-

year period, with an average of seventy-three books annually. In fact, the sixty-six books published in 2010 represent .05 percent of the 3,400 the CCBC received that year, a percentage that has remained virtually unchanged for quite some time.

Although lackluster, this publication data does show small variances, which are interesting when considered in light of U.S. educational politics and practices for Spanish-language students and demographic shifts of the Latino/Latina population. The initiation of three Latino/Latina book awards in the early 1990s, namely, the Américas Award for Children's and Young Adult Literature in 1993, the Tomás Rivera Mexican American Book Award in 1995, and the Pura Belpré Award in 1996, may have helped bump production high enough for the CCBC to count the total numbers of Latino-themed books published in the early 1990s. Yet this was followed by declining numbers from 1997 to a low of fifty-four books in 2000, around the same time as the demise of bilingual education in California under Proposition 227. The U.S. Census in 2000, with its report of high levels of growth for the Latino/Latina population, a seeming surprise for the popular media, was followed by small rises in publication rates in 2001 (seventy-seven books) and in 2002 (ninety-four books), with many of these texts being bilingual picture books. The elimination of the 1968 Bilingual Education Act and the passage of the No Child Left Behind Act in 2001 was followed two years later by a dip in Latino/Latina-themed book publication to sixty-three texts, with very few changes in publication rates thereafter until 2008, when the CCBC received a small increase to seventy-nine such books.

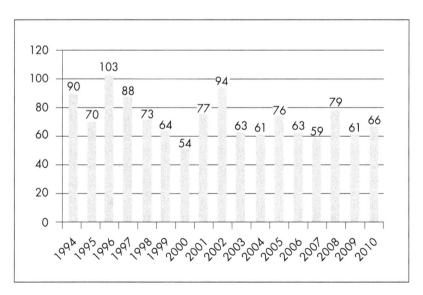

Figure 4.1: Statistics for Latino/Latina literature reported by CCBC, 1994–2010

PROBLEMATIC THEMES IN FICTIONAL TEXTS

Although a focus on publishing statistics may be revealing at one level, it does not address the actual literary and cultural quality of the books available from 1994 to 2010. However, these aspects have been documented as uneven over the years.[13] Another area that continues to present problems even within recently published texts is the manner in which Spanish words and phrases are included in primarily English-language books.[14] Here, spelling and grammatical errors still occur, together with concurrent translations, or paraphrase-like approaches used to explain and define the inclusion of Spanish terms. Such errors seem to infer a monolingual, English-language intended reader, given that she might not notice errors or that she must read the same content twice in one sentence, as is the case for a bilingual reader.

Another important consideration is that of the accuracy and "authenticity" of cultural content in individual titles, or the body of books as a whole. Notably, the three awards for books with Latino/Latina themes have resulted in increasingly positive portrayals of Latinos/Latinas in children's literature. Thus, Latino/Latina children and adolescents are "finally able to see their families, barrios, cultures, experiences, and lives reflected within the words and illustrations of their books," while students of other cultural backgrounds may get a glimpse into the windows of the "rich cultural experiences, languages, and traditions of their fellow Latino classmates."[15]

Unfortunately, stereotypic images and themes present in books published prior to 2000 still make their way into texts produced more recently.[16] As Cai notes, "the continued publication and popularity of books stereotyping oppressed groups carry the unmistakable message that the tradition of prejudice and racism is deep-rooted in the collective conscious of the dominant culture and entrenched in the cultural industry of children's literature."[17] He states that stereotypes cannot be ignored because of their cumulative nature, since repeated applications of over-generalized characteristics to a social group over time eventually morph into a deluded reality, damaging to students of Latino/Latina and other heritages alike. Thus, the very presence of such images within the limited number of new Latino/Latina-themed books produced annually is highly problematic, as each book has to count as an ambassador to those for whom it may serve as a window, or as an accurate, non-distorted mirror for those of similar backgrounds. Several of these long-standing, problematic themes and issues will be discussed here, together with recently published texts presenting more hopeful shifts in such trends.

The Barrio

One persistently insidious theme is that of urban barrios as solely undesirable, negative locales filled with crime and poverty. This perspective presents barrios as dangerous places, unfit for long-term residence, and offers negative, skewed images of the people living therein. In *Marisol,* the Chicago neighborhood of Pilsen is viewed as an unsafe community, so much so that the protagonist's family moves to a western suburb, even though this involves cutting cultural ties.[18] This particular book resulted in community outrage given that the neighborhood has undeniably rich resources, including cultural museums, history, and mural art, all of which were absent in the text.[19] In a similar manner, the picture book *Welcome to My Neighborhood!: A Barrio ABC* equates a barrio with broken glass, noisy neighbors, and burned-out buildings.[20]

Despite this persistently negative representation of the barrio, some recent publications highlight the strength and support of the Latino/ Latina community living in such sites. For example, Sofia, the protagonist of *Tequila Worm,* grows up in a barrio rich in cultural traditions and relationships.[21] As such, she receives strong support from her family, particularly from her mother's *comadres* and her own group of close female friends which helps her successfully navigate adverse situations at a boarding school, including racism. Recent picture books also provide more positive images of Latino/Latina barrios, as evidenced in *What Can You Do with a Paleta?/¿Qúe puedes hacer con una paleta?*[22] Here a young child describes all of the playful activities one can have with a *paleta* across richly colored illustrations set in a joyous Southwestern barrio. In addition, toddlers and preschool-age children gambol through a Latino/ Latina neighborhood, enjoying music, food, and a nap in *Fiesta Babies.*[23]

Images of Latin America

Another highly persistent stereotypic image is that of pajama-clad peasants living in Latin America, and particularly Mexico, often depicted with identical facial features and riding burros and wearing sombreros. For example, the images in a 1959 bilingual picture book entitled *Ramón Makes a Trade / Los cambios de Ramón* are still reflected in a text published thirty-eight years later, namely, *Day of the Dead.*[24] In *Ramón,* the characters are barefoot and wear generic white "traditional" attire with large sombreros, which changes little in *Day of the Dead,* except that the individuals now wear sandals and present even more pronounced similarities in terms of facial features and hair types. Such images most likely reflect the "indigenismo" present in the art of Diego Rivera, whose work served to popularize the image of the indigenous, particularly since the appearance of such elements in art and literature was either absent or presented in negative, stereotypical ways prior to that time.[25] Unfortunately, the proliferation of such images does not provide accurate reflections of present-day realities in Mexico and Latin America in general, and tends to promote the perception of individuals of indigenous heritage, or those living in rural areas, as backward and poor.

Several realistic and historical fiction texts published during the 2000s present more feasible images of individuals living in Latin American countries. For example, *The Composition*, set in an unidentified Latin American country, and *Before We Were Free*, set in the Dominican Republic, both weave aspects of daily life in countries with governments ruled by the military or a dictator.[26] In these books, children go to school, play soccer or chess, participate in family traditions, and eat meals together. Holiday and special traditions such as *quinceñeras* are embedded within the larger plot, rather than its sole emphasis, and time-appropriate clothing and fashions are mentioned or evidenced in the illustrations. Families live in cities and have high levels of education and professional careers, rather than only living in rural settings or in high-poverty regions.

Presentation of Gender

Gender presentation is a third problematic theme for Latino/Latina-themed children's and young adult books over the years. First, is the significant void of literature with GLBT themes, and second is the continuation of stereotypical images and roles assigned to Latinas.[27] For example, many books even in recent years depict mothers and grandmothers with rounded and even stooped figures, primarily wearing dresses and often in traditional-like clothing. This is true for notable books as well as those that are more lackluster in cultural content and literary themes. Females of all cultural and ethnic backgrounds represent a range of body types and skin/hair/eye colorings, a factor true of Latina women as well. The problem here is when the rounded, stooped figure is the primary way that mature Latina women are presented in illustrations for young children. In terms of employment, Latinas in fictional texts have been depicted as nannies, housekeepers, storytellers, cooks, nurses, and religious leaders rather than as lawyers, doctors, architects, or teachers and principals. They are also commonly presented as less intelligent or weaker than their male counterparts.

One example of such gender portrayal is evidenced in *The House of the Scorpion*, a highly lauded science fiction text.[28] Here women of Mexican origin take on the roles of an overweight, highly protective cook; a militantly religious leader in the fight against social ills; and a tear-stained and fearful, yet beautiful young adolescent girl. All of these female characters serve to enable the primary protagonist, Matteo, a clone, to survive the prospect of being farmed for his organs, so that he can begin to bring normalcy and justice to their dystopic world. At the same time, the realistic fiction text *Becoming Naomi Leon* portrays the increasing self-confidence of young Naomi in the face of her mother's rejection and betrayal, as well as her own agency in procuring the continuation of a safe home for her younger brother and herself through the U.S. legal system.[29] Naomi finds her voice without salvation or assistance from a

male character. She is neither seductive, militant, tear-stained, or caricatured, but rather a young girl who learns to find strength in the face of
difficulties.

Inclusion of Spanish

Another problematic aspect for even notable books is that of misspelled
Spanish words in illustrations or the awkward inclusion of more lengthy
Spanish phrases translated immediately into English using commas and
parentheses.[30] For example, *Grandmother's Gift* relates the story of the
protagonist Eric's tall, elegant Puerto Rican grandmother and the time
they spend together in preparation for the winter holidays. Despite positive portrayals of culture and gender, the text itself seems to be intended
solely for a monolingual English reader, as its lengthy, concurrent translation of Spanish phrases into English produces doublespeak for the
bilingual (Spanish/English) child. It also neglects to take into account
the comprehension strategies used by strong readers (even monolingual
readers) to make sense of unknown words and phrases through the use
of context clues. Additionally, in *90 Days to Havana*, the appalling number
of misspelled, well-known Spanish words negates its potential use with
students in terms of important historical content.[31]

On the other hand, the strategic and skillful inclusion of Spanish
terms in English-based books such as *Chato's Kitchen* or *Celemente!* serve
to enhance the literary merits of these texts by creating powerful images
of Latino/Latina settings, themes, and characters.[32] For example, the
description of Roberto Clemente in the latter text includes untranslated
Spanish words and phrases within the primarily English text. However, a
monolingual reader can ascertain Clemente's beliefs and character traits
without knowing every word because of the rich context in which these
terms are embedded. At the same time, the bilingual Spanish/English
reader can attain significantly deeper levels of aesthetic meaning due to
their lyrical inclusion.

PROMISING PORTALS AND SAFE PASSAGES

Despite the lingering problematic aspects in the body of Latino/Latina-
themed books for children and young adults, the following overview
of 2000–2010 books provides hope for the growth of positive, realistic
representations of individuals of Latino/Latina heritage in these texts.
This is critical since Latino/Latina-themed texts can open portals to new
or familiar worlds, and to better understandings of students and their
families. Such books are informative and thought-provoking, offering
the safety of a Latino/Latina child or adolescent perspective to consider
potentially different worlds and realities. With this in mind, the following discussion of trends and themes evidenced in texts published early in
the twenty-first century is meant to stir educators' and librarians' desire

to thoughtfully read, analyze, and enjoy these books, and to further personal and professional development so as to better serve the growing population of U.S. Latino/Latina students.

Overview

Between 2000 and 2010, several texts received recognition from Latino/Latina-themed and other awards, such as *The Surrender Tree: Poems of Cuba's Struggle for Freedom* (John Newbery Honor) and *Marcelo in the Real World* (Schneider Family Book Award).[33] In addition, the bilingual picture book *Poems to Dream Together/Poemas para soñar juntos* was awarded the Jane Addams Book Award in 2006 for promoting peace, social justice, world community, and the equality of the sexes and all races, as well as for literary excellence.[34] In addition, *Just a Minute: A Trickster Tale and Counting Book* was granted award status from all three Latino-themed book awards for children and adolescents.[35]

During this eleven-year period, authors from the 1990s continued to produce important works, namely, Gary Soto, Lulu Delacre, Pat Mora, Juan Felipe Herrera, and Francisco Jiménez, among others. Many new authors and illustrators dazzled readers with historically accurate books, filling gaps in the "standard" information provided in social studies or history textbooks. At the same time, picture books lent vibrant illustrations rich with humor and iconic or symbolic images. Several authors and illustrators produced multiple texts, namely Yuyi Morales, Francisco Alarcón, Carmen T. Bernier-Grand, Carmen Tafolla, Maya Christina Gonzalez, Amada Irma Perez, Monica Brown, Pam Muñoz Ryan, Julia Alvarez, Margarita Engle, and Benjamin Alire Sáenz, to name a few.

Some of the themes in chapter and picture books alike include joy and humor, untold history, important people, immigration/deportation, and protagonists with special needs. Woven throughout the majority of these books is the value of family, extended family, and community, which serves as the backdrop, or main subject, for stories in different genres. In fact, it is difficult to slot a specific book into only one or two of the themes above, since most effortlessly intertwine several topics together without detracting from their plot. At the same time, the themes listed serve as a useful way to organize this discussion of specific exemplary titles. It should be noted that the books highlighted are primarily drawn from those titles garnering award or honor status from one or more of the three Latino/Latina-themed book awards, although some titles from the annual Américas Award Commended lists are also included. In addition, effort was made to specifically feature titles published quite recently (2007–2010), given that these are easily accessible for purchase or through public and school libraries. Several titles are generally featured within each thematic category to serve as exemplars, rather than an exhaustive account of books carrying each of the various themes.

Some categories include more titles than others, simply because more such books in these areas seemed to be published in very recent years.

Family, Extended Family, and Community

The subject of family and extended family has consistently been a key theme of Latino/Latina-themed books.[36] This is particularly true for grandmothers, who featured in many titles, followed by the presence of mothers, siblings, fathers, and other relatives such as cousins, uncles, and aunts. Adult authors often seem to draw from their own fond childhood memories of a special relationship with an *abuelita* (grandmother), and recall the special foods she cooked and time spent together, as evidenced in *Grandma's Records; Grandma and Me at the Flea / Los Meros Meros Remateros*, and *Grandmother, Have the Angels Come?*[37] In the fantasy texts *Just a Minute: A Trickster's Tale and Counting Book* and *Just in Case: A Trickster Tale and Spanish Alphabet Book*, Grandma Beetle has a spunky humor and an extra touch of knowing, much like the Cuban Grandma overseeing her granddaughter's courting rituals in the traditional tale *Martina the Beautiful Cockroach*.[38] In *My Abuelita*, a young boy recounts the morning routines he partakes with his grandmother in preparation for her day at work as a storyteller.[39] In addition, Alma Flor Ada contrasts a young bilingual girl's experiences with each set of special grandparents—one of apparently Latino/Latina ancestry and the other of European American origins in *I Love Saturdays y domingos*.[40]

Relationships with family members are the fabric upon which Francisco Jiménez paints his semi-autobiographical books recounting memories from early childhood to young adulthood: *The Circuit, Breaking the Circuit,* and *Reaching Out*.[41] In other texts, family members help their children imagine possibilities and create new living spaces as in *My Very Own Room / Mi propio cuartito*; or live through difficult experiences such as immigration to the United States in *My Diary from Here to There / Mi diario de aquí hasta allá* and *Esperanza Rising*.[42] In addition, memoirs and biographies generally include family relationships when telling the stories of important Latinos/Latinas as evidenced in *Harvesting Hope* about César Chávez, or in *My Papa Diego and Me: Memories of My Father and His Art / Mi papa Diego y yo: Recuerdos de me padre y su arte*, in which the author shares memories of her father alongside images of his art.[43]

Joy and Humor

Celebrating noteworthy moments of life is a theme difficult to separate from that of family in Latino/Latina-themed books during the early 2000s. For example, the step-by-step creation of special foods to share with the family at a meal are commemorated in the poetic picture books *Sopa de frijoles/Bean Soup* and *Arroz con leche/Rice Pudding: Un poema para cocinar/A Cooking Poem*.[44] The previously mentioned Grandma Beetle is depicted creating a grand birthday feast to share with her grandchildren (*Just a Minute*), and family is prominent in Francisco X. Alarcón's four whimsical, seasonal poetry texts, two of which were published during the focal time period.[45]

Everyday life and love for people and the environment are featured in several books, as in *Arrorró mi niño: Latino Lullabies and Gentle Games*, a gentle text capturing traditional songs and games from fourteen Spanish-speaking countries, perfect for sharing with young children.[46] The loving relationship between a child and parent is also the focus of one poem in *Tan to Tamarind: Poems about the Color Brown*, a collection of poems celebrating the many wonderful hues of brown with references to Latino/Latina cultures, as well as to other ethnic groups.[47] Pat Mora's title, *Dizzy in Your Eyes: Poems about Love* is a collection of poems written in a variety of forms, some of which incorporate Spanish words and phrases, or are written entirely in Spanish and in English.[48] Mora compares the collection to a piece of music with four movements forming the cycle of love. Delight in the environment is central to *Animal Poems of the Iguazú / Animalario del Iguazú*, with its sparkling images of animals living in the Iguazú National Park shared by Argentina and Brazil, as well as in *I Know the River Loves Me / Yo sé que el río me ama*.[49]

Two new and equally humorous Chato books were produced during the focal time period, following the success of *Chato's Kitchen* in 1995.[50] Through humor and the skillful inclusion of Spanish in the text, as well as equally delightful illustrations with symbolic Latino/Latina images, the three texts provide the opportunity to see Chato mature as a character in relationship to himself, his community, and his world. Another book that focuses on themes of community, recounted with a gentle humor, is the literary tall tale titled *Doña Flor: A Tall Tale about a Giant Woman with a Great Big Heart* in which joy and community life go hand in hand.[51]

Untold History

Several authors emerged whose books helped to fill historical gaps in U.S. literature for children and adolescents. These texts are primarily intended for older readers with one particularly notable picture book, *The Composition*, originally published in Spanish.[52] Set in an unknown Latin American country, the main character Pedro finds himself learning about the impact of a new military government as people disappear in military trucks and his parents secretly listen to resistance radio stations in the evenings. Even at school the military requires participation in a writing contest that focuses on family activities after school, and Pedro must decide what to write about, particularly since a prize is attached to the winning essay.

Margarita Engle produced four novels in free verse poetry, all told through multiple voices or perspectives recounting different time periods in Cuba.[53] *The Poet Slave of Cuba: A Biography of Juan Francisco Manzano* details the life of Cuba's first poet, a slave in colonial times. *The Surrender Tree: Poems of Cuba's Struggle for Freedom* focuses on a woman who heals through natural herbs and plants. Her story crosses three wars for control of Cuba, and provides insight into slavery, the inception of reconcentration camps, and the struggles of the Cuban people. *The Firefly Letters: A Suffragette's Journey to Cuba* tells the story of Fredrika Bremer of Sweden who lived in Cuba for a time, and provides insights into the lives of women and slaves in 1851. Finally, *Tropical Secrets: Holocaust Refugees in Cuba* is set during World War II and chronicles the life of Daniel, a young Jewish refugee whose ship was not granted entry to the United States or Canada and finally disembarked in Cuba after some political debate.

In one of the very few books primarily set in the American Midwest, *Gringolandia* is a coming of age novel for teens that opens with the young protagonist, Daniel, witnessing his father's violent removal from the home by the military.[54] Shortly thereafter, the rest of his family immigrates to Madison, Wisconsin, and readers then meet Daniel as a sophomore in high school when his father is finally released from Chile after years of torture for involvement in a resistance movement. Daniel must now learn to deal with his own identity in the context of his father's lingering psychological and physical damage and its effects on family relationships.

Important People

Biographical award and honor books produced during this time period include the more standard subjects of César Chávez, Diego Rivera, Frida Kahlo, and Roberto Clemente; however, new individuals were added to this list, thus expanding the range of important Latinos/Latinas highlighted in quality literature.[55] Some of these included the Cuban American singer Celia Cruz, Mexican colonial scholar and poet Sor Juana Inés de la Cruz, Mexican potter Juan Quezada, Columbian novelist and Nobel Prize winner for literature Gabriel García Márquez, Chilean Nobel Prize winner for literature Pablo Neruda, Mexican American dancer José Limón, and newly appointed U.S. Supreme Court Justice Sonia Sotomayor of Puerto Rican descent.[56]

The majority of these books were produced as picture books in narrative form, although Carmen Bernier-Grand authored three biographical picture books comprised of a series of free verse poems: *César: Sí, se puede! Yes, We Can!; Frida: Viva la vida! Long Live Life!;* and *Diego: Bigger Than Life.*[57] In addition, *The Storyteller's Candle / La velita de los cuentos,* a notable historical fiction text, focused on the life of Pura Belpré, a Puerto Rican librarian in New York City.[58] Even though the majority of biographical books produced in recent years are likely intended for grades K–5, such texts are also helpful for middle-level and high school students, given that the illustrations and simpler text structures provide an overview that

is accessible to students with differing abilities, and can be highly moti-
vational at the inception of a unit of study. Additionally, Bernier-Grand's
Frida and *Diego* texts present content appropriate for adolescent readers
given that both closely follow the adult lives of these individuals.

Immigration/Deportation

Themes related to immigration and deportation have been present in
Latino/Latina-themed literature as early as the 1990s, if not before, in
books such as Gloria Anzaldúa's *Friends from the Other Side / Amigos del
otro lado.*[59] However, new stories with similar themes came to the forefront in 2009–2010, as in *From North to South / Del norte al sur.*[60] This text
chronicles the young protagonist José's emotional response to the recent
deportation of his mother to Mexico and his journey with Papá from
their home in San Diego, California, to visit her. Notably, author Laínez
is donating a portion of the proceeds from this book to El Centro Madre
Assunta, a refuge for immigrant women and children in Tijuana, Mexico.

Few Latino/Latina-themed chapter books for children in grades three
through five have included themes of undocumented immigration and
deportation, yet *Star in the Forest* tells the story of Xitlali (Nahuatl for
"Star") in the midst of her father's deportation to Mexico.[61] The realistic
child perspective of family relationships, friendships, and undocumented
immigration, together with the incorporation of Nahuatl language and
beliefs, make this a compelling read for intermediate-age children. A second important book for students in intermediate and middle-level grades
is that of *Return to Sender,* by Julia Alvarez.[62] Set in Vermont, this book is
recounted in two voices: that of Maria, the child of illegal immigrants,
and Tyler, whose parents own the farm where Maria's father and uncles
work. Alvarez carefully researched immigration laws and deportation
procedures in her home state of Vermont, particularly the fate of children following an Immigration and Naturalization Service raid and subsequent deportation of parents.[63] The adolescent text titled *La línea* cap-
tures the journey of Miguel and Elena as they struggle to travel from the
rural city of San Jacinto, Mexico, to find their parents in California.[64] The
siblings face police, the border patrol, death trains north, and the very
desert itself, giving the reader a sense of the range of emotions experienced during this journey.

Protagonists with Special Needs

The appearance of strong male and female protagonists with special
needs, or the siblings of such individuals, are themes long overdue in
Latino/Latina-themed books. One such book is *Marcelo in the Real World*,
with seventeen-year-old protagonist Marcelo, who describes himself
as on the high-functioning end of the autism spectrum, or "probably
Asperger's syndrome."[65] Told in first-person narrative, the reader follows

Marcelo through a summer of work in his father's high-power law-firm to prove his capability to make it in the "real world." This text incorporates more subtle cultural references than some books discussed here, although it clearly reveals the issues of racism faced even by individuals of Mexican origin in middle to upper socioeconomic levels. A second and equally strong text for intermediate grades is *Becoming Naomi León,* as Naomi lives with her great-grandmother and younger brother, whose special needs are not clearly identified other than some physical challenges, but which clearly impact the family and the story plot.[66] Author Pam Muñoz Ryan is able to pull many seemingly disparate themes together in ways that flow naturally into the plot, rather than serve to "teach" the reader, particularly in relation to Owen's special needs.

LOOKING FORWARD

As noted, the trends in publication rates for Latino/Latina-themed literature for children and adolescents continue to be quite dismal, with some lingering negative images, concepts, and manners of incorporating Spanish. However, the overall body of such texts does show increasing levels of quality in the twenty-first century, as evidenced in part by those books receiving multiple awards in recent years. Thus, there are reasons for hope for a future that includes higher numbers of Latino/Latina-themed books representing a wider range of themes and topics with strong literary aspects.

At some point in this country's growth trajectory, U.S. Latino/Latina children will move into the fields of authorship, illustrating, editing, and publishing in numbers commensurate with their growing population. With a stronger voice, it is hoped that there will finally be increased numbers of books produced that present positive, realistic images of Latino/Latina children and adolescents across a range of formats and genres. Teachers and librarians play important roles in ensuring this happens through the purchase and use of notable Latino/Latina-themed books in classrooms and libraries, as well as through their influence on the lives of their students. Familiarity with the trends and issues of this body of books, as well as with specific stellar titles, is a good beginning point toward ensuring that students have access to high-quality books, rich with Latino/Latina cultural content, that are also used in culturally responsive manners in classrooms and libraries.

NOTES

1. Jonda C. A. McNair, "The Representation of Authors and Illustrators of Color in School-Based Book Clubs," *Language Arts* 85, no. 3 (January 2008): 193–201. The year 1993 is selected as it was the first year that the Americas Award for Latino Children's and Young Adult Literature was presented and signifies the acknowledged need for high-quality Latino youth literature.

2. Jeffrey S. Passel, and D'Vera Cohn, "How Many Hispanics? Comparing Census Counts and Census Estimates 3.15.2011," Pew Research Center: Pew Hispanic Center, http://pewhispanic.org/reports/report.php?ReportID=139.

3. In 2010 the U.S. Census Bureau counted Latino/Latina heritage according to origin and not race, and used the terms *Hispanic origins* and *Latino, Hispanic or Spanish;* Jeffrey S. Passel, D'Vera Cohn, and Mark Hugo Lopez, "Hispanics Account for More Than Half of Nation's Growth in Past Decade 3.24.2011," Pew Research Center: Pew Hispanic Center, http://pewhispanic.org/reports/report.php?ReportID=140; United States Census Bureau, "Facts for Features: Hispanic Heritage Month 2010: September 15–October 15," www.census.gov/newsroom/releases/archives/facts_for_features_special_editions/cb10-ff17.html.

4. Karen R. Humes, Nicholas A. Jones, and Robert R. Ramirez, "Overview of Race and Hispanic Origin: 2010," United States Census Bureau, www.census.gov/prod/cen2010/briefs/c2010br-02.pdf.

5. United States Commission on Civil Rights, *Mexican American Education Study, Reports I-V* (New York: Arno, 1978), 30–31.

6. Council on Interracial Books for Children, "Special Issue on Puerto Rican Children's Literature and Materials," *Interracial Books for Children: Bulletin* 4, no. 1/2 (Spring 1972); Council on Interracial Books for Children, "Special Issue on Chicano Children's Literature and Materials," *Interracial Books for Children: Bulletin* 5, no. 7/8 (1974).

7. Council on Interracial Books for Children, *Bulletin* 5, no. 7/8 (1974): 7.

8. Rosalinda B. Barrera, "The Mexican American Experience in Children's Literature: Past Present, and Future," *Oregon English Journal* 14, no. 1 (Spring 1992): 14.

9. Kathleen T. Horning, Ginny Moore Kruse, and Michele A. Seippe, *CCBC Choices 1983* (Madison, WI: Cooperative Children's Book Center, 1984), 1, http://minds.wisconsin.edu/handle/1793/6603; Kathleen T. Horning and Ginny Moore Kruse, *CCBC Choices 1984* (Madison, WI: Cooperative Children's Book Center), 1985, 13, http://minds.wisconsin.edu/handle/1r793/6605.

10. Kathleen T. Horning, Ginny Moore Kruse, Megan Schliesman, and Merri V. Lindgren, *CCBC Choices 1993* (Madison, WI: Friends of the CCBC, 1994), 2.

11. Kathleen T. Horning, Ginny Moore Kruse, and Megan Schliesman, *CCBC Choices 1994* (Madison, WI: Friends of the CCBC, 1995).

12. University of Wisconsin-Madison, "Children's Books by and about People of Color Published in the United States: Statistics Gathered by the Cooperative Children's Book Center, School of Education, University of Wisconsin-Madison," www.education.wisc.edu/ccbc/books/pcstats.asp.

13. Rosalinda B. Barrera and Oralia Garza de Cortes, "Mexican American Children's Literature in the 1990s: Toward Authenticity," in *Using Multiethnic Children's Literature in Grades K-8,* ed. Violet J. Harris (Norwood, MA: Christopher-Gordon, 1997), 129–54; Rosalinda B. Barrera, Ruth E. Quiroa, and Cassiette West-Williams, "*Poco a poco:* The Continuing Development of Mexican American Children's Literature in the 1990s," *New Advocate* 12, no. 4 (Fall 1999): 315–30; Jamie C. Naidoo, "Opening Doors: Visual and Textual Analysis of Diverse Latino Subcultures in Américas Picture Books," *Children and Libraries: The Journal of the Association for Library Service to Children* 6, no. 2 (Summer/Fall 2008): 27–35; Jamie C. Naidoo, ed., *Celebrating Cuentos: Promoting Latino Children's Literature and Literacy into Classrooms and Libraries* (Westport, CT: Libraries Unlimited, 2010); Nina L. Nilsson, "How Does Hispanic Portrayal in Children's Books Measure Up after 40 Years? The Answer Is 'It Depends,'" *Reading Teacher* 58, no. 6 (March 2005): 534–48.

14. Rosalinda B. Barrera and Ruth E. Quiroa, "The Use of Spanish in Latino Children's Literature in English: What Makes for Cultural Authenticity?" in *Stories Matter: The Complexity of Cultural Authenticity in Children's Literature,* ed. Dana L. Fox and Kathy G. Short (Urbana, IL: National Council of Teachers of English, 2003), 247–65.

15. Jamie C. Naidoo, Jennifer Battle, and Orelia Garza de Cortés, "Celebrating Cultures and Cuentos: Three Awards for Latino Children's Literature," in *Celebrating Cuentos: Promoting Latino Children's Literature and Literacy Into Classrooms and Libraries,* ed. Jamie C. Naidoo, 79–98 (Westport, CT: Libraries Unlimited, 2010), 97.

16. Jamie C. Naidoo, "Reviewing the Representation of Latino Cultures in U.S. Children's Literature," in *Celebrating Cuentos: Promoting Latino Children's Literature and Literacy Into Classrooms and Libraries,* ed. Jamie C. Naidoo (Westport, CT: Libraries Unlimited, 2010), 59–78.

17. Cai Mingshui, *Multicultural Literature for Children and Young Adults: Reflections on Critical Issues* (Westport, CT: Greenwood, 2002), 21.

18. Gary Soto, *Marisol* (Middleton, WI: Pleasant Company, 2004).

19. Yolanda Perdomo, "Marisol in the Middle," *Hispanic* 18, no. 4 (April 2005): 12.

20. Alegria Hudes Quiara, *Welcome to My Neighborhood!: A Barrio ABC*, ill. Shino Arihara (New York: Arthur A. Levine Books, 2010).

21. Viola Canales, *The Tequila Worm* (New York: Wendy Lamb Books, 2005).

22. Carmen Tafolla, *What Can You Do with a Paleta? / Qué puedes hacer con una paleta?* ill. Magali Morales (Berkeley, CA: Tricycle, 2009).

23. Carmen Tafolla, *Fiesta Babies,* ill. Amy Córdova (Berkeley, CA: Tricycle, 2010).

24. Barbara Ritchie, *Ramón Makes a Trade / Los cambios de Ramón,* ill. Earl Thollander (Berkeley, CA: Parnassus, 1959); Tony Johnston, *Day of the Dead,* ill. Jeanette Winter (San Diego, CA: Voyager Books, 1997/2000).

25. David Craven, *Art and Revolution in Latin America, 1910–1990* (New Haven, CT: Yale University Press, 2002).

26. Antonio Skármeta, *The Composition,* ill. Alfonso Ruano (Toronto: Groundwood, 2000); Julia Alvarez, *Before We Were Free* (New York: Knopf Books for Young Readers, 2002).

27. Naidoo, "Reviewing the Representation of Latino Cultures in U.S. Children's Literature."

28. Nancy Farmer, *The House of the Scorpion* (New York: Atheneum, 2002).

29. Pam Muñoz Ryan, *Becoming Naomi León* (New York: Scholastic, 2004).

30. Eric Velasquez, *Grandma's Gift* (New York: Walker Books for Young People, 2010).

31. Enrique Flores-Galbis, *90 Miles to Havana* (New Milford, CA: Roaring Brook, 2010).

32. Gary Soto, *Chato's Kitchen,* ill. Susan Guevarra (New York: Putnam Juvenile, 1995); Willie Perdomo, *Clemente!,* ill. Bryan Collier (New York: Henry Holt, 2010).

33. Margarita Engle, *The Surrender Tree: Poems of Cuba's Struggle for Freedom* (New York: Henry Holt, 2008); Francisco X. Stork, *Marcelo in the Real World* (New York: Arthur A. Levine Books, 2009).

34. Francisco X. Alarcón, *Poems to Dream Together / Poemas para soñar juntos,* ill. Paula Barragán (New York: Lee and Low Books, 2005).

35. Yuyi Morales, *Just a Minute: A Trickster Tale and Counting Book* (San Francisco: Chronicle Books, 2003).

36. Barrera, Quiroa, and West-Williams, *"Poco a poco."*

37. Eric Velasquez, *Grandma's Records* (New York: Walker, 2001); Juan Felipe Herrera, *Grandma and Me at the Flea / Los Meros Meros Remateros,* ill. Anita de Lucio-Brock (San Francisco: Children's Book Press, 2002); and Denise Vega, *Grandmother, Have the Angels Come?* ill. Erin Eitter Kono (New York: Little, Brown, 2009).

38. Morales, *Just a Minute;* Yuyi Morales. *Just in Case: A Trickster Tale and Spanish Alphabet Book* (New Milford, CT: Roaring Brook, 2008); Carmen Agra Deedy, *Martina the Beautiful Cockroach / Martina una cucarachita muy linda: Un cuento Cubano,* ill. Michael Austin (Atlanta: Peachtree, 2007).

39. Tony Johnston, *My Abuelita,* ill. Yuyi Morales (Orlando: Harcourt Children's Books, 2009).

40. Alma Flor Ada, *I Love Saturdays y domingos,* ill. Elivia Savadier (New York: Atheneum, 2002).

41. Francisco Jiménez, *The Circuit* (Albuquerque: University of New Mexico Press, 1997); Francisco Jiménez, *Breaking the Circuit* (Boston: Houghton Mifflin, 2001); and Francisco Jiménez, *Reaching Out* (Boston: Houghton Mifflin, 2008).

42. Amada Irma Pérez, *My Very Own Room / Mi propio cuartito,* ill. Maya Christina-González (San Francisco: Children's Book Press, 2000); Amada Irma Pérez, *My Diary from Here to There / Mi diario de aquí hasta allá,* ill. Maya Christina Gonzalez (San Francisco: Children's Book Press, 2002); and Pam Muñoz Ryan, *Esperanza Rising* (New York: Scholastic, 2000).

43. Kathleen Krull, *Harvesting Hope,* ill. Yuyi Morales (New York: Harcourt, 2003); and Guadalupe R. Marín, *My Papa Diego and Me: Memories of My Father and His Art / Mi papa Diego y yo: Recuerdos de me padre y su arte* (San Francisco: Children's Book Press, 2009).

44. Jorge Agrueta, *Sopa de frijoles / Bean Soup,* ill. Rafael Yockteng. (Toronto: Groundwood Books, 2009); Argueta, *Arroz con leche / Rice Pudding: Un poema para cocinar / A Cooking Poem,* ill. Fernando Vilela (Toronto: Groundwood Books, 2010).

45. Francisco X. Alarcón, *Laughing Tomatoes and Other Spring Poems / Jitomates risueños y otras poemas de primavera,* ill. Maya Christina Gonzalez (San Francisco: Children's Book Press, 1997); Francisco X. Alarcón, *From the Bellybutton of the Moon and Other Summer Poems / Del ombligo de la luna y otros poemas de verano,* ill. Maya Christina Gonzalez (San Francisco: Children's Book Press, 1998); Francisco X. Alarcón, *Iguanas in the Snow and Other Winter Poems / Iguanas en la nieve: Y otros poemas de invierno,* ill. Maya Christina Gonzalez (San Francisco: Children's Book Press, 2001); Francisco X. Alarcón, *Angels Ride Bikes: And Other Fall Poems / Los Angeles Andan en Bicicleta: Y otros poemas de otoño,* ill. Maya Christina Gonzalez (San Francisco: Children's Book Press, 2005).

46. Lulu Delacre, *Arrorró, mi niño: Latino Lullabies and Gentle Games* (New York: Lee & Low Books, 2004).

47. Michelle Iyengar Malathi, *Tan to Tamarind: Poems about the Color Brown,* ill. Jamel Akib (San Francisco: Children's Book Press, 2009).

48. Pat Mora, *Dizzy in Your Eyes: Poems about Love* (New York: Knopf Books for Young Readers, 2010).

49. Francisco X. Alarcón, *Animal Poems of the Iguazú / Animalario del Iguazú,* ill. Maya Christina Gonzalez (San Francisco: Children's Book Press, 2008); Maya Christina Gonzalez, *I Know the River Loves Me / Yo sé que el río me ama* (San Francisco: Children's Book Press, 2009).

50. Soto, *Chato's Kitchen;* Gary Soto, *Chato and the Party Animals,* ill. Susan Guevarra (New York: Putnam, 2000); Gary Soto, *Chato Goes Cruisin','* ill. Susan Guevarra (New York: G. P. Putnam's Sons, 2007).

51. Pat Mora, *Doña Flor: A Tall Tale about a Giant Woman with a Great Big Heart,* ill. Raul Colón (New York: Alfred A. Knopf, 2005).

52. Skármeta, *The Composition.*

53. Margarita Engle, *The Poet Slave of Cuba: A Biography of Juan Francisco Manzano*, ill. Sean Qualls (New York: Henry Holt, 2006); Engle, *The Surrender Tree;* Margarita Engle, *Tropical Secrets: Holocaust Refugees in Cuba* (New York: Henry Holt, 2009); Margarita Engle, *The Firefly Letters: A Suffragette's Journey to Cuba* (New York: Henry Holt, 2010).

54. Lyn Miller-Lachtmann, *Gringolandia* (Willimantic, CT: Curbstone, 2009).

55. Krull, *Harvesting Hope;* Illan Stavans, *César Chávez: A Photographic Essay* (El Paso, TX: Cinco Puntos, 2010); Marín, *My Papa Diego and Me;* Amy Novesky, *Me, Frida*, ill. David Diaz (New York: Abrams, 2010).

56. Monica Brown, *My Name Is Celia / Me llamo Celia: The Life of Celia Cruz / La vida de Celia Cruz*, ill. Rafael López (Flagstaff, AZ: Rising Moon, 2004); Pat Mora, *A Library for Juana*, ill. Beatrice Vidal (New York: Knopf, 2002); Nancy Andrews-Goebel, *The Pot That Juan Built*, ill. David Diaz (New York: Lee & Low, 2002); Monica Brown, *My Name Is Gabito: The Life of Gabriel García Márquez / Me llamo Gabito: La vida de Gabriel García Márquez*, ill. Raul Colón (Flagstaff, AZ: Rising Moon, 2007); Pam Muñoz Ryan, *The Dreamer*, ill. Peter Sís (New York: Scholastic, 2010).

57. Carmen T. Bernier-Grand, *César: ¡Sí, Se puede! Yes, We Can!* (Tarrytown, NY: Marshall Cavendish, 2005); Carmen T. Bernier-Grand, *Frida: ¡Viva la vida! Long Live Life!* (Tarrytown, NY: Marshall Cavendish, 2007); Carmen T. Bernier-Grand, *Diego: Bigger Than Life*, ill. David Díaz (Tarrytown, NY: Marshall Cavendish Children, 2009); Susanna Reich, *José! Born to Dance*, ill. Raul Colón (New York: Simon & Schuster, 2005); Jonah Winter, *Sonia Sotomayor: A Judge Grows in the Bronx / Sonia Sotomayor: La juez que creció en el Bronx*, ill. Edel Rodríguez (New York: Atheneum, 2009).

58. Lucia M. González, *The Storyteller's Candle / La velita de los cuentos*, ill. Lulu Delacre (San Francisco: Children's Book Press, 2008).

59. Gloria Anzaldúa, *Friends from the Other Side / Amigos del otro lado*, ill. Consuelo Méndez (San Francisco: Children's Book Press, 1993).

60. René Colato Laínez, *From North to South / Del norte al sur*, ill. Joe Cepeda (San Francisco: Children's Book Press, 2010).

61. Laura Resau, *Star in the Forest* (New York: Delacorte Books for Young Readers, 2010).

62. Julia Alvarez, *Return to Sender* (New York: Alfred A. Knopf, 2009).

63. Library of Congress, "Webcasts: 2010 Américas Award," www.loc.gov/today/cyberlc/feature_wdesc.php?rec=5128.

64. Ann Jaramillo, *La línea* (New Milford, CT: Roaring Brook, 2006).

65. Stork, *Marcelo in the Real World*.

66. Muñoz Ryan, *Becoming Naomi León*.

SLIDING DOOR 1

The Politics of Publishing Latino Children's Books

ORALIA GARZA DE CORTÉS AND JENNIFER BATTLE

WHILE THE WORLD OF American children's literature has become increasingly more representative since the days of Nancy Larrick's seminal article "The All-White World of Children's Books," the dramatic increase in the population of Latinos in the United States should compel publishers to find quality manuscripts for this fast-growing reading market. Regrettably, stereotypes that negatively reflect Latino culture and language persist despite an abundance of knowledge and information to the contrary.[1] Whether due to a lack of cultural sensitivity or a failure to recognize the importance of finding and publishing stories that reflect an insider perspective, or perhaps because the staff and editorial boards of publishing houses lack cultural knowledge about Latino culture, uninformed publishers continue to miss the mark when it comes to producing literature respectful of Latinos and their cultures.

As mentioned in other parts of this book, it is imperative for children from all cultural backgrounds to encounter authentic and culturally accurate representations of all cultures, the Latino ones notwithstanding. Publishing houses are called to assume editorial responsibility in carefully selecting manuscripts for publication. They should seriously weigh editorial decisions based on manuscripts with Latino protagonists who face life's challenges and solve their own problems using their own rich Latino cultural and language resources (e.g., Spanish, English, Portuguese, bilingualism, and caló), rather than presenting them with familiar mainstream stereotypical representations and contrived Anglicized expressions in Spanish.

In their formative years and throughout their social and intellectual development, Latino children deserve access to a flood of books that strengthen, affirm, and validate their identities. Like all children, Latino children need opportunities to find their heritage, experiences, and familiar language within the pages of the books they read.[2] Rudine Sims Bishop writes: "Literature transforms human experience and reflects it back to us, and in that reflection we can see our own lives and experiences as part of the larger human experience. Reading, then, becomes a means of self-affirmation, and readers often seek their mirrors in books."[3] These personal connections to their world and their role in the universe intensify children's motivation and serve them well when acquiring the technical skills for reading, writing, and other aspects of the literacy process. Learning through literature is a scaffolding process, beginning with what is known and familiar while at the same time introducing new and unfamiliar concepts. Culture, heritage, and ways of speaking are assets for learning and provide the motivation precisely because they validate one's own life and experiences. They provide Latino children with the impetus for meaningful engagement in learning through quality literature that validates and affirms their humanity.

Inasmuch as publishers of children's books pride themselves on the quality of their publications, in a market-driven industry, however, editorial decisions about children's book publishing are ultimately based on a publisher's ability to sell books and make a profit. The "sellability" of a book and its ultimate appeal to a broader buying public are compelling driving forces that result in the publication of inflammatory titles that, while holding broad appeal to white, middle-class kids who consume the humor, actually insult and demean Latino cultures.

A close examination of a popular children's book, Judy Schachner's *Skippyjon Jones*, sheds light on an example of stereotypes that popularizes already negative images and gives legitimacy and credence to their continued use for demeaning rather than affirming Mexican culture.[4] Based on well-known stereotypical media images like the Frito Bandito, Speedy Gonzales, and El Zorro, the predominantly "white" protagonist is a mischievous kitten that goes to Mexico ("a faraway desert land") disguised as El Skippito Bandito. His goal is to save a group of "bean eaters" (a reference to the pejorative "beaners") named "Chimichangos" from the bee that has stolen their frijoles. The author/illustrator attempts to use creative language play, which requires a reader to enunciate the words with an Anglo-Saxon pronunciation in order for the rhyme and rhythm to work. She contrives certain Spanish-like endings by adding an "o" or an "ito" to many words in both English and Spanish like "Skippito" and "Bumblebito" to create a repeated rhyme. The result is a distortion and misuse of semantics, originally designed in Spanish to mean small or with affection.

Reinforced by a professional book review that extolled the book's humor and recommended it in particular for Spanish-speaking children, this title is the first in a series that perpetuates these stereotypical themes and appropriated speech forms.[5] Despite its cultural insensitivities, *Skip-*

pyjonJones received the inaugural E. B. White Award for best read-aloud picture book from the American Booksellers for Children in 2004. Both the positive review and the award falsely credential the book and serve to mislead teachers, parents, and librarians who rely on these tools to select good literature, be it for a read-aloud, storytime, or other programming activities based on the book. The result is a continued perpetuation of demeaning, stereotypical images that serve to debase Mexicans even further.

Such misguided, stereotypical depictions in children's literature only serve to further distort and negatively impact Latino children's own self-image, identity, and literacy development during their formative years. In an era of immigrant bashing, "Juan Crow" laws, and hatred toward "the other," such attitudes fuel anger and resentment of Mexicans, further reinforcing children's misconceptions of what a Mexican is or should be and falsely perpetuating myths and other distorted, harmful views about Mexicans.

In complete contrast to Schachner's outsider-generated stereotypical images, children's author and illustrator Yuyi Morales has created the beloved children's character Señor Calavera, a charming skeleton who first debuted in children's literature in Morales's multiple award-winning title *Just a Minute: A Trickster Tale and Counting Book*.[6] In the sequel, *Just in Case: A Trickster Tale and Spanish Alphabet Book*, Señor Calavera is again the main protagonist, an engaging, clever fellow who is equally charming.[7] He is culled from Morales's own storehouse of local knowledge based on her childhood experiences growing up in a culture steeped in traditions associated with *Dia de los Muertos* (Day of the Dead). Together, the text and illustration form a rich iconic litany of elements familiar to many children from Mexican culture. From the accordion to the jaguar to Lotería games and much more through the letters of the Spanish alphabet, the writer/illustrator engages children in a visually delightful journey. Indeed, with creative language involving both English and Spanish, Señor Calavera uses both humor and *corazón* (heart) in his search for just the right gift to take to Grandma Beetle for her birthday. Additionally, the end pages of the book are skillfully decorated with Morales's own original icons that give credence to new cultural symbols that highlight the importance of artists and books in the life of children. Children unfamiliar with Mexican culture can participate and become engaged in meaningful, fun, and respectful ways while at the same time learning about other cultures and traditions in the Mexican heritage.

In an industry currently straddled with financial market pressures coupled with the rapid changes in the book industry, decisions about which books to publish as hardcover, paperback, or e-book dominate editorial boardroom conversations to the seeming exclusion of more pressing unresolved issues like authentic representation and increasing the production of children's books that reflect the changing face of America and Latino cultures in particular. Publishing houses need to seriously address issues such as diversifying their own staff and challenging their editorial boards to deepen their understanding of the nuances of Latino cultures in order to create a more representative and inclusive selection of books that include quality titles free of contrived, demeaning, and offensive characters like Skippyjon Jones and his exploits.

Young children deserve high-quality reading materials with positive characters and messages that reflect the richness of their diversity and that will ultimately engage and motivate them to want to read. Publishers would do well to expand their mission to ensure that their corporate and social responsibility includes publishing books for all children. Additionally, they must recognize their important role in the continuing development of a new "nation of readers" who deserve access to quality stories that respect rather than mock one's culture and ethnicity and help children to thrive as they develop and grow as readers and learners.

NOTES

1. Nancy Larrick, "The All-White World of Children's Books," *Saturday Review* no. 48 (September 11, 1965): 63–65.
2. Cai Mingshui, "Can We Fly across Cultural Gaps on the Wings of Imagination? Ethnicity, Experience and Cultural Authenticity," in *Stories Matter: The Complexity of Cultural Authenticity in Children's Literature*, ed. Dana L. Fox and Kathy G. Short (Urbana, IL: National Council of Teachers of English, 2003), 167–81.
3. Rudine Sims Bishop, "Mirrors, Windows, and Sliding Glass Doors," *Perspectives* 1, no. 3 (1990): ix–xi.
4. Judy Schachner, *Skippyjon Jones* (New York: Dutton, 2003).
5. Judith Constantinides, "Review of Skippyjon Jones," *School Library Journal*, January 2004, 106.
6. Yuyi Morales, *Just a Minute: A Trickster Tale and Counting Book* (San Francisco: Chronicle Books, 2000).
7. Yuyi Morales, *Just in Case: A Trickster Tale and Spanish Alphabet Book* (New York: Roaring Book, 2008).

SLIDING DOOR 2

Re-Storying Nuestro Barrio

Mentoring Children's Picture Book Writing with Latino/Latina Children's Literature

JESSE GAINER, ANGIE ZAPATA, AND NANCY VALDEZ-GAINER

WHAT CAN YOU DO WITH A PALETA? The simplicity of the question carries profound implications for some, particularly in a diverse classroom of fourth-graders in central Texas. The question is the title of an award-winning children's book written by Carmen Tafolla and illustrated by Magaly Morales.[1] Its cover depicts a whimsical scene of children designing colorful patterns on the ground with melting popsicles. In the background a man appears to be flying while pushing his *paleta* cart as other members of the community enjoy *paletas* in the shade on a warm afternoon. The saturated yellows, pinks, and greens that compose the illustration communicate a warm and friendly tone as the characters' expressions prepare the reader for a playful narrative that will answer the question: What *can* you do with a *paleta*? Tafolla and Morales not only answer this question in pictures and words, but also re-story a *barrio* in political and artful ways that can mentor students' writing and illustrations.

Why did author Carmen Tafolla choose the word *paleta*, Spanish for "popsicle," in her title? Sipe maintains that all art reflects the sociocultural and political contexts in which it is made, and the languages and images within picture books are no exception.[2] As an adult artist, Tafolla is informed by her social conscience. She uses her voice to author stories for present generations of Latino/Latina children to have what she longed for as a child—quality literature that respectfully depicts the story of her barrio. In a discussion at the

Rivera Book Award Tafolla stated, "I wrote this book as an affirmation of the power of *comunidad,* of *barrio,* to heal and nurture and create a beautiful world regardless of one's socio-economic level."[3] Tafolla views her book as a testament to the wealth of cultural resources offered to Latino children living in the barrio, a distinct area often characterized by its history, poverty, and Latino cultural specificity. The author's decision to integrate the term *barrio* in lieu of "neighborhood" signals an understanding of the barrio stories missing from her childhood. She wanted to create a narrative of affirmation in *Paleta,* one that embraces the lives, languages, and literacies of Latino students and clearly communicates the barrio as a context replete with important and desirable seeds for writing and illustrating.

Paleta stories a child's view of life in her barrio. On each page she takes readers on a multi-sensory tour of the sights, smells, and sounds of her neighborhood, demonstrating imaginative uses of a *paleta.* From paintbrush to mini-air conditioner to a way to win a baseball game or a way to say "I love you," a simple treat gives life to everyday events in the barrio. On each page, Morales's illustrations draw on a Latino-influenced palette and style to further develop Tafolla's themes of a caring and loving barrio. The rich colors of the serape and detailed scenes of community further the story's tone and message of a supportive and vibrant neighborhood. The art of Tafolla's writing and Morales's illustration work together to create a counter-narrative—one that addresses a history of deficit-oriented representations of Latino networks in mainstream texts. Though the picture book is not didactic in its approach to addressing issues of essentializing, or reducing all Latino communities to characteristics based in deficit-driven stereotypes, the purposeful and selective lens used by the author and illustrator shapes their resulting picture book. Tafolla and Morales embrace the ideology of power in *comunidad.* As Tafolla states, "it takes a *pueblo* to make a person," and in this book she foregrounds her childhood memories of growing up in the barrio of West San Antonio where "the people of the neighborhood called everyone *mijita.*"[4]

Many educators recognize the incredible value of quality Latino/Latina children's literature as part of a language and literacy curriculum, as does Nancy Valdez-Gainer. Nancy is a fourth-grade bilingual teacher in a school that is predominantly Latino and bilingual in English and Spanish. The authors of this chapter shared this book with her class during a larger author and illustrator study that enjoyed and examined *Paleta* as a potential mentor to guide students in their work as picture book makers and storytellers of their lives and communities. Through a series of interactive read alouds and mini-lessons, we read and reread the book, focusing on different aspects of the craft of writing and illustrating with purposeful intentions to communicate cultural knowledge and experiences. This recursive process conducted with the class allowed students to engage in a deep study of written text, illustrations, and the ways in which text and illustrations work together in picture books to create something bigger than the sum of their parts, what Sipe calls synergy.[5]

The fourth-grade students both appreciated and deconstructed Tafolla's prose and Morales's illustrations while analyzing how synergy communicated meaning, specifically as it related to culture and community. Mini-lessons included exploring specific vocabulary (in English and Spanish), layering of color and language to create tone, designing text and image to show perspective, and styling facial expressions and gesture. We invited students to examine similar artistic practices and incorporate them in their own writing. We also collaborated to design a collective story that included a mural and poem of *nuestra comunidad*. Students wrote in English, in Spanish, and in Spanglish and created detailed illustrations of the sights, sounds, smells, experiences, and feelings of life in their community, much in the spirit of Tafolla and Morales.

With *Paleta* as their guide, students collaboratively re-storied their neighborhood and fashioned a barrio identity as a loving network of caring relationships between children and their parents and among neighbors and others who together make up an extended family. This story, like that of Tafolla and Morales, stands in unambiguous contrast to mainstream depictions of the barrio as "the wrong side of the highway," or the "bad side of town." The students celebrated their work at the Tomás Rivera Book Award celebration by sharing it, and juicy *paletas*, with Tafolla and Morales.

We started with the question: what can you do with a *paleta*? Had Tafolla substituted *paleta* with "popsicle" and Morales illustrated the book in black and white, we might have a different answer. For Nancy and her students and for us, the researchers, *Paleta* functions as a metaphor for the rich cultural and linguistic capital of the Latino community that is often excluded, or distorted and treated as deficit, in mainstream texts. Like many, we contend that all texts are ideological and communicate powerful sociocultural and political messages and that quality Latino literature can mentor students' creations of counter-narratives affirming their communities and the wealth of important stories we all have to share.[6]

NOTES

1. Carmen Tafolla, *What Can You Do with a Paleta?*, ill. Magaly Morales (Berkeley: Tricycle, 2009).
2. Lawrence Sipe, "The Art of the Picturebook," in *Handbook of Research on Children's and Young Adult Literature*, ed. Shelby Wolf, Karen Coats, Patricia Enciso, and Christine Jenkins (New York: Routledge, 2011), 238–52.
3. Carmen Tafolla, "What Can You Do with a Paleta?" (presentation, Tomás Rivera Mexican American Children's Book Award Celebration, San Marcos, TX, October 14, 2010).
4. Ibid.
5. Sipe, "The Art of the Picturebook."
6. Patricia Enciso and Carmen Medina, "Some Words Are Messengers/Hay Palabras Mensajeras: Interpreting Sociopolitical Themes in Latino/a Children's Literature," *New Advocate* 15, no. 1 (2002): 35–47.

Beyond Sari, Hindu Monkey God, and Divali

A Critical Analysis of South Asian Cultures and Childhoods Represented in Picture Books

EUN HYE SON AND YOO KYUNG SUNG

ASIA IS NOT ONE SINGLE COUNTRY, but the world's largest and most populous continent. It is comprised of 46–50 countries, depending on political and geographic definitions, and has a variety of cultures that each country has developed and uniquely celebrates. However, images that many non-Asians have of Asia seem to stem from a few countries in East Asia. This trend is also shown in the representation of Asian countries in children's literature. Over 70 percent of children's books about Asian cultures focus on the countries China, Korea, and Japan.[1] These are the mainstream Asian cultures that dominate the overall images of Asia in children's books.

We started to wonder about other parts of Asia that are not well-represented in children's literature. With this thought lingering in our minds, we looked at a few books about South Asian Indian culture. We were pleasantly surprised to see the depiction of South Asian children's reactions to the sari, a traditional garment worn by females in South Asian countries: the children were captivated by it (see Pooja Makhijani's *Mama's Saris*, Sandhya Rao's *My Mother's Sari*, and Kashmira Sheth's *My Dadima Wears a Sari*). This instantly grabbed our attention because of the difference that we observed in an example from our own culture, from young Korean protagonists who are portrayed constantly resisting the traditional dress their grandmothers wear in *Halmoni and the Picnic* and *Halmoni's Day*. We also found that books about South Asian cultures depict more male figures (e.g., grandfathers and uncles) involved in sharing with the children stories about heritage, while it is usually portrayed as a grandmother's role to "educate" the children about Korean culture. Discussing these differences, we became more curious about the representations of South Asian cultures and children's experiences and attitudes toward their heritage shown in children's literature.

In this chapter, we examined thirty-seven picture books about South Asian countries, such as Afghanistan, Bangladesh, Bhutan, India, Maldives, Nepal, Pakistan, and Sri Lanka. As outsiders of South Asian cultures, we did not focus on exploring the accuracy and authenticity of the representation of South Asian cultures. Rather, we seek to analyze elements and patterns of cultural representation and children's experiences within and around the cultures based on the theories we will discuss in the following section. We believe that South Asia is an important but missing piece of the puzzle necessary to create more comprehensive understandings of Asian cultures through children's literature.

THEORETICAL FRAMEWORKS

The analysis of the representations of cultures and childhood in picture books about South Asian cultures was informed by concepts of culture as thick description and interpretive reproduction in childhood studies and colonialism.[2]

Culture as Thick Description

Culture is defined differently by a variety of scholars. Some consider culture external, observable, and describable, yet something they claim not to have.[3] Others define culture as something ordinary that is part of life at all levels.[4] Critical theorists argue that the dominant society has defined what is of cultural worth and has marginalized people and ways of knowing.[5] In this study we adopted Geertz's concept of culture as thick description that is beyond observable and describable. According to Geertz, culture is "the shared patterns that set the tone, character and quality of people's lives."[6] These patterns include language, religion, gender, relationships, class, ethnicity, race, disability, age, sexual orientation, family structures, nationality, and rural/suburban/urban communities. They go beyond external characteristics to include the values, symbols, interpretations, and perspectives held by a group of people.

Interpretive Reproduction

Interpretive reproduction is a concept of socialization in which children participate to create or maintain memberships in those societies.[7] It claims socialization does not consist of mere actions of adaptation and internalization of the adult's world but requires a process of appropriation, reinvention, and reproduction.[8] It emphasizes children's practical activities in their production of and participation in their own peer cultures.[9] Peer culture is "a stable set of activities or routines, artifacts, values, and concerns that children produce and share in interaction with peers."[10] Corsaro claims that children create and participate in their own unique peer cultures by creatively taking or appropriating information from the adult world to address their own peer concerns.[11]

Colonialism

Loomba states that "knowledge about 'the Orient' as it was produced and circulated in Europe was an ideological accompaniment of colonial 'power.'"[12] Said argues that Europe characterizes the Orient as alien and features it on a theatrical stage that is established and arranged for and in service to Europe.[13] Just as the power structure is set against the Orient, Nodelman maintains that images of childhood in children's literature are constructed and controlled by adults who produce, distribute, analyze, and purchase children's books.[14] Authors who are most likely adults suggest what childhood should be like based on their definitions and perceptions of childhood experiences. Nodelman states that "contemporary children's literature is filled with images of childhood experience that accord more with Wordsworth's visions of idyllic childhood innocence than with the realities of modern children's lives."[15]

BOOK SELECTION AND ANALYSIS

We started our search of picture books about South Asia at a website (www.poojamakhijani.com/sakidlit.html) owned by the author Pooja Makhijani. It provides a comprehensive list of children's books about South Asian culture. In order to ensure a thorough search, we searched other databases and websites, including the Children's Literature Comprehensive Database, Novelist, WorldCat, and Amazon. We used names of countries (e.g., Bangladesh, India, Nepal) as keywords to locate the books. After locating picture books about South Asia, we narrowed them down to thirty-seven contemporary realistic fiction pieces ranging from 1987 to 2010 by reading the synopses of the stories.

To systematically examine thirty-seven books, we implemented three layers of analyses. First, we wrote down our first responses to the books. We wanted to record them so that we did not lose our initial thoughts, emotions, and connections to the books after multiple rounds of analysis. The initial responses guided us to find emerging patterns and themes. Then we conducted literary analysis by closely examining plots, characters, and settings. Doing the literary analysis helped us devise our own three categories (i.e., diaspora literature, global literature, and touristic literature) that we organize the books into. Lastly, we reanalyzed each group of books focusing on the two aspects, representations of culture and the young protagonists' childhood experiences within and around the cultures. For the cultural representation analysis, we collected all the cultural elements presented in the books and searched for patterns in each group of books. Employing Geertz's theory, we further investigated which elements of culture are emphasized and which are silenced. Then we explored childhood experiences that South Asian children have within the cultures, situated in the concept of interpretive reproduction. We employed colonialism to interpret and discuss our findings about images of childhood portrayed in the books.

THREE TYPES OF BOOKS IN
LITERATURE ABOUT SOUTH ASIAN CHILDREN

We grouped the thirty-seven books into eight countries and three categories (shown in figure 5.1) and found that two countries, Bhutan and Maldives, were not included in the collection. Because twenty-five of the thirty-seven books portrayed India, it follows that most of the other represented countries were not adequately portrayed. The limited number of the books made it difficult to show the diverse facets of rich cultures and lives of the people in these countries. For instance, both books about Nepal describe the Sherpa, a small ethnic group from the most mountainous region in Nepal who guide trekkers to the Himalayas, yet there are many other ethnic groups that could also have been depicted. The three books about Afghanistan are limited to children's lives in a war or refugee camp, providing one important but limited aspect of life for Afghan children.

Our three categories are different from those of Rudine Sims Bishop, which she discusses in *Shadow and Substance: Afro-American Experience in Contemporary Children's Fiction*.[16] Her three categories are social conscience books, melting pot books, and culturally conscious books. Stemming from a thorough analysis of the books about African American community and culture, Bishop's categories are based on the books' purposes, their depictions of African Americans, and their target audience. For example, the social conscience books are written mainly to help white people know the state and lives of blacks in the United States. The melting pot books written for any group of readers show that African American children are not different from other American children except for their skin color. The culturally conscious books are written for African American readers to reflect their experiences that are unique as well as universal from the perspective of an African American child or family.

On the other hand, our categories are broader since we investigated books about a region of Asia that consists of multiple countries. In order to be more inclusive, we employed settings and characters as a guideline in grouping our collections. First, diaspora literature is set outside of South Asian countries, mostly in the United States. Books in this category describe the experiences of South Asian diasporas including immigrants, their descendants, and biracial children. Second, *global literature*

	Diaspora Literature	Global Literature	Touristic Literature
Afghanistan		Nasreen's Secret School Four Feet, Two Sandals The Roses in My Carpet	
Bhutan		Yasmin's Hammar	
Bhutan			
India	Bringing Asha Home Mama's Saris Chachaji's Cup The Closet Ghosts The Happiest Tree Ashok by Any Other Name Lights for Gita A Gift for Gita Roses for Gita My Mother's Sari My Name Is Bilal My Dadima Wears a Sari The Road to Mumbai Romina's Rangoli Siddharth and Rinki Divali Rose	Monsoon Monsoon Afternoon Kali and the Rat Snake Cherry Tree Trash! On Ragpicker Children and Recycling	Audrey and Barbara Lily's Garden of India Finders Keepers?
Maldives			
Nepal		Kami and the Yaks Pemba Sherpa Namaste!	
Pakistan	Nadia's Hands	Silly Chicken Ruler of the Courtyard King of the Skies	
Sri Lanka		Umbrella Thief Tea Leaves	

Figure 5.1: Picture books about South Asia

is set in South Asian countries and portrays the lives of South Asians who reside in their home countries. Global literature is often understood as world literature that is set outside the United States or written by persons other than Americans with settings that are unidentified.[17] Third, touristic literature, coined by us, refers to the books about non-South

Asian characters who travel to South Asian countries and introduce the cultures in their perspectives. In the following section, we will discuss the three categories of the collections—diaspora, global, and touristic literature—and how each portrays children's experiences and South Asian cultures. Then, we will focus on diaspora literature to examine how children's lives intersect with cultural events or cultural practices.

Diaspora Literature

Diaspora literature describes the lives of South Asians who are dispersed outside their traditional homelands, as well as their children who were born and raised in the United States and other countries. We collectively refer to them as diaspora to be inclusive of South Asian populations who do not resides in their motherlands or maintain their heritage in one way or another. The books in this group portray the diaspora's daily lives and conflicts navigating among multiple cultures; adoption; celebration of traditional festivals and weddings; and learning more about their own heritage.

Our analysis indicates diaspora literature includes a variety of cultural elements such as holidays, traditional practices, names, food, history, clothing, geography, and so on. Almost all cultural elements we found fall into the 5F level of cultures: festivals, food, folktales, fashion, and famous people.[18] Applying Stuart Hall's cultural iceberg model, they belong to the tip of the iceberg, which are visible and easily identifiable parts of the culture.[19] The invisible part of the cultural iceberg, which is similar to Geertz's concept of culture as thick description, is important because it underlies and explains the external aspects of culture. Focusing too much on the visible culture may result in a loss of depth of cultural understanding. However, the books in this category rarely convey cultural values, beliefs, or perspectives behind the external cultural practices.

Global Literature

The books in this category illustrate South Asians in their homelands. These stories portray children located in their original homelands and involved in diverse experiences such as reading the weather, herding yaks, catching snakes, kite fighting, living in refugee camps, and overcoming fear. Most stories are specific to South Asian cultures and are family-oriented, but rarely portray children interacting with peers.

The superficial level of cultural elements shown in diaspora literature is not emphasized in global literature. In fact, these cultural elements are portrayed as a part of their everyday lives in the illustrations. Many South Asian women are illustrated wearing saris, and the pictures show elephants and cows roaming around the streets. Nevertheless, they are not the main aspect of the stories. Global literature rather focuses on exploring local cultures or unique political situations in South Asian countries. *Kali and the Rat Snakes* depicts a village that is well known for catching snakes. Kali, in the beginning, is ashamed of his village because it is different from other typical ones, but later learns to take pride in it after saving the day by catching a snake that invaded his classroom. Two books, *Pemba Sherpa* and *Kami and the Yaks*, portray the lives and experiences of Sherpas who guide and help trekkers in the Himalayas. *King of the Skies* describes a young kite fighter's exciting experience in Pakistan. Three books about Afghanistan illustrate children's experiences, friendships, and struggles in a war and refugee camp. Since global literature tends to focus on local culture and unique situations, the stories are often set in rural areas. This reveals "exotic" and foreign aspects of South Asian cultures, but at the same time suppresses contemporary understandings. This unbalanced portrayal may reinforce primitive assumptions about South Asian cultures.

Touristic Literature

The third group, touristic literature, revolves around introducing South Asian cultures. The three books in this category use travel as a main theme to provide a brief overview of the target culture. Because of the limited length of picture books, the cultural representations usually end up as surface-level surveys of cultures. Information is not embedded in the context but straightforwardly provided because there is not much storyline. *Lily's Garden of India* presents information about South Indian culture in relation to the cultural practices, lives, and beliefs of Indians regarding plants. *Barbara and Audrey* describes the process of two friends getting ready to take a trip from the United States to India. Audrey's excitement reveals brief, but somewhat stereotypical, information about India, for example, turbans, snake in the pot, and greetings. *Finders Keepers* follows an American tourist taking a bus trip in India. His journey takes readers to different places such as a village and Mt. Abu in the state of Rajasthan, giving a glimpse of daily lives in northwest India (e.g., language, religion, clothing, and lifestyles).

SOUTH ASIAN CHILDREN'S CHILDHOODS REPRESENTED IN DIASPORA LITERATURE

In the three categories of books, children's lives are intertwined with cultures. Especially in diaspora literature, children show more interest in culture because it is their heritage that makes them different from the mainstream. In this section, we discuss how children's lives and cultures are represented in diaspora literature, or more specifically what aspects of diaspora children's experiences are emphasized or omitted when they interact with others both inside and outside their cultures.

South Asian Children Interacting with Culture

Despite different facets of cultures presented in diaspora, global, and touristic literature, young protagonists have overall similar attitudes toward them: they do not resist them, but are willing to accept them (many of them have already accepted them as their proud heritage). Their affirmative attitudes toward their heritage are shown in most diaspora literature about South Asian cultures. Neel loves drinking tea, listening to folktales about the monkey god, family history, and Indian history in *Chachaji's Cup*, and Gita is eager to celebrate the Divali festival with her friends in *Light for Gita*. In the three books *Mama's Sari*, *My Mother's Sari*, and *My Dadima Wears a Sari*, children are excited about the sari. Firmly founded in positive attitudes toward heritage, South Asian children appropriate culture to solve the problems they encounter. In *The Happiest Tree*, Meena, a clumsy Indian American girl, has a hard time becoming a still tree in the class play. By taking yoga class, she learns to calm herself down and stay still on the stage. In *Ghosts in the Closet*, Anu, who is new to town, becomes scared of ghosts in the closet. In order to overcome the fear, she asks Hanumanji, the monkey god, for help. In these two stories, Meena and Anu make an interpretive reproduction of South Asian culture.[20] They take yoga and Hanumanji contextualized in Indian culture and reinterpret the meanings of them to address their own concerns. They do not consider culture an abstract tradition, but adopt it to be a part of their daily lives.

In addition, South Asian children with strong cultural pride do not hesitate to share their culture with non-South Asian American friends. We call them "disciples of tradition" because of their faithful devotion to their heritage. They have internalized pride in their heritage and actively employ it to solve problems. They are also enthusiastic about sharing their traditions with others. In *Bringing Asha Home*, *Light for Gita*, and *Chachaji's Cup*, all of the young protagonists provide their friends with information about cultural practices; invite them over for the feast of Divali; and enjoy chai tea and South Asian food together. Their non-Asian friends do not resist unfamiliar cultural elements, but support them by joining the celebrations.

Unfortunately, but more realistically, the disciples of tradition are not always welcome, but sometimes confront "persecution" from the mainstream culture. They are conscious of the differences that their heritage creates in their lives and peers' perceptions of the dissimilarities. Nadia in *Nadia's Hands* is concerned that the *mehndi*, the art of applying henna to the hands, that she got at her aunt's wedding will distinguish and isolate her from her peers at school. Other characters, such as Bilal in *My Name is Bilal* and Ashok in *Ashok by Any Other Name*, undergo similar situations. They want to fit in, but their unique names make it difficult to blend in with their peers' culture.

South Asian Children Interacting with Others around the Culture

Culture is not an isolated unit that an individual can make available, but is embodied in public symbols that members of a society communicate through.[21] South Asian children maintain their memberships in a range of affiliations through interacting with multiple members of different groups. Among them, elders are portrayed as the most significant group that South Asian children interact with. They are physically close to the children, as well as actively involved in their cultural practices and experiences. Elders in families are internal cultural experts who provide knowledge and experiences of culture to children who are curious about their heritage. In *Elephant Dance* and *Chachaji's Cup,* an uncle and grandfather share many stories about the Indian culture. They also support young family members with comfort and sentiments based on their previous experiences, which makes cultural experiences more comforting and enjoyable for the children. In *Monsoon Afternoon,* Dadima (grandfather) shares with his grandson a story about a peacock that confirms their connection, and at the same time enjoys playing with the boy in monsoon rains. Shared membership in the family enhances mutual understanding of cultural practices, experiences, and problems.

Community elders, including teachers and neighbors, open doors for children to learn more about their heritage. Using their roles as teachers, they create opportunities for confused protagonists to confirm pride in their heritage and cultural identity. For example, a teacher in *Romina's Rangoli* gives an assignment to construct symbols that represent her half-Mexican and half-Indian heritage. Teachers in *Ashok by Any Other Name* and *My Name Is Bilal* guide the children to learn the meanings of their names. The yoga instructor who runs a grocery store in *The Happiest Tree* provides yoga skills for Meena to be a still tree in her class play. While teachers guide the children to gain more understanding of their heritage, neighbor elders in *Roses for Gita* and *Divali Rose* provide more subtle help for children to get closer to their heritage. They cause tensions and misunderstanding in the beginning but lead to successful celebration of Divali and Indian Rose.

The emphasis on interactions with elders sacrifices another important culture—peer culture—for children. Compared with elder groups, peer group relationships are not portrayed much in South Asian children's lives. Except for the main characters, other children are hardly visible in the books. Peer interactions, when they appear, are often used as a tool to promote cultural experiences. For example, friends are invited to be part of heritage learning. Peers' marginalized status makes it difficult to contribute to constructing South Asian children's childhood experiences. We speculate this may reflect adult writers' agenda of controlling and romanticizing childhood, as Nodelman argues.[22] They determine that young disciples of tradition are ideal images for South Asian children, ignoring other varied and authentic aspects of childhood. This agenda also portrays South Asian children as exotic beings, which distinguishes them from the children of the West. The "otherness" imposed on them may create distance for readers and limit a chance to read about the diverse diaspora's voices.

CONCLUSION

We examined thirty-seven picture books depicting South Asian cultures based on Geertz's concept of culture, Corsaro's interpretive reproduction, and Said and Nodelman's colonialism. Examining three categories (diaspora, global, and touristic literature), we found that each category displays different issues, conflicts, and cultural elements. One of the recurring patterns we observe is that the young protagonists' childhood is centered on traditional features of South Asian cultures. This naturally focuses more on the interactions between the children and family elders, that is, cultural experts, which strengthen adults' contributions to the stories. When the existence of cultural experts is prevalent, other aspects of childhood experiences may be minimized. Even though this is a realistic depiction of a close-knit family culture in South Asian community, when it is excessively emphasized it may lead to overrepresenting traditional contexts of childhood and at the same time underrepresenting children's own peer culture. Literature for children where older cultural experts replace child peers can teach young readers otherness with the absence of their own culture. This appears to contribute to the neglect of contemporary peer culture, as well as reinforcing the images of young disciples of tradition, which we suspect reflect adults' preference for young South Asians to maintain their close cultural, familial connections.

CHILDREN'S LITERATURE

Arnett, Robert A. *Finders Keepers? A True Story*. Illustrated by Smita Turakhia. Columbus, GA: Atman, 2003.

Bercaw, Edna C. *Halmoni's Day*. Illustrated by Robert Hunt. New York: Penguin, 2000.

Bond, Ruskin. *Cherry Tree*. Illustrated by Allan Eitzen. Honesdale, PA: Caroline House, 1991.

Choi, Sook R. *Halmoni and the Picnic*. Illustrated by Karen Dugan. Boston: Houghton, 1993.

Cohn, Diana. *Namaste!* Illustrated by Amy Córdova. Great Barrington, MA: Steiner-Books, 2009.

Cossi, Olga. *Pemba Sherpa*. Illustrated by Gary Bernard. Longmont, CO: Odyssey Books, 2009.

English, Karen. *Nadia's Hands*. Illustrated by Jonathan Weiner. Honesdale, PA: Boyds Mills, 1999.

Farmer, Addy. *Siddharth and Rinki*. Illustrated by Karin Littlewood. London: Tamarind, 2009.

Gilmore, Rachna. *A Gift for Gita*. Illustrated by Alice Priestley. London: Mantra, 1998.

———. *Lights for Gita*. Illustrated by Alice Priestley. Gardiner, ME: Tilbury House, 1994.

———. *Roses for Gita*. Illustrated by Alice Priestley. Toronto: Second Story.

Heine, Theresa. *Elephant Dance: Memories of India*. Illustrated by Shella Moxley. Cambridge, MA: Barefoot Books, 2004.

Iyengar, Malathi M. *Romina's Rangoli*. Illustrated by Jennifer Wanardi. Fremont, CA: Shen's Books, 2007.

Jeyaveeran, Ruth. *The Road to Mumbai*. Boston: Houghton Mifflin, 2004.

Khan, Ruksana. *King of the Skies*. Illustrated by Laura Fernandez and Rick Jacobsen. Canada: Scholastic, 2001.

———. *The Roses in My Carpets*. Illus. Ronald Himler. New York: Holiday House, 1998.

———. *Ruler of the Courtyard*. Illustrated by Gregory R. Christie. New York: Viking, 2003.

———. *Silly Chicken*. Illustrated by Yunmee Kyong. New York: Viking, 2005.

Krishnaswami, Uma. *Bringing Asha Home*. Illustrated by Jamel Akib. New York: Lee & Low Books, 2006.

———. *Chachaji's Cup*. Illustrated by Sourmya Sitaraman. San Francisco: Children's Book, 2003.

———. *The Closet Ghosts*. Illustrated by Shiraaz Bhabha. San Francisco: Children's Book, 2006.

———. *The Happiest Tree: A Yoga Story*. Illustrated by Ruth Jeyaveeran. New York: Lee & Low Books, 2005.

———. *Monsoon*. Illustrated by Jamel Akib. New York: Farrar, Straus, and Giroux, 2003.

Lawson, Janet. *Audrey and Barbara*. New York: Atheneum Books for Young Readers, 2002.

Lipp, Frederick. *Tea Leaves*. Illustrated by Lester Coloma. New York: Mondo, 2003.

Makhijani, Pooja. *Mama's Saris*. Illustrated by Elena Gomez. New York: Little, Brown, 2007.

Malaspina, Ann. *Yasmin's Hammer*. Illustrated by Doug Chayka. New York: Lee & Low Books, 2010.

Mobin-Uddin, Asma. *My Name Is Bilal*. Illustrated by Barbara Kiwak. Honesdale, PA: Boyds Mills, 2005.

Rahaman, Vashanti. *Divali Rose*. Illustrated by Jamel Akib. Honesdale, PA: Boyds Mills, 2008.

Rao, Sandhya. *My Mother's Sari*. Illustrated by Nina Sabnani. New York: North South Books, 2006.

Sheth, Kashmira. *Monsoon Afternoon*. Illustrated by Yoshiko Jaeggi. Atlanta, GA: Peachtree, 2008.

———. *My Dadima Wears a Sari*. Illustrated by Yoshiko Jaeggi. Atlanta, GA: Peachtree, 2007.

Smith, Jeremy. *Lily's Garden of India*. Illustrated by Rob Hefferan. Columbus, OH: Gingham Dog, 2003.

Stryer, Andrea S. *Kami and the Yaks*. Illustrated by Bert Dodson. Palo Alto, CA: Bay Otter, 2007.

Wettasinghe, Sybil. *The Umbrella Thief*. Illustrated by Cathy Hirano. New York: Kane/Miller, 1987.

Whitaker, Zai. *Kali and the Rat Snake*. Illustrated by Srividya Natarajan. La Jolla, CA: Kane/Miller, 2006.

Williams, Karen. L., and Khadra Mohammed. *Four Feet, Two Sandals*. Illustrated by Doug Chayka. Grand Rapids, MI: Eerdmans Books for Young Readers, 2007.

Winter, Jeanette. *Nasreen's Secret School: A True Story from Afghanistan*. New York: Beach Lane Books, 2009.

Wolf, Gita, and Anushka Ravinshankar. *Trash! On Ragpicker Children and Recycling*. Illustrated by Orijit Sen. India: Tara, 2003.

Yamate, Sandara. S. *Ashok by Any Other Name*. Illustrated by Janice Tohinaka. Chicago: Polychrome, 1992.

NOTES

1. Shwu-yi Leu, "Reimagining a Pluralistic Society through Children's Fiction about Asian Pacific Americans, 1990–1999," *New Advocate* 14, no. 2 (2001): 127–42.
2. Clifford Geertz, *Interpretation of Cultures* (New York: Basic Books, 1973); William A. Corsaro, *The Sociology of Childhood*, 3rd ed. (Los Angeles: SAGE, 2011); Edward Said, "Imaginative Geography and Its Representations: Orientalizing the Oriental," in *Race Critical Theories*, edited P. Essed and D. T. Goldberg (Oxford: Blackwell, 2000), 15–37; and Ania Loomba, *Colonialism/Postcolonialism* (London: Routledge, 2005).
3. Matthew Arnold, *Culture and Anarchy* (New York: Macmillan, 1882).
4. Nelson Brooks, "Culture—A New Frontier," *Foreign Language Annuals* 5, no. 1 (1971): 54–61; Geertz, *Interpretations of Culture*.
5. Antonia Darder, *Culture and Power in the Classroom: A Critical Foundation for Bicultural Education* (Cambridge, MA: Bergin & Garvey, 2000); Antonio Gramsci, *Selections from the Prison Notebooks* (New York: International, 1971).
6. Geertz, *Interpretation of Cultures*, 216.
7. Corsaro, *Sociology of Childhood*.
8. Allison James, Chris Jenks, and Alan Prout, *Theorizing Childhood* (New York: Teachers College, 1998).
9. Barbara Rogoff, "Developmental Transitions in Children's Participation in Socio-Cultural Activities," in *The Five to Seven Year Shift: The Age of Reason and Responsibility*, ed. A. Sameroff and M. Haith (Chicago: University of Chicago Press, 1996), 273–94.
10. Corsaro, *Sociology of Childhood*, 21.
11. Corsaro, *Sociology of Childhood*.
12. Loomba, *Colonialism/Postcolonialism*, 42.
13. Said, "Imaginative Geography."
14. Perry Nodelman, "The Other: Orientialism, Colonialism, and Children's Literature," *Children's Literature Association Quarterly* 17, no. 1 (1992): 29–35.
15. Ibid., 31.
16. Rudine Sims Bishop, *Shadow and Substance: Afro-American Experience in Contemporary Children's Fiction* (Urbana, IL: National Council of Teachers of English, 1982).
17. Barbara A. Lehman, Evelyn B. Freeman, and Patricia L. Sharer, *Reading Globally, K–8: Connecting Students to the World through Literature* (Thousand Oaks, CA: Corwin, 2010).
18. Elsie Begler, "Global Cultures: The First Steps toward Understanding," *Social Understanding* 62, no. 5 (1998): 272–75.
19. Edward T. Hall, *Beyond Culture* (New York: Doubleday, 1976).
20. Corsaro, *Sociology of Childhood*.
21. Geertz, *Interpretation of Cultures*.
22. Nodelman, "The Other."

"That's So Chamorro"

Representations of Culture in Chamorro Realistic Fiction

MONIQUE STORIE

THE CHAMORROS OF THE Mariana Islands have been invisible members of the United States community for more than a century. Even though Guam became associated with the United States in 1898 and the other Mariana Islands followed suit in 1947, what most Americans have heard about these Pacific islands is their impact on American history, such as Guam was a spoil in the Spanish-American War and Tinian was a key battle site for World War II. This focus and the archipelago's geographic distance from the continental United States have kept these Native Pacific Islanders' presence essentially hidden a half a world away. As the Chamorro population within the nation continues to grow (the U.S. Census approximates there are about 92,000 Chamorros nationwide, including 24,820 children), the need to understand the Chamorro sense of reality increases.[1] Given the vast distance between the Mariana Islands and the United States mainland, stories are an effective way of learning about one of the nation's fastest-growing populations.[2] This chapter focuses on how Chamorro realistic fiction not only reminds the mainland Chamorros of home but also creates their voice within the American community.

THE CHAMORRO PEOPLE

Chamorros are the indigenous people from the Mariana Islands, a thirteen-island archipelago in the western Pacific Ocean, and the third largest Native Pacific Islander group in the United States.[3] There are about 177,000 Chamorros, but only 84,000 members reside in the home islands of Guam, Saipan, Tinian, and Rota.[4] The other half have taken up residence in the U.S. mainland, with most congregating in the West Coast, where Chamorro social organizations have developed to maintain social ties and practice the culture.

Today's Chamorro culture has Pacific, Asian, and Western roots. The ancestors of the Chamorro people are said to have been seafaring explorers of Indo-Malayo descent who settled in the islands between 2000 B.C. and 1500 B.C. By the time of first contact with European explorers in 1521, this group had developed a subsistence economy and culture characterized by gender-based division of labor and a complex network of reciprocal exchanges. Spain formally claimed the Mariana Islands and, by 1668, established its first Catholic mission in Guam. Under the Spanish crown, the Chamorro people developed a bilingual/bicultural society where islanders exhibited Spanish mannerisms in public but Chamorro ones in the home.[5] Native observances gave way to Catholic rites, but oral traditions and social customs remained focused on the Pacific ideals of interdependence and cooperation.

The end of the Spanish-American War separated the Mariana Islands both politically and culturally. The Treaty of Paris ceded Guam to the United States while the other Mariana Islands became possessions of Germany and then Japan. Over the next century, each island's cultural practices were influenced by the groups with which they interacted, that is, Guam's Chamorro culture was imbued with American practices, while the Chamorro culture in the northern islands exhibited significant influence by the Carolinian people (who had settled into the islands during a period of Spanish *reducción*) and a smattering of German and Japanese influence. Today, the Chamorro culture is described as having two parts: the core values that trace back to pre-contact society and social practices that were influenced by external cultures.[6]

IMAGES OF CULTURE IN CHAMORRO REALISTIC FICTION

Storytelling and oral traditions remain a relatively rich component of many Pacific cultures. Micronesian, Polynesian, and Melanesian cultures use oral traditions to entertain, teach proper behavior, and highlight important social values. Storytelling is used to strengthen communal ties and express identity. In many cases, the written form of Pacific literature began with stories from American or European authors who emphasized the exoticism of the region rather than with stories that evolved from traditional storytelling practices.[7] Described as "one of the youngest in the world," Pacific literature grew out of the movement by indigenous scholars to include native voices and realities in the region's literary canon.[8] The simultaneous presence of these literary styles has resulted in Pacific Islanders' literary expectations changing to include both Western and indigenous storytelling techniques.[9] As a result, contemporary Pacific children's literature is defined on one side by this synthesis of literary expectations and on the other by the islanders' cultural worldviews.

The Chamorros are a prime example of how literature has developed in the Pacific. They have oral traditions and customs that reflect almost

4,000 years of existence, but their written literary heritage is only about a hundred years old, considered young even by Pacific standards.[10] Until about the mid-twentieth century, Chamorros relied on oral traditions for entertainment and cultural instruction before they began to write down stories with the idea of sharing them with future generations. With only a scant half-century of history to its name, Chamorro children's literature is best described as being emergent. Interestingly, its brief existence has been rich enough to create a sense of an authentic Chamorro voice and acceptable cultural representations.

Imagery plays a role in creating that initial credibility in a story. Since the Mariana Islands are considered home to the Chamorros, images of tropical environments and local landmarks help to create a believable sense of place. Local place names (e.g. Agana/*Hagåtña*, Double Reef), familiar pastimes (swimming, barbecuing, hiking through *halom tano*), flora (orchids, coconut trees), and fauna (carabaos, crabs, pigs, geckos) help establish an island setting, while a Chamorro sense of place is drawn out through little details connected to the characters. For instance, the box of envelopes Toni's grandmother uses for funeral donations and Tata's angst in trying to figure out an appropriate donation after the loss of their *chenchule* book—the family's record of who have assisted them and their donations—are meaningful cultural images in *Attitude 13: A Daughter of Guam's Collection of Short Stories*.[11] They show characters in real-life situations and allude to the importance of helping and supporting one another in times of need. Similarly, *Dolphin Day* illustrates the familiar sight of children wearing *zoris*, or flip-flops, to the beach while their stateside cousin wears sneakers.[12] The way names are used also can increase or decrease the sense of realism. Given names within the family, such as the names Aunt Bernadette or Aunt Minerva in *Keeper of the Night*, seem inauthentic.[13] Instead, nicknames, for example, Kiko for Francisco in *Duendes Hunter* and Deding for Mercedes in *Lola's Journey Home*, indicate the level of intimacy that family shares, creating that sense of realism.[14]

Chamorro personalities are diverse but a few archetypes exist. For example, grandparents, especially grandmothers, play an important role in Chamorro childhood. The grandmother archetype is a strong-willed woman who manages a household with a firm hand but shows her love through small acts like cooking. Chamorro children tend to have dual personalities: reserved and respectful among adults but carefree and boisterous among their peers. So the Chamorro cousin archetype would be a companion, an advisor, and an immediate link to family. The Chamorro sense of place is also revealed through themes that reflect cultural issues. Themes of resiliency and "being Chamorro enough" are extremely poignant as islanders try to find a balance between tradition and progress and between their past and their present.[15]

Until recently, Chamorro society has not had a strong material culture. Instead, culture was maintained through people's actions.[16] Since Pacific literary theory suggests that evaluation of literature should be grounded in the value system of the community depicted, it stands to reason that the presentation of cultural values and practices within a story would be an integral part of evaluating a Chamorro story. While some disagreement exists regarding the overall composition of the Chamorro value system, the irrefutable core values are *inafa'maolek*, family, and respect. Therefore, authentic Chamorro literature should include appropriate reflections or meaningful explorations of these attributes.

Inafa'maolek *and Family*

The concepts of *inafa'maolek* and family are considered central to the Chamorro value system and are often explained together. A difficulty in explaining them separately is that "many of the expectations and actions used to describe *inafa'maolek* [such as everybody working together at the ranch or family coming together to support a family member in need] applies to family." In distinguishing between the two, "*inafa'maolek* is concerned with how a person behaves and family focuses on who a person is."[17] In tandem, the two values create a blueprint of how Chamorros carry themselves when interacting with others.

Inafa'maolek, the most basic building block of the Chamorro value system, encourages cooperation and seeks to put community needs above individual desires. *Inafa'maolek* is learned from an early age through familial interactions, such as when an older sibling helps a younger one with homework. It is seen when a man shares tomatoes, avocados, or fish with his cousin or when neighbors help put up a canopy for a party. Within the community, it can take many forms; but, in all of its forms, *inafa'maolek* demonstrates that "each person is mutually responsible for the well-being of others."[18] Within the realm of story, *inafa'maolek* is best shown through depictions of togetherness, such as characters sharing, characters taking care of one another, or a character keeping quiet rather than boast loudly about a personal success or triumph.

Inafa'maolek is carried out by acts of sharing. In *Grandma's Love* the narrator reminds her grandchildren about the importance of sharing while the illustrations capture ways of sharing, such as going to church as a family, visiting relatives, or spending time with a grandparent.[19] The families in Evelyn Flores's "Island Cousins" series demonstrate how this value is important in everyday activities as well as in times of tragedy. In *Dolphin Day*, the characters are constantly interacting with each other, from going off-roading to visiting the beach to visiting each other's houses. In *Isa's Avocado Tree*, family members work together to prepare for the upcoming typhoon: Isa's mom prepares food, her father and Davy board up the house, and Isa takes care of the clothes.[20] As the storm nears, Isa's father invites their neighbors to wait out the storm with them. Throughout the story, Isa's family is shown sharing the workload as well as sharing what they have (food and shelter) with others.

Inafa'maolek is present when characters perform acts of kindness. For example, Davy brings Isa an avocado seedling after hers is destroyed in the storm in *Isa's Avocado Tree*. His action is considered a sign of *inafa'maolek* because Davy is trying to help Isa move beyond her grief and start over. In the short story "Resurfacing" from *Attitude 13*, the character Maia gives Raina, a girl she has just met, a set of clothes and a ride to *Hagåtña* so Raina can look for her family. Maia's actions are *inafa'maolek* because they demonstrate genuine concern and a sense of responsibility for another person.

Interestingly, not all acts of providing assistance are a part of *inafa'maolek*. While Chamorros might talk about helping each other as a family obligation, they make a clear distinction between obligation and *inafa'maolek*. Acts of assistance are considered an obligation when there is an expectation that these services will be repaid through monetary compensation, a favor returned later, or by public praise. In contrast, *inafa'maolek* is performed "willingly and [with] sincere concern or affection for another person."[21] It is this distinction that weakens *Keeper of the Night* as a Chamorro story. Two prominent characters in the story are the protagonist's aunts Minerva and Bernadette. Aunt Bernadette is depicted as a happy-go-lucky woman who will go anywhere or do anything for her sister's children. In contrast, Aunt Minerva is depicted as a Catholic zealot who takes in her grieving brother and his kids because it was expected. Minerva's stern and unforgiving attitude towards the children suggests that she did not feel any affection for them. Within the Chamorro community, some might be able to see Minerva as a plausible character, but others see her attitude as so far removed from acceptable Chamorro behavior that Minerva becomes an inauthentic representation.[22]

Inafa'maolek is also about keeping peace and harmony. In *Isa's Avocado Tree*, the character of Mama exemplifies how Chamorros use humor to maintain harmony within a community. When she makes a joke about Tony Boy keeping the bread warm by sitting on it, Mama discreetly saves him and his family from further embarrassment. In *Dolphin Day*, Little Girl tries to help her cousins end their rivalry. Similarly, the *suruhana* (Chamorro traditional female healer) in *Lola's Journey Home* demonstrates how maintaining harmony with nature is just as important as keeping peace between family members.

For most Chamorros, maintaining peace in the family is important because family is their source of support and identity. Within a story, family should be a constant. Good depictions show grandparents as actively involved in their grandchildren's upbringing, such as Grandma Deding in *Lola's Journey Home* and Nana in *Duendes Hunter* sharing stories with their granddaughters, or the grandfather in *Grandpa's Love* telling his grandkids about being Chamorro while fixing his net. Likewise, cousins are an important part of the Chamorro family structure. For example, in the short story "Sand" from *Attitude 13*, Captain Mom's comfort in knowing Ha'ani's cousins will help her through another deployment reinforces the idea that cousins play a special role in the family structure. Similarly, Georgie and Frankie figure out that they need to rely on each other in order to survive their ordeal at Double Reef in *Dolphin Day*. In other words, cousins are more than the companions depicted in *Endless Summer* and *Lola's Journey Home*; rather, they also act as the next generation of support. By interacting with their cousins, Chamorro children learn that the whole family ensures companionship, love, support, and a sense of identity. In essence, Chamorros see family as the social structure that reminds them of what is important and who they are.

Respect

The value of respect is so deeply embedded in the Chamorro way of life that respectful behaviors are often carried out without much thought about their meaning. Chamorros explain respect as the kissing of a relative on the cheek or an elder on the hand. Succinctly, respect is easy to demonstrate but difficult to define. What can be surmised is that respect is connected to *inafa'maolek* in that it ensures that younger Chamorros develop a sense of humility so that they work towards community goals rather than individualistic needs and they develop an appreciation for older members for the knowledge and wisdom they possess.[23] Within a story, actions of respect are central to developing the strong feeling of community and interdependency of the characters.

Chamorros show respect through formal and informal actions. The ultimate demonstration of respect is the *manginge'*, or "taking [an] elder's right hand upon meeting and kissing it."[24] Two stories include powerful examples of *manginge'*. In *Grandma's Love*, a young girl, holding an older woman's downturned right hand in her own upturned right hand, bends down to bring the older woman's hand up to her nose. This illustration depicts the way the *manginge'* is properly carried out. The illustration of the *manginge'* in *Lola's Journey Home* is a little more complex because it shows Lola using her left hand to Grandma Deding's right, which results in them being in an awkward-looking position. A first glance suggests that it is not an appropriate illustration. However, the text indicates that it is the first time Lola meets Grandma Deding after arriving from the U.S. mainland. The combination of words and illustration suggest that Lola is still unfamiliar with this tradition, giving the illustration a new yet appropriate meaning.[25]

While the *manginge'* is the most recognized form of respect for characters to engage in, informal acts of respect can be just as important. For example, holding one's tongue in the presence of an elder demonstrates just as much respect as the *manginge'*. The character of Toni in the story "By Any Other Name" exemplifies this form of respect in *Attitude 13*. As the story opens, Toni has enrolled in college in Hawai'i, where the reader infers she has "escaped" the family rather than stay and silently endure her grandmother's stern presence and unkind comments. Later in the story, Toni learns that her grandmother's treatment is based on the older Antonia's understanding that "anger . . . could not be stronger than . . . obedience."[26] In *Isa's Avocado Tree*, the neighbor children call Mama "Auntie" since they do not know her name. Finally, Lola takes care of the chickens after Grandma Deding passes away as a sign of love and respect in *Lola's Journey Home*.

Actions of respect are not limited to people but also extend out to the natural environment. The narrator in *Grandma's Love* demonstrates that respect includes being "kind to everything" and paying attention to nature.[27] *Endless Summer*'s Daniet teaches his boys that they have a responsibility to care for all living things, even those that are smaller than they are. Basically, respect gives Chamorros a means by which the individual remains conscientious of the impact his or her actions might have on family, friends, community and nature. Through these examples it becomes clear that Chamorro literature requires a setting that is familiar to what today's Chamorros see, a plot that resonates with what they experience, and has characters whose actions express their feelings and concerns.

ISSUES RELATED TO LOCATING
CHAMORRO CHILDREN'S LITERATURE

Chamorro stories are being written, but finding them is the challenge. Chamorro literature is difficult to find through standard acquisition methods because of its limited nature. While nonfiction is published with some regularity, realistic fiction is not. Very few titles have been published and the numbers of volumes have been scant. In the 1970s, two works of realistic fiction were published and in the 1990s there were five. Currently, the total number of realistic fiction books hovers at about fourteen titles.

Chamorro realistic fiction faces a problem familiar to many parallel cultures,[28] specifically the perceived ability to market these stories to various audiences. Very few stories with a Mariana Island setting have been published recently by large publishing houses, e.g., *Songs of Papa's Island, Keeper of the Night, Code Talker: A Novel about the Navajo Marines of World War Two,* and *Warriors in the Crossfire*.[29] A look at these titles reveals two easily marketable topics: World War II in the Pacific and family.

World War II was a pivotal moment in Marianas history, so World War II-type stories would be significant to Chamorro readers, especially since this period of time is still a part of living cultural memory. Most Chamorro families know what their great-grandparents and grandparents endured under the Japanese occupation. However, the published stories present the experiences of other native communities. For instance, Bruchac's *Code Talker* shares the Navajo code talkers' experience in the Pacific and Flood's *Warriors in the Crossfire* is centered on the Refaluwasch (Carolinian) experience in Saipan. By that token, neither qualifies as Chamorro realistic fiction, leaving the Chamorro experience unexpressed.

Family stories comprise the other half of the titles mentioned. The breadth of family situations in Guam and the Marianas as well as their importance to culture provide for endless possibilities of rich storylines. *Songs of Papa's Island* is about a mother and father's island adventures. The story is descriptively written, but it should be regarded as an island story because the island and the characters are depicted in such a way that it could be about any resident on any island.[30] On the other hand, *Keeper of the Night* is about a Chamorro family coming to terms with the loss of their mother and wife. Unfortunately, this story is not an exemplary piece of Chamorro literature. The way the story is constructed has made this novel contentious because Chamorro readers are split between seeing it as being acceptable (relevant social issues and familiar characters create credibility) or a completely unacceptable representation (unfamiliar narrative voice, unfamiliar places, and stereotypical characterizations are detracting enough to make readers question if the author knew local culture).[31]

While these stories demonstrate the array of other cultural communities represented within the islands, namely Carolinians and non-Chamorro residents, they also highlight the fact that so few Chamorro stories make it to major publishing houses. Local stories are more likely to be self-published or published through small-scale/print-on-demand printing houses. Chamorro authors, like Evelyn Flores, Victoria Lola Leon Guerrero, and Tanya Chargualaf Taimanglo, have produced exemplary works through this method of publication that sets the tone and standard for Chamorro stories. By going this route, they have had more liberty in customizing the text and images to reflect what islanders encounter regularly. For example, Taimanglo's characters in *Attitude 13* slip easily and fluidly between the respectful conversations with family members and the more colorful phrases—colloquial phrases, local slang, as well as profanities— that are usually said only among peers. Similar, even though the text in *Lola's Journey Home* describes how Tita performs her ritual healing, the image of the *suruhana* visiting the sick Lola may seem unusual to outside audiences. Thus, control over the entire artistic process has been advantageous towards developing a uniquely local literature.

One significant disadvantage to this method of publishing is the absence of an editorial team that can push a novice author to think about a deeper purpose of literature. For example, *Si Isa Yan Si Napu* resembles the didactical Dick and Jane books, and the plot in *I Kandet Gi Langet* does not crescendo into a climax that younger Chamorro readers have come to expect from a story.[32] Editorial guidance with these types of stories would create more meaningful stories exploring the island's natural beauty to complement Evelyn Flores's *Duendes Hunter*. Another disadvantage is the small quantities of readily available books. Many local authors underwrite the cost of publishing their works, which means small print runs and fewer opportunities to reprint. These factors result in smaller areas of dissemination, thereby limiting access to these stories.

CONCLUSION

Authentic representations rely upon appropriate reflections or explorations of the core values of *inafa'maolek* (where characters demonstrate mutual concern for each other), family (where membership ensures companionship, love, support, and a sense of identity), and respect (where an individual remains conscientious of his or her impact on family, friends, community, and nature). Unfortunately, the number of Chamorro stories published is few and the number published by large publishers is even fewer. Instead, most titles are self-published or made available through book-on-demand publishing houses. This publishing method has actually been advantageous to the development of an authentic literature. It has allowed local authors to share stories they want to tell and according to what looks right, resulting in books that have allowed the Chamorro community to find representations of themselves within the written word.[33] As a result, Chamorro children's literature has begun opening up new avenues of literary exploration that will encourage further development in a local Chamorro literature.

NOTES

1. "2000 Census of Population and Housing" (U.S. Summary File 1, Population and Housing Profile: Guam, Population and Housing Profile: CNMI) (Washington DC: USGPO), www.spc.int/prism/country/gu/stats/census/chamorros_in_us.htm; Phillip M. Harris and Nicholas A. Jones. *We the People: Pacific Islanders in the United States* (Washington, DC: U.S. Dept. of Commerce, U.S. Census Bureau, 2005), www.census.gov/prod/2005pubs/censr-26.pdf, p.6, figure 3.

2. Nicholas A. Jones, "2010 Census Data Results for the Asian Population and the Native Hawaiian and Other Pacific Islander Population: Presentation to the White House Initiative on Asian Americans and Pacific Islanders," May 19, 2011, www.apiidv.org/files/2010Census-WHIAAPI-2011.pdf, slide 12: Percent Change: 2000 to 2010.

3. Davina McGregor and Edmund Moy, "Native Hawaiians and Pacific Islander Americans," *Asian-Nation: The Landscape of Asian America* (2003), www.asian-nation.org/hawaiian-pacific.shtml.

4. "2000 Census of Population and Housing" (Guam, Population and Housing Profile: CNMI).

5. Paul Carano and Pedro Sanchez, *The Complete History of Guam* (Rutland, VT: Tuttle, 1964).

6. Dipåttamenton I Kaohao Guinahan Chamorro, *Chamorro Heritage: A Sense of Place: Guidelines, Procedures, and Recommendations for Authenticating Chamorro Heritage* (Guam: Dipåttamenton I Kaohao Guinahan Chamorro, 2003), 23.

7. Evelyn Flores, "Rewriting Paradise: Countering Desire, Denial and the Exotic in American Literary Representations of the Pacific" (Ph.D. Diss., University of Michigan, 2002); Robert Torres, "Post-Colonial and Modern Literature of the Marianas: A Critical Commentary," *Micronesian Journal of Humanities and Social Sciences* 3, no. 1 and 2 (2004): 26–44. http://marshall.csu.edu.au/MJHSS/Issue2004/MJHSS2004_04.pdf.

8. Rob Wilson, "Introduction: Toward Imagining a New Pacific," in *Inside Out: Literature, Cultural Politics and Identity in the New Pacific*, ed. V. Hereniko and R. Wilson (Lanham: Rowman & Littlefield, 1999), 1.

9. Torres, "Post-Colonial and Modern Literature of the Marianas," 26–44.

10. Subramani, *South Pacific Literature: From Myth to Fabulation* (Suva, Fiji: University of the South Pacific, 1985).

11. Tanya Chargualaf Taimanglo, *Attitude 13: A Daughter of Guam's Collection of Short Stories* (Bloomington, IN: Authorhouse, 2010).

12. Evelyn Flores, *Dolphin Day*, ill. Vivian Lujan Bryan. (Guam: Green Island, 1988).

13. Kimberly Willis Holt, *Keeper of the Night* (New York: Henry Holt, 2004).

14. Flores, *Dolphin Day*; Victoria Lola Leon Guerrero, *Lola's Journey Home*, ill. Maria Yatar (Guam: Estorian Famagu'on, 2005).

15. Rob Wilson, "Introduction: Toward Imagining a New Pacific," in *Inside Out: Literature, Cultural Politics and Identity in the New Pacific*, ed. V. Hereniko and R. Wilson. (Lanham: Rowman & Littlefield, 1999), 1–14.

16. Laura Thompson, *Guam and Its People* (Princeton, NJ: Princeton University Press, 1947).

17. Monique C. Storie, "All Fifty Ka-Thousand Cousins: Chamorro Teachers Responding to Contemporary Children's Literature Set in Guam" (diss., 2009), 217–18.

18. Storie, "All Fifty Ka-Thousand Cousins," 53.

19. Dottie Winterlee, *Grandma's Love*, ill. Judy Flores, trans. Ann Rivera and Hirose Sakae et al. (Hong Kong: Knowledge Craft, 2002).

20. Evelyn Flores, *Isa's Avocado Tree*, ill. Vivian Lujan Bryan (Guam: Green Island, 1988).

21. Storie, "All Fifty Ka-Thousand Cousins, "207.

22. Ibid., 211, 255–330.

23. Dipåttamenton I Kaohao Guinahan Chamorro, *Chamorro Heritage*.

24. *The Official Chamorro-English Dictionary: Ufisiåt na Diksionårion Chamorro-Engles. Hagåtña* (Guam: Dept. of Chamorro Affairs, Depåttamenton I Kaohao Guinahan Chamorro, 2009), 299.

25. Storie, "All Fifty Ka-Thousand Cousins," 231.

26. Taimanglo, *Attitude 13*, 15.

27. Winterlee, *Grandma's Love*.

28. Rudine Sims Bishop, "Books from Parallel Cultures: Celebrating a Silver Anniversary," *The Horn Book* 69, no. 2 (1993): 175.

29. Barbara Kerley, *Songs of Papa's Island*, ill. Katherine Tillotson (Boston: Houghton Mifflin, 1995); Joseph Bruchac, *Code Talker: A Novel about the Navajo Marines of World War Two* (New York: Penguin, 2005); Nancy Bo Flood, *Warriors in the Crossfire* (Honesdale, PA: Front Street, 2010).

30. Storie, "All Fifty Ka-Thousand Cousins," 255–330.

31. Ibid.

32. Eddie L. G. Benavente, *Si Isa yan si Napu* (Hagatna, Guam: Eddie L.G. Benavente, 2009); Dolores I. Marciano. *I kandet gi Langet* (Saipan: Version Certified, 2005).

33. Rudine S. Bishop, "Reframing The Debate about Cultural Authenticity," in *Stories Matter: The Complexity of Cultural Authenticity in Children's Literature,* ed. Dana L. Fox and Kathy G. Short (Urbana, IL: NCTE, 2003), 25–37; Wanda Brooks, "Reading Representations of Themselves: Urban Youth Use Culture and African American Textual Features To Develop Literary Understandings," *Reading Research Quarterly* 41, no. 3 (2006): 372–92.

Growing Mixed/Up

Multiracial Identity in Children's and Young Adult Literature

AMINA CHAUDHRI

"MIXED-RACE," "BIRACIAL," "multiracial," "interracial," "hapa," "mestizo," "mulatta": the multitude of labels for people whose parents are of different races belies a concept with which Americans have grappled since the first instances of colonial contact. Yet despite, or perhaps because of this long history of racial intermingling, our national understanding of race tends to focus on discrete classifications with monoracial labels (black, white, American Indian, etc.) and an adherence to the one-drop rule that determined that anyone with even a single drop of non-white blood belonged to a non-white racial category. Despite anti-miscegenation laws, people with multiple racial connections have existed for centuries, but legal institutions that provide the language that shapes our ideology have only recently made room for individuals who see themselves belonging to multiple racial groups. In 1967 the U.S. Supreme Court overturned the law banning interracial marriage between non-whites and whites. In the year 2000, the U.S. Census allowed Americans to choose more than one of the five prescribed racial categories, and 6.8 million people did. A decade later this number increased to 9 million.

In the world of children's and young adult (YA) literature, the inclusion of mixed-race experiences has been slow and sporadic. Even the multicultural movement that recognizes the function of literature to affirm identities, diversify perspectives, and promote appreciation of difference seems to have missed the transformational possibilities of including mixed-race stories and voices. Identity categories are at once useful and problematic. While they replicate the model of otherizing and naturalize discrete racial categories, they also serve to validate, include, and assert a presence of identities otherwise made invisible. Labeling and classification practices in textbooks, libraries, schools, and bookstores enable readers to easily locate so-called multicultural books. But unless defined by their titles, such as *Half and Half, Mexican WhiteBoy, How to Salsa in a Sari, Emily Goldberg Learns to Salsa, Marisol McDonald Doesn't Match,* and *Chloe Lieberman (Sometimes Wong),* books about mixed-race experiences tend to be swallowed up in the larger realm of multicultural literature.

The purveyors of children's and YA literature are responding to national events and shifts in cultural attitudes. Gradually, librarians and scholars have been turning their attention to mixed-race issues in children's and young adult literature. In 2002 *Book Links* published an article by Junko Yokota and Sharon Frost titled "Multiracial Characters in Children's Literature"; librarians at the Cooperative Children's Book Center in Madison, Wisconsin, have created an online list of recommended picture books for interracial families; and author Cynthia Leitich Smith's website features a bibliography of children's and YA books with interracial family themes.[1]

Since 1991, the Library of Congress has used the subject heading "racially-mixed people: fiction" and currently identifies 161 children's fiction titles bearing it. These include picture books and young adult fiction. A separate subject heading, "racially-mixed people: biography," includes 52 titles. Of the fiction titles, 25 were published between 1973 and 1999 and the rest since 2000. Of these 25, only 8 came out before the mid-1990s. Thus it appears that the majority of children's books with mixed-race characters were published around or after the time when the change in the U.S. Census standards allowed Americans to identify themselves as multiracial. This pattern suggests a growing literary awareness of a change in the racial make-up of the country. This is not to say that racially mixed people and books about racially mixed people did not exist before the mid-1990s; rather, the shift from singular to multiple racial classification possibilities has provided a label and a presence for a mixed-race identity in America and in the world of children's and young adult literature.

Unfortunately, one response to the publication of information about the growing numbers of mixed-race Americans was the public media's distortion of social reality by promoting the idea that we are now in a "post-race" society in which people like Tiger Woods, Halle Berry, Mariah Carey, and even Barack Obama represent a new, race-free identity for American youth. But post-race does not mean post-*racism*, and advertising the faces of beautiful, racially ambiguous celebrities cannot erase centuries of prejudice. Contemporary researchers of mixed-race experiences and writers of children's and young adult literature attest to the many ways in which racial attitudes remain bound to discrete categories with their associated power structures.

One of the features of multicultural literature is that it exposes the ways in which racial hierarchies privilege and oppress different groups of people. Readers are familiar with stories depicting cross-burnings, slavery, internment camps, and other vivid images set in earlier time periods.

The result is that racism is marked as a thing of the past. Critical analysis of mixed-race literature enables us to look beyond obvious and familiar acts of racism and see the subtle, persistent ways in which it functions on a daily basis *now*. Whether real or fictional, anyone who has to answer the "what are you?" question, who must explain appearance, cultural connection, linguistic difference, struggle to prove group membership, has been socially and emotionally isolated because of difference, or been denied voice and agency, does so because of deeply embedded limited perceptions of race and culture. Rudine Sims Bishop's metaphor of literature serving as windows and mirrors is all the more relevant when it comes to awareness of mixed-race experiences.[2]

In her recent book *Mixed Heritage in Young Adult Literature,* Nancy Thalia Reynolds provides a clear picture of trends and themes in this body of work.[3] Not surprisingly, she found that mixed-heritage issues in YA literature repeat the kinds of issues in adult literature with mixed characters. Thus the tragic mulatto/mulatta, the search for the Missing Half, the outcast Native American, the perpetual Asian immigrant, internalized racial confusion, abject isolation, self-doubt, and so on, reappear in both historical and contemporary YA fiction. While the validity of these issues for some mixed-race individuals is not to be underestimated, it is problematic when the repetition of these themes creates a one-dimensional, essentialized representation that ends up being understood as inherent to mixed-race identity. Scholars in mixed-race studies have demonstrated how scientific research in the early twentieth century pathologized mixed-race subjects and disseminated ideas that fed into a racist ideological paradigm. The overall picture was a bleak one, ranging from mental insanity and sexual impotence at one end to socially and emotionally maladjusted individuals with no community who often ended up alone or dead at the other. The impact of such images was to create the impression that racial mixing was a terrible idea, with evidence embodied in the unfortunate products of mixed unions. The survival of this idea, repeated in a variety of iterations, renders it natural and inevitable rather than a social construction.

A review of contemporary realistic and historical fiction for middle-grade readers reveals a singular theme recurring consistently, reifying the stereotype of the socially maladjusted child struggling to fit in. Conventional literary patterns have monoracial characters in coming-of-age stories emerge from transformative experiences wiser and more self-confident. Mixed-race characters are also transformed, but the site of both conflict and resolution is the fact of being mixed, and the transformation process is private, internal, and usually solitary. Once characters understand their racial identity, all problems are solved. In this way the problem *is* the mixed-race subject, not the attitudes of society. Often such racial identity struggle is the focus of the story. Protagonists tend to be socially isolated, victims of racism, introverted, and hurt. They often come from abusive or unstable homes and rarely have two parents. In other instances, racial identity negotiation is combined with supplemental conflicts, such as winning a competition, making friends, or connecting with an estranged family member. In these situations, mixed-race identity is closely tied to the obstacles keeping the characters from resolution. Moving slightly away from that trend, other novels depict protagonists who must resolve conflicts not centered on their racial identity, but complicated because of it in ways that would not pertain to monoracial characters. A few recent novels portray mixed-race characters in nurturing environments, having non-traumatic racial-identity experiences, negotiating social expectations in nurturing contexts. Harder to identify are the stories in which mixed-race heritage is incidental to the plot and/ or character development. These books are not labeled by the Library of Congress and only sporadically appear in bibliographies or themed library lists. Pam Muñoz Ryan's *Becoming Naomi León,* and Blue Balliett's *Chasing Vermeer* series include protagonists whose mixed-race identities are descriptive and only briefly mentioned. Of the titles identified with the "racially-mixed people" Library of Congress subject heading, most books are about black-white biracial characters, followed by Native American-white, Asian-white, Latino-white, and fewer than ten titles about non-white mixed characters. There are likely to be many more of this latter description, but they are harder to identify by title, review, jacket blurb, or summary.

Given the inevitability of encountering stereotypes, readers need to consider the extent to which the literature resists or reinforces those paradigms. Questions can be asked, for example, about how biracial characters respond to racism. Are readers led to believe that the reason for a character's real or perceived lack of group membership is *because* he or she is mixed, or because of the rigidity of his or her environment? Do characters have to change in order to be accepted, or are they able to enact change in their environments and remain true to themselves? Does the task of explaining/performing racial identity rest only with the mixed-race character while monoracial characters are rendered more "natural"? Are clearly defined racial identities portrayed as stable and "normal" while mixed-race ones are unstable and "freakish"? What kind of language is used in describing racial identity? Terms like "pure," "only half," "100%," and the more pejorative "mongrel," "mutt," and so on are value-laden and directly inform a reader's understanding.

With such questions in mind, the next section looks at three different approaches in the literary construction of mixed-race identity. In *Mexican WhiteBoy,* by Matt de la Peña, being mixed is the cause of the protagonist's self-hatred. In *The Other Half of My Heart,* by Sundee Tucker Frazier, the protagonist negotiates her identity within a supportive environment and forms a positive sense of self. In *After Tupac and D Foster,* Jacqueline Woodson shows that mixed-race identity disrupts convention but does not have to be an obstacle in relationships. These books are by no means representative of *all* literature about mixed-race experiences. Instead they are presented here as examples of different ways in which realistic characters negotiate mixed-race identity. Readers searching for literature on the topic are likely to find these titles, as they come up repeatedly in library and online searches. The books are well reviewed (by *School Library Journal, Booklist, VOYA,* and *The Horn Book Magazine*), and the American Library Association (ALA) has recognized all three authors. Woodson's other works have received numerous awards, and *After Tupac and D Foster* won the Newbery Honor in 2009, *Mexican Whiteboy* was on the ALA's Top Ten Best Books for Young Adults in 2009, and Sundee Tucker Frazier was awarded the Coretta Scott King/John Steptoe New Talent Author Award for her first novel, *Brendan Buckley's Universe and Everything in It,* in 2008.

MEXICAN WHITEBOY: MISSING HALF

Mexican WhiteBoy is a classic Missing Half story. The protagonist, sixteen-year-old Danny Lopez, is too brown for his hometown and too white for the barrio. In response to the racism of his hometown and school, and anger at his mother whom he blames for his father's absence, he stops speaking and turns deeply inward to nurse his depression, while inflict-ing physical pain by digging his nails into his arm to remind himself that he is real.

The story takes place over the summer when Danny chooses to live with his father's Mexican family in the barrio, rather than with his white mother and her boyfriend in San Francisco. Danny's discomfort with his mixed-race identity is established right from the start of the novel. He hates the racism of his elite high school peers and his isolation in his hometown, where the only other Latinos are undocumented landscap-ers. Being with his Mexican relatives, distancing himself from his white mother, Danny feels, brings him closer to his father, even though he feels like he doesn't entirely belong there either. Danny is sure that the fail-ure of his parents' marriage was due to their being an interracial couple. In one imaginary letter to his father, he says he can relate: "You were telling me you were going to Mexico. You were sick of living in a city with so many white people, with a white wife, with two kids who were half white. You wanted to be around more Mexicans . . . But what I've wanted to tell you, Dad, is how much I've changed since that day. How much better I am. How much stronger and darker and more Mexican I am."[4] This sounds like wishful thinking because Danny is constantly self-conscious about his light skin and lack of Spanish. He doesn't "feel" Mexican at all, but occasionally being left out is preferable to being the target of racism. In National City Danny is the focus of a different kind of attention, which he dislikes almost as much. Girls think he is attractive, while older relatives turn to him to explain unfamiliar English-language concepts and put him on an intellectual pedestal that reminds him of his privilege and magnifies the gap between him and his Mexican family. In *Mexican WhiteBoy*, straddling cultures means negotiating power and privilege as well as language, culture, and difference. The difficulty of this is made abundantly clear through Danny's self-image.

While the racism at his high school is real, Danny's isolation in National City is self-imposed. Gradually, he comes to realize this. His cousin, Sofia, and her friends include him in their social life with all the teasing and ribbing that goes with the territory. Danny is withdrawn and silent, but very much accepted: "Barely ever talking. Mexican as anybody else in the 'hood but dressed like some kind of skater dude."[5] In a motif familiar in many novels of mixed-race identity, Danny relates to two other marginalized characters who are similarly isolated and seeking connections with absent parents.

For most of the novel, mixed-race identity is the source of unhappiness. Danny believes that he will be complete only when he is far from his mother and reunited with his father. We can understand this as a perpetuation of the master narrative of the problem of interracial unions, or as a critique of the ways accepted attitudes about race have no place for multiraciality and make people unhappy. The ending is somewhat positive, but the message about the difficulty of mixed-race experience is firmly established.

THE OTHER HALF OF MY HEART: BLENDING IN

Like many stories in this genre, *The Other Half of My Heart* focuses on physical appearance as the source of conflict for mixed-race characters. Having to explain or defend racial group membership is part of the reality of mixed-race individuals in life and in literature.[6] Kiera and Minni King are twins with an African American mother and a German-Irish father. Kiera resembles her mother in that she has brown skin and dark curly hair; Minni's features are closer to her father's. Her blue eyes, pale skin, and red hair make her feel less connected to her mother and sister when they are together outside their home, and people question or stare. The story focuses on Minni's negotiation of her racial identity. The twins spend ten days with their maternal grandmother in Raleigh, North Carolina, at her insistence that they participate in the Miss Black Pearl Preteen Program—"not just a pageant . . . it's a *scholarship* program."[7] Minni is anxious that people might not believe she is African American. She asks her mother, "Am I black or white or what?" and is not convinced when her mother points out the variety of features she and Kiera share with both sides of their family.[8] She also tells Minni about her own upbringing in Raleigh, where she was surrounded by African Americans "who were as dark as licorice and as light as cream."[9] Most important, she points out, was that despite physical differences, their community was "united by a common struggle."[10] It is this "common struggle," Minni learns, that matters more than skin color.

Periodically we see that the girls have been raised with a strong sense of their African American heritage. The book hits all the hot-button issues from famous people and historical events to hair care. Minni envies her sister's dark skin and curly hair, but she is blind to the racism that Kiera experiences. Part of Minni's development includes learning about her own privilege—the many ways in which her appearance allows her to fit in to her home and school environment. An incident in a store in which a salesperson treats Minni and Kiera very differently shakes Minni to the core, particularly because her silence made her complicit in the racism. At the competition, she feels alone and different, which Kiera reminds her is how she feels all the time at home.

Ultimately, *The Other Half of My Heart* spotlights the arbitrariness of racial identity as a social construct. People who appear white can have proud and close connections to black culture, while some who look black might internalize the shame bred by a racist society. The characters embody their cultural connections, traditions, appearance, and self-worth in a variety of ways so that Minni's mother's assertion "there are many ways to be black," and Ms. Oliphant's celebratory comment "I contain multitudes" ring true in this context.[11] At the end Minni admits that she knows what "fits my soul . . . I'm a mixture. Of black and white, Mama and Daddy, and all the people who came before me."[12] Most significantly, she acknowledges that her sister may feel differently, but that their relationship trumps those differences.

AFTER TUPAC AND D FOSTER: STRANGERS IN OUR MIDST

Jacqueline Woodson's *After Tupac and D Foster* is a story of a friendship that develops among three girls, Neeka, D Foster, and the nameless narrator. D Foster, a melancholy, mixed-race young girl appears in the neighborhood and leaves a few years later as suddenly as she arrived. During their time together the girls are drawn together mostly by the lyrics in Tupac's songs. As the title indicates, after D leaves and Tupac dies, the two girls are left to think about the impact of such brief but meaningful relationships on their lives. Their sadness at D's departure is compounded by the fact that her mother is white. Prior to this, D's appearance marked her as different, but her mother's presence is a stark reminder. In response to their bewilderment and anger at this news, D responds, "I didn't think it mattered . . . what difference would it make? You gonna like me more or less because I got a white mama?"[13] Thus as readers we too must ask ourselves if it matters that this character is biracial. If so, why? What do we learn about mixed-race identity from this character?

Readers familiar with Jacqueline Woodson's writing will appreciate the complexity and detail with which she creates her characters. So it is safe to assume that yes, it does matter that this enigmatic character is biracial. Furthermore, it matters that we don't know this for sure until the very end. Throughout the course of the novel we are given glimpses of her life, details about loneliness and sadness that draw us, and the other characters, in, so that when D reveals that her name is Desiree Johnson, not D Foster, and that her mother is white, the bonds are too strong to be broken by news that could establish her as too different to belong to this new community. The girls are stunned though, in their realization that they never really knew their friend—her mysteriousness is amplified by her whiteness, her access to experiences far removed from their block in Queens. Subsequent to this "discovery" the narrator cannot help but think of D in terms of her biracial heritage. She refers to her "green eyes that were her white mama's green eyes" and recalls how when they first met her, she and Neeka were struck by her appearance: "She was tall and skinny and looked like she thought she was cute with her green eyes and pretty sort of half way of smiling at us. Her hair was in a bunch of braids . . . were long, coming down over her shoulders and across her back . . . and her hair was this strange dark coppery color I'd never seen on a black girl—not *naturally* . . . She had on white-girl clogs like you saw on the girls on TV . . . Everything about her was screaming *I'm not from around this way*."[14] D's racial heritage is never an issue among the friends, but we are reminded that she often has to respond to other people's curiosity: "Her skin wasn't brown like mine or light brown like Neeka's—it was kinda *tan* brown in that way that made people always ask her what she was mixed with. When she said, 'I'm half black and half your mama!'. . . D hated people asking what she was."[15] Through cultural, linguistic, and historical references, D seems to identify as black, though she does not say so directly. Perhaps one way to understand this aspect of the book is that it is an example of how sometime mixed-race people identify monoracially, especially when appearance is a strong marker and the absence of family of the other racial group make it "easier" or more logical to identify with those who are present than those who are not.

As such D's mixed-race subjectivity seems to be crafted to bring the unknown in to the otherwise circumscribed world of the girls. Readers are reminded that there are always things we don't know about people we think we know well. Relationships can flourish when socially constructed obstacles are ignored or unknown. Unlike other mixed-race novels in which characters struggle to fit in with one or both of their racial groups, *After Tupac and D Foster* does not locate D's isolation in her racial identity. Instead it is because she is the product of a heartless foster care system and a mother who cannot take care of her. Her yearning to belong is not to a particular racial or cultural group, but to a caring family.

CONCLUSION

These three novels remind us that we still live in a very racialized society. Seemingly minor markers of difference such as names, skin tone, or language have a tremendous impact on people who are called to explain themselves or combat social expectations on a daily basis. The examples above are part of a small body of literature that has much room to explore the myriad ways in which race is experienced by individuals and groups. In selecting books that focus on mixed-race experiences, care should be taken to examine how they reinforce or interrupt stereotypes. Book talks and discussions with children that account for historical context and current attitudes can encourage consideration of the realities of mixed-race individuals. The difficulty of embodying multiple racial identities in a culture that only recognizes a few has found its voice in many stories for children and young adults. What is needed now is representation of a diverse range of experiences that include non-traumatic circumstances. There is also a scarcity of books in which mixed-race characters belong to multiple minority groups, since the bulk of this corpus is about white and non-white mixes. Mixed-race people are a rapidly growing demographic, and there is certainly a need for representation of their experiences showing the ways they shape and are shaped by the world we live in today.

YOUTH LITERATURE BIBLIOGRAPHY

Balliett, Blue. *Chasing Vermeer.* New York: Scholastic, 2004.

Brown, Monica, and Sara Palacios. *Marisol McDonald Doesn't Match/Marisol McDonald no combina.* New York: Children's Book Press, an imprint of Lee & Low Books, 2011.

Frazier, Sundee Tucker. *Brendan Buckley's Universe and Everything in It.* New York: Yearling, 2007.

———. *The Other Half of My Heart.* New York: Delacorte, 2010.

Namioka, Lensey. *Half and Half.* New York: Delacorte, 2003.

Ostow, Micol. *Emily Goldberg Learns to Salsa.* New York: Razorbill, 2007.

Peña, Matt de la. *Mexican WhiteBoy.* New York: Delacorte Press, 2008.

Rosten, Carrie. *Chloe Leiberman (Sometimes Wong).* New York: Delacorte, 2005.

Ryan, Pam Muñoz. *Becoming Naomi León,* New York: Scholastic, 2004.

Sarkar, Dona. *How to Salsa in a Sari.* Buffalo, NY: Kimani, 2008.

Woodson, Jacqueline. *After Tupac and D Foster.* New York: G. P. Putnam's Sons, 2008.

NOTES

1. Junko Yokota and Sharon J. Frost, "Multiracial Characters in Children's Literature," *Book Links* (December 2002): 51–57; "CCBC Booklists," University of Wisconsin-Madison School of Education; "Exploring Diversity: Children's and Young Adult Books with Interracial Themes," official author site of Cynthia Leitich Smith and home of Children's & YA Lit Resources, www.cynthialeitichsmith.com/lit_resources/diversity/multiracial/multi_race_intro.html.

2. Rudine Sims Bishop, *Shadow and Substance: Afro-American Experience in Contemporary Children's Fiction* (Urbana, IL: National Council of Teachers of English, 1982), 2.

3. Nancy Thalia Reynolds, *Mixed Heritage in Young Adult Literature* (Lanham, MD: Scarecrow, 2009).

4. Matt de la Peña, *Mexican WhiteBoy* (New York: Delacorte, 2008), 28.

5. Ibid., 140.

6. Maria P. P. Root, *The Multiracial Experience: Racial Borders as the New Frontier* (London: SAGE, 1996).

7. Sundee Tucker Frazier, *The Other Half of My Heart* (New York: Delacorte, 2010), 16.

8. Ibid., 55.

9. Ibid., 59.

10. Ibid.

11. Ibid., 220, 249.

12. Ibid., 290.

13. Jacqueline Woodson, *After Tupac and D Foster* (New York: G. P. Putnam's Sons, 2008), 128.

14. Ibid., 131, 24.

15. Ibid., 13.

The Door Has Never Opened for Us

The Roma in Recent Children's Fiction for Grades 4–6

BRIAN W. STURM AND MEGHAN GAHERTY

THE ROMA, ALSO KNOWN AS GYPSIES, are among the most persecuted ethnic groups of Europe, and the impact of that prejudice can be seen in literature dating back centuries. Initially misunderstood, the origin and culture of the Roma is now far better known by experts, though still distorted and mysterious to most people. Estimates indicate that there are approximately 8–10 million Roma living in Europe today, and at least several hundred thousand in North America.[1] They have been denied property, education, and jobs, and they suffered enslavement and attempted extermination in the Holocaust of World War II. Despite this grim history, prejudice and bigotry about the Roma are still common, and in countries where the Roma population is small, their culture is nearly unknown. This lack of knowledge has been filled with images and myths that distort Roma culture to portray them as thieves, kidnappers, fortune-tellers, and vagabonds. In the United States, there is little to no exposure to accurate information about the Roma as an ethnic group.

The origin of the Roma can be traced back to a mass migration out of northern India in the tenth century. Pushed into Europe in front of the Ottoman invasions of the Middle Ages, the Roma became associated with the Turks, and their nomadic lifestyle and unique traditions set them apart wherever they were. Early stories and theories about the Roma included an origin from Egypt, hence "gypsies," and ties to biblical sins such as being descended from Cain and the forgers of the nails used to crucify Christ.[2]

During the Middle Ages, the Roma were enslaved in what is now Romania, expelled from England, France, and Spain, and forbidden to own property across the continent. As a marginalized population, the Roma turned to underground economies to survive and became associated with petty thievery and fortune-telling, which fed the superstitions of European villagers.[3] The Roma have an oral, rather than written, tradition and strongly value separation from non-Roma or *gadje*, which most likely contributed to the misunderstandings and perversions of their culture that began to appear in European literature.[4] After the abolition of slavery in Romania in 1865, many Roma managed to circumvent immigration restrictions and enter the United States.[5]

Discrimination against the Roma continued through the nineteenth and twentieth centuries. In the middle of the twentieth century, the Roma were targeted for extermination by Hitler, and in what they call "Porajmos," or "The Devouring," at least two million Roma were killed. Because of their liminal position in European society and exclusion from most state censuses, it is especially difficult to estimate the number of casualties, but the 70–80 percent loss of the population was devastating.[6] By the end of the twentieth century, the Roma began to organize and demand rights, beginning with their attempt to change their name from the misunderstood and often pejorative term "gypsies" to Roma, or Romani, which derives from their native word *rom*, meaning "man."[7] Today there are at least 12–15 million Roma living around the world, and "discrimination continues in every aspect of their lives, particularly in education, health care, and employment."[8] The new century presents a new opportunity for tolerance and understanding, but persistent myths and misunderstandings threaten that progress.

The population of Roma in the United States may be small compared to other marginalized minorities, but many of the assumptions and prejudices against them have continued because of the lack of education and understanding. The treatment of gypsies as a behavioral group, rather than an ethnicity, has allowed this imagery to persist with little modification, even by publishers seeking to modernize biased texts.[9] For example, the updated version of Shel Silverstein's classic "The Gypsies are Coming" replaces "gypsies" with "googies" and leaves everything else, including a pictorial caricature of a Roma woman with a bag of children over her shoulder, intact.[10]

This historical context draws attention to the need to show children accurate and current images of Romani culture and life. An examination of currently available juvenile novels demonstrates the current state of the portrayal of the Roma to American children and casts light on the unique function of gypsy imagery in children's literature and its development over time.

LITERATURE REVIEW

The use of gypsy imagery in literature has been common for years. Ian Hancock, a leading scholar on the Roma, notes that "Black's Gypsy Bibliography, which includes nothing later than 1914, lists 351 novels, 199 plays, and 133 ballads in the English literary tradition alone."[11] He identifies three specific roles for gypsy characters in children's literature: a liar or thief, a witch or caster of spells, and a romantic figure. Many of the common associations with the Roma come from the Victorian period of British literature, when imperialism was at its peak and the Roma were associated with the savages being conquered. Literary representations of gypsies as tramps, thieves, and beggars flourished as authors exaggerated the image of the Roma to create images of a romantic, dangerous people living outside the laws of polite society.[12] Ronald Lee describes the process:

> The mythical "Gypsy" stereotype took on a life of its own and the same hackneyed clichés were used over and over again . . . the Victorian and post-Victorian novelists fed on previous works and their own fertile minds to create a composite "Gypsy" in their works of fiction, combining bits and pieces of many unrelated Romani groups and cultures—the colorful caravans of the English Romanies, the fiddles of the Hungarian Romungere, the costumes of the Romanian Vlach-Romani women . . . until this ludicrous, composite creation replaced the genuine Romanies in the minds of the reading public.[13]

This effort to define the gypsies as "other" was mirrored by British laws, which were being adapted to identify gypsies as a behavioral group rather than an ethnicity. British literature was able to marginalize the Roma by describing their behavior as primitive. The Roma did not have the power to combat this image in part because they lacked a nation-state and refused to participate in the modern wage market. Yahev-Brown notes, like Hancock, that gypsies frequently appear in literature as stock characters rather than individuals, notable only for being gypsies who play merely the symbolic role of the mysterious—and often villainous—other.[14]

Nancy Drew and her predecessors in series novels with a female lead demonstrate the importance of the gypsy in defining the "other" in order to define the norms and expectations for the main characters in the novel.[15] Gypsies in *Nancy Drew* are romanticized and eroticized, wearing scandalous clothing and embodying freedoms off-limits to young girls of the time. The temporary flirtation with the gypsy lifestyle enforces boundaries while giving the white women of the novels a taste of primitivism and excitement. The "fascination with gypsies and exoticism is manipulated and transformed into a cautionary tale about the limits of independence."[16] By extension, this cautionary tale can be applied to other social or political anxieties, such as the association between the gypsies and communists in *The Clue in the Old Album*, written in 1947. In this story, "the evil gypsy king, Zorus, and his female accomplice, Nitaka, are hatching a plot to overthrow the American government. The king is a communist, in practice if not in name, who compels his people to turn all their earnings over to 'the cause.'"[17]

The persistent misrepresentation of the Roma in the United States during the middle of the twentieth century is problematic, and whether or not it has continued into the twenty-first century is the focus of this research.

METHODOLOGY

Content analysis was used to analyze currently available children's literature featuring Roma characters or themes. The sample for this analysis was created by searching *Children's Books in Print* from 1996 to 2010 for "gypsies-fiction" and "romanies-fiction" to create a list of books first published in the United States since 1995.[18] This list was then augmented by a subject and title search of the Chapel Hill (NC) Public Library catalog for "Juvenile literature" and "gypsies" or "romanies," and a subject search of the online review database NoveList using the search term "romanies," limited to fiction for ages 9–12 and published since 1995.

The result was a sample of twenty-four books. As the focus of this research study was text novels for the third- to sixth-grader, two books for young adults, a graphic novel, and a picture book were eliminated from the sample. A fifth book (*Tyso's Promise*) was removed from the list since no libraries in the United States own it. Finally, three books first published in the late nineteenth and early twentieth centuries were added for historical comparison, leaving a total of twenty-two books. (See table 8.1.)

Characteristics associated with the Roma and their roles in children's literature were identified using the academic literature. One book was then read by both researchers and a complete list of quotes pertaining to the Roma was compiled. Each researcher then assigned these quotes to categories independently to assess how reliable the categories were. Inter-coder reliability was assessed using Cohen's Kappa, with a resulting score of 0.89, well above the recommended 0.7 threshold. The remaining books were then analyzed, coded, and compiled into Excel data tables.

ANALYSIS OF CONTEMPORARY FICTION

The contemporary fiction (since 1995) was analyzed separately from the early twentieth-century fiction to enable a historical comparison. Table 8.2 summarizes the clusters of Romani stereotypes identified in the literature, in order of decreasing prevalence.

As table 8.2 shows, stereotypes of the Roma abound in these children's novels. The typical depiction is of a nomadic musician dressed in bright clothing, whose goal is to tell your fortune, steal your belongings, or, worse, kidnap your children. They are described by other characters as dirty ("I would so hate my dear old daddy to hear I've been hobnob-

Table 8.1: Children's novels analyzed in this study

BOOK# CITATION

Late 20th century and early 21st century titles

1 Forsyth, Kate. *The Gypsy Crown*. New York: Hyperion, 2008.

2 Duey, Kathleen. *The Unicorn's Secret #5: The Sunset Gates*. New York: Aladdin, 2002.

3 Duey, Kathleen. *The Unicorn's Secret #6: True Heart*. New York: Aladdin, 2003.

4 Hicyilmaz, Gaye. *Pictures from the Fire*. Dolphin Paperbacks, 2003.

5 Vande Velde, Vivian. *A Coming Evil*. Houghton Mifflin, 1998.

6 DiLiberto, Frank. *Gypsy Kids: The Adventures of Colby Myers and Mark Howard*. Frankfort, NY: Crystal Ball, 2002.

7 McCusker, Paul. *Glennall's Betrayal*. Carol Stream, IL: Tyndale House, 1999.

8 King-Smith, Dick. *Mr. Ape*. New York: Crown, 1998.

9 Roos, Stephen. *The Gypsies Never Came*. New York: Simon and Schuster Young Readers, 2001.

10 Snyder, Zilpha Keatley. *The Gypsy Game*. New York: Delacorte, 1997.

11 Spalding, Andrea. *Phoebe and the Gypsy*. Olympia, WA: Orca Books, 1999.

12 Zach, Cheryl. *Mind over Matter #4: The Gypsy's Warning*. New York: Avon, 1997.

13 Alexander, Lloyd. *Gypsy Rizka*. New York: Dutton Children's Press, 1999.

14 Bradley, K. B. *One-of-a-Kind Mallie*. New York: Delacorte, 1999.

15 Matthews, L. S. *A Dog for Life*. New York: Delacorte, 2006.

16 Kent, Trilby. *Medina Hill*. Plattsburgh, NY: Tundra Books, 2009.

17 Morgan, Jill M. *Blood Brothers*. New York: HarperCollins, 1996.

18 Lawton, Wendy. *The Tinker's Daughter: A Story Based on the Life of Mary Bunyan*. Chicago: Moody Press, 1996.

19 Lawlor, Laurie. *Come Away with Me*. New York: Pocket Books, 1996.

Late 19th century and early 20th century titles

20 Molesworth, Mrs. *Us: An Old Fashioned Story*. London: Macmillan, 1900.

21 Sherwood, Mrs. Mary Marthal. *Shanty the Blacksmith: A Tale of Other Times*. Utica: O. Hutchinson, 1841.

22 Penrose, Margaret. *The Motor Girls through New England; or Held by the Gypsies*. New York: Cupples and Leon, 1911.

---

bing with those dreadful dirty Gypsy children. I might spoil my velvet coat"),[19] ignorant ("none of her family and very few of their neighbors or relatives could read or write"),[20] troublemakers ("'What was a family of gypsies doing up there anyway? You can't trust 'em. Sly bunch they are. Dirty diddikais. Shouldn't be surprised if they started the fire'").[21]

Table 8.2: Romani stereotypes evident in late 20th and early 21st century children's novels

BOOK#	1	2	3	4	5	6	7	8	9	10	11	12	13	14	15	16	17	18	19	TOTALS	%
STEREOTYPES																					
Nomad	x	x	x	x	x		x	x	x	x	x		x	x	x	x	x	x	x	17	89%
Intolerance	x	x	x	x	x			x		x	x		x	x	x	x	x	x		14	74%
Dishonest/Thief	x	x	x	x		x			x	x	x	x	x	x		x	x			13	68%
Outsider	x	x	x	x	x	x		x					x	x	x	x		x		12	63%
Unschooled	x		x	x	x	x							x				x		x	8	42%
Magic/Curses	x										x		x				x	x	x	6	32%
Kidnapping						x	x		x		x						x		x	6	32%
Animals—Affinity	x	x	x										x							4	21%
Dancing Bear	x									x								x	x	4	21%
Ungodly	x																	x		2	11%
TOTALS	9	5	6	5	4	4	2	3	3	4	5	1	7	4	3	4	6	6	5	86	
OCCUPATION																					
Fiddler/Musician	x	x	x	x		x			x	x	x		x	x		x		x		12	63%
Fortuneteller	x				x	x				x	x		x	x		x				8	42%
Adventurer	x		x			x													x	4	21%
Dancer	x																	x	x	3	16%
Blacksmith										x			x			x				3	16%
Street Vendor											x		x							2	11%
TOTALS	4	1	2	1	1	3	0	0	1	3	3	0	4	2	0	3	0	2	2	32	

PHYSICAL TRAITS

Trait	Count	%
Colorful Clothing	13	68%
Ethnic Features	13	68%
Poor Hygiene	9	47%
Gold Earring	6	32%
Flower behind Ear	2	11%
TOTALS	**43**	

Per-column totals: 5 0 1 3 4 2 3 2 4 1 2 2 3 1 0 4 2 0 4

POSITIVE FEATURES

Feature	Count	%
Roma Character (present in story)	16	84%
Rom	8	42%
Difference Celebrated	5	26%
Holocaust	4	21%
Origin	2	11%
Tolerance	1	5%
TOTALS	**36**	

Per-column totals: 2 2 2 2 0 2 2 3 0 2 2 3 2 3 1

Their magical abilities include fortune-telling ("Fortune Telling [the sign] proclaimed in large letters, Palm Reading and Crystal Ball"),[22] magical charms ("And like any Gypsy door would be, it was enchanted to protect the home"),[23] curses ("With the other [hand] she pointed three fingers at the startled crowd, 'Curse the voices that cry for blood?' Emilia called. 'Curse this town, which lives by fire and iron and death?'"),[24] and even voodoo ("She took another pin from the box and jabbed it cruelly into the rag doll, again and again.").[25]

They are musically gifted, with the violin or fiddle being the instrument of choice, though accordions, guitars, and mouth-organs are also evident. The predominant physical portrayal is of "nut brown skin,"[26] dark eyes ("her eyes were so dark, they were almost black")[27] with an intense gaze ("her black gaze piercing"),[28] and black hair ("He was a dark-skinned fellow with black hair").[29] They wear colorful, though often ragged, clothing ("Emilia . . . was dressed in her vivid Gypsy skirt, with a gaudy scarf tied over her head"),[30] golden earrings ("Augie sees the ring the man wears in his ear. It's gold"),[31] and other jewelry ("'And the women wear these bright-colored head scarfs and all kinds of weird jewelry'").[32]

These books create an image of the Roma that mirrors and perpetuates the negative stereotypes discussed in the literature. In fact, despite having subject headings that include "Romanies" or "Gypsy," three of these books do not even include true Roma characters. The characters in *Glennall's Betrayal* are assumed to be gypsies because they completely fit the stereotype, but they are never identified. In *The Gypsies Never Came*, the main character only meets his presumed gypsy father in his dreams, and in *The Gypsy's Warning*, the thieving villain is dressed as a stereotypical gypsy fortune-teller, but is not Roma. This shows just how deeply the gypsy stereotype is ingrained in social consciousness and how attractive their "mysterious allure" remains, in that catalogers will assign Romani subject terms to these books even when Roma characters are not present.

There are, however, some mitigating circumstances, as can be seen in the "Positive Features" in table 8.2. The inclusion of Roma characters (84 percent) in children's stories is positive, though the number is skewed due to our inclusion criteria, and the depiction is largely negative. One could argue that no representation is better than an ongoing negative one, but there are glimmers of hope in some of the more recent novels.

For example, 42 percent of these recent novels used the correct term for this ethnicity: Rom. While many of the books still use the outdated term *gypsy*, and some use both, there seems to be a growing consciousness of the Roma's preference for this name, though there is certainly room for improvement. While details of Roma history are often disregarded in fiction, the Roma Holocaust was mentioned in four novels (21 percent), and their origin in India was mentioned in two (11 percent).

While the depiction of Roma characters in these novels is certainly stereotypical, one must be careful not to vilify the authors or assume that they, too, hold these stereotypical beliefs because the "authorial voice" in many of these novels is *strongly positive*. This may seem at odds with this analysis which shows an overall negative portrayal of the Roma in these books, but what manifests here is the difference between the occurrence of stereotypes in a text and the authors' underlying perceptions of the Roma. For example, while Forsyth's *The Gypsy Crown* has the "worst" representation according to the analysis above—with eighteen of the negative stereotypes evident in the text and only two of the positive features—the Roma protagonists in this story are thoughtful, caring children who struggle against the oppression they encounter in a race to save their relatives from death. As in many of these novels, the author seems to put the stereotypes into the speech and actions of secondary characters so that the protagonists can *refute* them. We identify with the children despite their stereotypical portrayal, and, as readers, we leave with a deep sense of connection with these characters; we understand our common humanity beneath the trappings of the "other."

ANALYSIS OF EARLY TWENTIETH-CENTURY FICTION

Table 8.3 summarizes the findings for the three early twentieth-century books. Many of the stereotypes evident in the recent literature were also present in the late nineteenth and early twentieth centuries, showing that in many ways little has changed over the last 100–150 years in the depiction of the Roma people in children's literature. All three of these early books showed the Roma as nomadic, traveling the roads in caravans or wagons. They were depicted as disheveled, lazy, or "dirty and ragged,"[33] and one novel reduced Roma characters to the level of animals, claiming, "the *Comet* [car] . . . was placed just where the young men could hear the girls whisper should any gypsies appear, or rather be scented."[34]

All three books included the negative stereotype of the Roma as thieves. The evil gypsy in *Us* steals a child's money box, and the claim is made that "no doubt wherever they stopped the farm-yards and poultry-yards in the neighbourhood were none the better for it."[35] Sherwood's villains are "gipsies (*sic*) (who, among other thieves, always have their eyes on those who are supposed to carry valuables about them)."[36] In *The Motor Girls*, a gypsy posing as a waiter "made away with a lot of the silver and with money from the men's pockets."[37] Indeed, the overall attitude of these early books is best summed up by Cora in *The Motor Girls* when she exclaims, "Bess, all gypsies are supposed to steal."[38]

A third negative stereotype evident in all of these early books is the relation of the Roma to kidnapping, as all of these protagonists are abducted by gypsies. On trial for attempting to steal a landowner's fortune, a gypsy woman reveals how she stole jewelry from her employer

Table 8.3:

Romani stereotypes evident in late 19th and early 20th century children's novels

BOOK#	20	21	22	TOTALS	%
STEREOTYPES					
Nomad	x	x	x	3	100%
Kidnapping	x	x	x	3	100%
Dishonest/Thief	x	x	x	3	100%
Magic/Curses		x	x	2	67%
Ungodly		x		1	33%
Outsider	x			1	33%
Unschooled	x			1	33%
Intolerance			x	1	33%
Dancing Bear				0	0%
Animals—Affinity				0	0%
TOTALS	5	5	5	15	
OCCUPATION					
Fortuneteller	x		x	2	67%
Fiddler/Musician			x	1	33%
Street Vendor	x			1	33%
Dancer				0	0%
Blacksmith				0	0%
Adventurer				0	0%
TOTALS	2	0	2	4	
PHYSICAL TRAITS					
Poor Hygiene	x	x	x	3	100%
Ethnic Features	x		x	2	67%
Colorful Clothing	x		x	2	67%
Gold Earring				0	0%
Flower behind Ear				0	0%
TOTALS	3	1	3	7	
POSITIVE FEATURES					
Roma Character (present in story)	x	x	x	3	100%
Rom				0	0%
Difference Celebrated				0	0%
Holocaust				0	0%
Origin				0	0%
Tolerance				0	0%
TOTALS	1	1	1	3	

and admits "that her cupidity was so much excited by these ornaments, that she fixed her eye immediately on the family, and resolved, if possible, to get possession of the child."[39] The two children in *Us* are also abducted by the evil gypsy Mick and are kept for over a week until a caring gypsy woman helps them escape, claiming, "'he [Mick] may steal horses and poultry and what he likes, but I'll have no more to do with stealing children.'"[40] In *The Motor Girls*, Cora is abducted so that she may not testify at the hearing of another gypsy who is in court on charges of theft.

Descriptions of the Roma in these books emphasize their dark skin tone, black hair, and eyes that are often like "sword points."[41] *The Motor Girls* also comments on the Roma character's teeth: "She smiled and showed that wonderful set of teeth. Cora thought she had never before seen such human pearls."[42] Whether the girl's teeth are noticeable in contrast to her dark skin or because they are considered unusual in a race thought to be so dirty and unkempt, it is an ethnic feature that recurs in contemporary novels as well, though infrequently, and it recalls the grinning caricatures of African Americans from the same era, such as the minstrels of the mid-nineteenth century, the Aunt Jemima caricature dating back to the late nineteenth century, or Helen Bannerman's (1899) *Little Black Sambo* character.[43] By aligning with pervasive black stereotypes of that era, these ethnic descriptions of the Roma reinforce the role of the Roma as the "other."

Several other stereotypes were evident, including the depiction of the Roma as unschooled outsiders who deserve to be persecuted and harried from their homesteads. They were depicted as dancers, fortune-tellers, and adventurers who wore colorful clothing. There was also mention of their "ungodly" natures (not surprising, given the strong religious overtones and morality in early American children's novels). Interestingly, the contemporary "gold earring" stereotype was not seen in these three books, and may indicate a later association of the Roma with the romantic and "lawless pirate and cutthroat" stereotype developed in such books as Robert Louis Stevenson's *Treasure Island* (1883) and Rafael Sabatini's *Captain Blood* (1922).[44] Not one of the positive features for which we coded the texts was seen in these early novels other than the presence of a Roma character, though at least in *The Motor Girls* and *Us*, one of the gypsies helps the protagonists escape.

USES IN CLASSROOMS AND LIBRARIES

Due to the large number of negative stereotypes in these novels, their use in classrooms and libraries is best limited to negative examples of the prevalence of cultural stereotypes. Older children could explore the distinction—mentioned earlier—between the presence of stereotypes and the author's voice. Given their history of ostracism and oppression, it is unsurprising that there are few examples of online lesson plans for using children's literature about the Roma with young people. The Texas State Historical Association has a website about the Romani in Texas, but it does not include lesson plans for educators.[45]

The United Kingdom is the leader in trying to provide accurate information and creative ideas for including the Roma in modern curricula. The University of Manchester, England, for example, has created a website to help educators and children learn the facts about Romani life, and there are a few other lesson plans on Roma inclusion for elementary school-aged children, but these tend to rely on supplemental British publications and cannot stand alone.[46] The U.K.-based Roma Education Network is dedicated to "exploring . . . the experience of Roma/Romany/Romani/ Gypsy identity through the medium of music and the arts in general," and their website provides information and lesson plans about Romani culture.[47] The Center for Learning offers a set of fifteen lesson plans exploring Roma culture in Snyder's *The Gypsy Game,* but these must be purchased.[48] In short, the Roma are as invisible in educator resources as they are in American culture, a situation that requires immediate attention if Roma-Americans are to have the voice they deserve in today's society.

CONCLUSION

In general, American children's literature has done little over the last 150 years to change the literary portrayal of the Roma. Many of the attributes cobbled together by the Victorian writers remain prevalent in today's literature, including nomadism, thievery, and poor hygiene. There appears to be an increased emphasis on magic and curses, perhaps as the romantic, fortune-telling gypsy becomes more evolved as a stereotype. There is, however, a decreased prevalence of the Roma's association with kidnapping, an increase in the positive features used to portray this ethnicity, and a subtle change in authorial perspective from treating Roma characters as stock villains to creating sympathetic Roma protagonists, despite their stereotypical portrayal.

Despite these changes, the Roma continue to serve as an outlet for American society to fantasize—and demonize—the "other." It is time we corrected this literary misrepresentation and opened the door to accurate and culturally authentic depictions of the Roma in children's literature. As Lloyd Alexander claims in *Gypsy Rizka,* "Gorgios? Gypsies? At the end, it comes to the same. No one's as bad as they seem, or as good as they think they are."[49]

NOTES

1. Anne Hartley Sutherland, "Roma in the United States and Europe," in *Encyclopedia of Medical Anthropology,* ed. Carol R. Ember and Melvin Ember (New York: Kluwer Academic, 2004), 923–29.
2. Isabel Fonseca, *Bury Me Standing: The Gypsies and Their Journey* (New York: Knopf, 1995).

3. Ibid.
4. Ian Hancock, "The Origin and Function of the Gypsy Image in Children's Literature," *The Lion and the Unicorn* 11, no. 2 (1987): 47–59.
5. Fonseca, *Bury Me Standing*.
6. Ronald Lee, "Roma in Europe: 'Gypsy' Myth and Romani Reality—New Evidence for Romani History," in *"Gypsies" in European Literature and Culture*, ed. Valentina Glajar and Domnica Radulescu (New York: Palgrave Macmillan, 2008), 1–28.
7. Ibid.
8. Anne Wallace Sharp, *The Gypsies* (San Diego, CA: Lucent Books, 2003), 12.
9. Hancock.
10. Shel Silverstein, *Where the Sidewalk Ends* (New York: Harper Collins, 1974).
11. Hancock, "Origin and Function," 47.
12. Ibid.
13. Lee, "Roma in Europe," 10.
14. Amit Yahav-Brown, "Gypsies, Nomadism, and the Limits of Realism," *MLN* 121, no. 5 (2007): 1124–47.
15. Nancy Tillman Romalov, "Lady and the Tramps: The Cultural Work of Gypsies in Nancy Drew and Her Foremothers," *The Lion and the Unicorn* 18, no. 1 (1994): 25–36.
16. Ibid., 29.
17. Ibid., 33.
18. *Children's Books in Print* changed from the subject heading "gypsies-fiction" to "romanies-fiction" in 2009.
19. Kate Forsyth, *The Gypsy Crown* (New York: Hyperion, 2008), 17.
20. Gaye Hicyilmaz, *Pictures from the Fire* (London: Dolphin Paperbacks, 2003), 18.
21. Dick King-Smith, *Mr. Ape* (New York: Crown, 1998), 112–13.
22. Andrea Spalding, *Phoebe and the Gypsy* (Custer, WA: Orca Books, 1999), 26.
23. Frank DiLiberto, *Gypsy Kids: The Adventures of Colby Myers and Mark Howard* (Crystal Ball, 2002), 19.
24. Forsyth, *The Gypsy Crown*, 275.
25. Ibid., 224–25.
26. Ibid., 158.
27. Vivian Vande Velde, *A Coming Evil* (New York: Houghton Mifflin, 1998), 15.
28. Trilby Kent, *Medina Hill* (Plattsburgh, NY: Tundra Books, 2009), 75.
29. Paul McCusker, *Glennall's Betrayal* (Carol Stream, IL: Tyndale House, 1999), 11.
30. Forsyth, *The Gypsy Crown*, 275.
31. Stephen Roos, *The Gypsies Never Came* (New York: Simon and Schuster Young Readers, 2001), 88.
32. Zilpha Keatley Snyder, *The Gypsy Game* (New York: Delacorte, 1997), 9.
33. Mrs. Molesworth, *Us: An Old Fashioned Story* (London: Macmillan, 1900), 51.
34. Margaret Penrose, *The Motor Girls through New England; or Held by the Gypsies* (New York: Cupples and Leon, 1911), 101.
35. Molesworth, *Us*, 95.
36. Mary Martha Sherwood, *Shanty the Blacksmith: A Tale of Other Times* (Utica, NY: O. Hutchinson, 1841), 135.
37. Penrose, *The Motor Girls*, 136–37.
38. Ibid., 67.
39. Sherwood, *Shanty the Blacksmith*, 127.
40. Molesworth, *Us*, 155.

41. Penrose, *The Motor Girls*, 77.

42. Ibid., 159.

43. Robin D. G. Kelley, "There Are No Coons Here," *History Teacher* 31, no. 3 (1998): 399–402; Helen Bannerman, *Little Black Sambo* (London: Grant Richard, 1899).

44. Barb Karg and Arjean Spaite, *The Everything Pirates Book* (Avon, MA: Adams Media, 2007); Robert Louis Stevenson, *Treasure Island* (London: Cassell, 1883); Rafael Sabatini, *Captain Blood* (New York: Houghton Mifflin, 1922).

45. www.tshaonline.org/handbook/online/articles/pxrfh.

46. www.childrensuniversity.manchester.ac.uk/interactives/literacy/wordclasses/ discovermore/romaniproject.asp; www.re-net.ac.uk/ViewArticle2.aspx?contentId= 14488;www.google.com/url?sa=t&source=web&cd=1&sqi=2&ved=0CBYQFjAA& url=http%3A%2F%2Fwww.school-portal.co.uk%2FGroupDownloadFile.asp%3 FGroupID%3D926232%26ResourceId%3D2774531&ei=GfvGTbQQie7SAe25qK EI&usg=AFQjCNHlek4adb6_po5tNtX87ZnJl1ePbA; www.schools.norfolk.gov.uk/ myportal/custom/files_uploaded/uploaded_resources/4529/StoryTellingLesson-PlansKS2.pdf.

47. www.re-net.ac.uk/ViewArticle2.aspx?contentId=14376.

48. www.centerforlearning.org/p-499-the-gypsy-gamethe-trumpeter-of-krakow.aspx.

49. Lloyd Alexander, *Gypsy Rizka* (New York: Dutton Children's Press, 1999), 182.

Building a Core Collection

Muslim Experiences in English-Language
Children's Books, September 2001–September 2011

ANNA L. NIELSEN

WHEN DIFFERENCES BETWEEN cultural or religious experiences are pointed to as something to exalt as romantic and exotic otherness or as problems to be solved or protected against, the prejudicial and xenophobic constructions of the authoring culture tend to be supported. When these representations of romanticizing exoticism, prejudice, and xenophobia are presented in youth literature, the presentations function to create contact zones between the authoring culture and reading child that are fields of damaging and destructive messages and models of appropriation and disappearance, rendering the reader of the other culture in the text invisible and the reader of the authoring culture inequitably empowered. In effect, the literature becomes part of the propaganda of keeping the dominant cultural powers firmly dominant. What is the librarian to do? One answer lies in a pluralistic approach to book selection and collection development.

TOWARD PLURALISM

Edward Said defines Orientalism in his groundbreaking text of the same name as the pervasive and persistent Western tradition of prejudicial outsider interpretation of cultural artifacts and behaviors not stemming from within the Western tradition itself.[1] Fault lines include attitudes of constructed superiority and treating what is different as exotic, creating a wrangling between the realness of the other and the naming decisions of the Western tradition. In effect, the battle disappears the culture in question in favor of the culture as interpreted by Western tradition. When the so-called exotic tradition of the perceived other begins to cross boundaries into Western everyday life and gain prominence and visibility, the reactions of those on the receiving field of the cultural boundary crossing often remain responses of imposed interpretation of exoticism, and so on, that continue to function to disappear the other. Responses also include assimilation and appropriation, with varying degrees of respectful and benevolent intent.

bell hooks posits cannibalism as the rather problematic appropriation of minority cultures in her seminal piece, "Eating the Other: Desire and Resistance."[2] She uses the term to refer to dominant cultures assimilating minority cultures to such extremes that the minority culture is disappeared under the newly recognized and supposedly shared cultural experience. The minority culture is melted into the pot of the majority culture, lost under the more powerful presence. The cultural invisibility that results is a loss of identity. Which brings to point Geertz's notion that what we build from shared cultural systems, be they imposed definitions or appropriations or assimilations, are in effect shared impositions of what common sense is for all who live under them, which in turn become our shared cultural presuppositions that become our shared stories through which we create operating identities.[3]

What this means for English-language youth literature of Muslim experiences is that when peoples of different geographic, cultural, and religious locations and traditions are forced together, there are, invariably it often seems, conditions of dominance and sublimation, coercion, inequality, conflict, and misrepresentation. In youth literature this is already a defining feature because the literature is written by adults for children, a relationship of parties that is not remotely equitable in power or communication but is purely the imposed will and creation of one group over another.[4] When cultural hegemony is added to this mix of adult over child, texts become problematic indeed. Maria Tatar refers to these inevitable conditions as contact zones that must be navigated by children as they engage with stories and reading in the process of growing up and forming their own identities.[5]

This is not to say the project of collection development in a subject with which the librarian is culturally and religiously inexperienced is impossible. It isn't. It simply requires a certain amount of care and a pluralistic approach to selection.

PLURALISM IN PRACTICE

Cultural pluralism is the idea that the cultural practices and identities of all groups, minority and majority, have an integrated and defining place within the wider cultural construct of the dominant culture. No cultural practices and identities are disappeared and no cultural group is invisible. All have a valid and invaluable unique identifying faction of the whole. Philosophically, it can be defined as American pragmatist William James explains it, in opposition to monism. That is, if a person is a monist, he or she behaves according to a belief in the one and the only, the single belief representing a notion of unity. That is, if we are all one, we are the same, and thus we are in union. There is no texture of difference. If a person is a pluralist he or she behaves according to a belief in the many and the various. That is, if we are many, union is in multiplicity. The texture of all our differences defines us. James proposes that it is the "variety in things" that must be considered alongside the monist unity of things to understand and embrace a "totality," and "acquaintance with reality's diversities is as important as understanding their connection."[6] Culturally, and in terms of selecting diverse literature for youth, pluralism is the idea that the pratfalls of intended and unintended disappearance can and should be avoided while developing a collection. "For pluralistic pragmatism, truth grows up inside all of the finite experiences."[7]

COLLECTION DEVELOPMENT: EVALUATION MODEL

Rudine Sims Bishop, in her foundational study *Shadow and Substance: Afro-American Experience in Contemporary Children's Fiction*, offers a three-part approach to finding pluralistic texts, examining representations of African American characters in children's books published in the fifteen years following the Civil Rights Act of 1964.[8] Her divisions are "social conscience" books, which point to African Americans as a problem to be understood, disappearing people and experience in judgment; "melting pot" books, which insist that the experience and identity of African American children are indiscernible and therefore the same as other Americans, disappearing people in what hooks would later label cannibalistic assimilation and appropriation; and "culturally conscious" books, which recognize African American youth experiences as unique and universal, as part of what is now called a pluralistic interpretation of the human experience. It is used here as a departure point to build a pluralistic model of evaluating and selecting books concerning Muslim experiences in English-language children's books published since the hugely confrontational and controversial contact zone of September 11, 2001.

ISLAM ACROSS THE GLOBE

The immediate setback, of course, is what exactly do we mean by Muslim experiences? It is not static or monolithic or singular; one definition does not and cannot represent every Muslim or Muslim experience. There are nuances and variety of integral importance of Islam and Islamic culture as there is in every religious and cultural tradition that must be recognized and respected. For example, the Shii Muslims believe that the blood male relative of the Prophet should have ruled after the passing of the Prophet Muhammad, while the majority Sunni Islam support the Rashidun, the four caliphs who were the immediate successors of the Prophet Muhammad, and the resulting and current hierarchy.[9] Another example of annual note are the discrepancies concerning the celebration of Eid al-Fitr, the Muslim holiday that marks the end of Ramadan, the Muslim period of fasting. The Muslim calendar is lunar-based, and calculations of religious holidays are made by lunar sightings according to region and further individuated by weather and technology of moon sightings, making the end of Eid one day and moment in one part of the world and a slightly different day and moment in another part of the world.[10]

According to the Pew Research Center's Forum on Religion & Public Life report, "Mapping the Global Muslim Population," 1.57 billion people identify as Muslim out of the estimated 6.8 billion people who constitute the world population, which means that more than one in five global citizens is a practitioner of Islam.[11] Sixty percent of Muslims live in the Asia-Pacific region, a mere 20 percent in the Middle East and North Africa combined, 15 percent in sub-Saharan Africa, 2.7 percent in Europe, and 0.3 percent in the Americas. The world Muslim population is expected to grow 35 percent, or twice the rate of non-Muslims, to 2.2 billion by 2030.[12] According to 2010 numbers, there are almost 2.6 million Muslims living in the United States, 0.8 percent of the population, a group that is expected to more than double by 2030 to 6.2 million.[13] In 2010, Islam was the religion most frequently mentioned in news media within the United States.[14] In the midst of this growth, the Muslim experience is acknowledged as facing more discrimination than any other religion in the United States.[15]

THE LITERATURE

The non-commensurate representation in youth literature of real-life populations and minority groups is a reality of publishing and reading. Muslim experiences, frustratingly, are not exempt from this tradition of exclusion. However, the number of books published in the decade since 2011 that speak to Muslim experiences has increased, and with that increase comes the joyous difficulty of a complete survey project. Surveys are rarely absolute. A text can always be missed, and the ruling parameters of one researcher and another will often differ. For the purposes of this project I read and reviewed English-language children's books published in the decade following 9/11 that overtly include the mention of Islam and Islamic culture. I included fiction only, in picture book, middle reader, and young adult novel form. I avoided reprints of previously published titles, information texts, and fairy tales, reserving all three for separate projects. The titles I read totaled 105.

COLLECTION DEVELOPMENT:
THEMES, TREATMENTS, AND SELECTION CRITERIA

Of the books that fit the survey criteria, repeated themes include the let's-learn-from-the-children-and-all-get-along syndrome, an imagined and romanticized ideal, to say the least; stereotyping and prejudice, depicting Muslims as villainous; terrorism and war; identity through religious practice and attire; and chirpy-perky-super-positive-all-is-resolved girl teen fiction. Most have treatments that range from socially conscious to melting pot to culturally conscious with contact zones of misrepresentation, cannibalism, appropriation, and assimilation. All point to the qualitative alternative of a pluralistic approach. Selection rules are provided throughout.

Exemplifying the unfortunate practice of disappearance through romantic simplification in an uncomfortable blend of socially conscious and melting pot treatments is the picture book *Snow in Jerusalem*. It diminishes and effectively disappears the very real complexity and boundary war of the Palestinian-Israeli conflict to the absurdly simplified metaphor of children learning to share. Two gently but shallowly rendered boys, one Muslim and one Jewish, fight over who owns the cat they've both been feeding. The cat conveniently has an even number of kittens, whom the boys promptly divide and take across their respective borders, one to Palestine territory and one to Israel territory. The mother cat proceeds to travel across Jerusalem each night in ease and safety, visiting each in turn, bringing peace and satisfaction to all. The story is an idealistic parable of the power and possibility of friendship. While the intention to simplify and normalize may be well meant, it is deeply damaging in that it disappears the real experience in favor of a sanitized, common, and romanticized fallacy. To sublimate an experience in a metaphor is a disappearing act no matter the kindness of gesture, since to make something like or as something else makes it not itself. And what is that but imposed invisibility on cultural and religious identity?

Continuing in this vein is *Drita, My Homegirl*. Ten-year-old Kosovo refugee Drita is teased in her new fourth-grade classroom in Brooklyn, New York, especially by the popular African American Maxie. The girls are forced to bond and so they do, becoming friends. Maxie gives an oral presentation on Kosovo, spreading the feeling of companionship and common ground across the classroom. Again, racial and ethnic identity is insultingly simplified and solved through the metaphor of childhood friendship.

Selection Rule No. 1: Avoid Simplification and Romantic Metaphor

The misrepresentation of the young adult novel *The Flame Tree* is reactionary and perilous in its stereotyping of Muslims as villainous terrorists. A twelve-year-old son of American missionaries in Indonesia is kidnapped after the attacks of September 11 by anti-American Islamic fundamentalists, and none of the local Muslims the bereaved family considers friends will help rescue him. The boy is forcibly circumcised and attempts are made to convert him to Islam. Eventually, he and his mother forgive those who trespassed against him.

Selection Rule No. 2: Avoid Villainous
Stereotyping and Simpering Superiority

Eve Bunting's *One Green Apple*, illustrated by Ted Lewin, is about recent émigré Farah, a girl of indiscriminate country and unmentioned cultural and religious heritage but who is pictured in a *hijab*, inappropriately referred to as a *dupatta*. She goes on a field trip with her new classmates, hoping to learn English soon. She finds a green apple while everyone else finds red, but she is comforted by the fact that together the apples will make sweet cider. Another tale of complex global issues solved through the simplicity of childhood friendships, the bigger issue here is the knowing misuse of the word *dupatta*.

Before Farah has all her problems about immigration and cultural assimilation solved by sweet apple cider, she worries, "I am different, too, in other ways. My jeans and T-shirt look like theirs, but my dupatta covers my head and shoulders. I have not seen anyone else wearing a dupatta, though all the girls and women in my home country do."[16]

Correspondence between Bunting and her editor at Clarion indicate that there was editorial concern over the misappropriation of the word *dupatta* to refer to a head scarf, and that the concern was mentioned to the author, along with a provision of research showing that a *dupatta* is not, in truth, synonymous with head scarf. The South Asian *dupatta* is a long, rectangular shawl worn mainly in Pakistan and India, most commonly draped over one shoulder, though sometimes used to loosely cover the head and neck. It is customarily worn as part of the South Asian traditional feminine ensemble *shalwar kameez*, which includes a long tunic and loose pants. Moreover, illustrator research showed that "young girls in Pakistan don't wear the dupatta over their heads but arranged around their shoulders like a scarf."[17]

Bunting's response is cavalier and reproachable. "About the dupatta . . . I'm not really sure of the problem. In the text no country is mentioned." Bunting goes on to write, "My feeling is that it's not important as we have left the country unnamed. If [the illustrator] wants to use a Pakistani model, it doesn't really matter. The model could be assumed to be from any middle eastern country." To be so casual, almost flippant, about the synonymous nature of all countries in the Middle East and to use an item of traditional attire from South Asia to do so, not even an item from the Middle East, is to succumb to cultural disregard and outsider prejudice of the most regressive kind. It is predicated on a Western styling of all things Middle Eastern as the same in their otherness. It is, especially in a book messaging tolerance and cultural blending, disingenuous. It disappears cultural tradition into one cloth of difference. It is unacceptable. Bunting does suggest, "Another solution would be to eliminate the word and call it simply a head scarf." If the word were changed, the text would be tenable, begging the question of why it wasn't. Or the word could have been exchanged for *hijab,* a word that comes from the Arabic for veil and is used to describe the head scarves worn by Muslim women. As the text stands, it misrepresents with imposed blanket interpretation of all things other.

Selection Rule No. 3: Avoid Misrepresentation

Fortunately, there are many books that engage with a pluralistic viewpoint and avoid the contact zones of misinterpretation, appropriation, and assimilation to create culturally conscious pluralistic reading. The books satisfy cultural and literary aesthetics and present Muslim experiences in a manner that is accurate, respectful, and natural. The characters and plots are well developed. Picture books are fully realized, issues are fully integrated into stories, and in perhaps one of the surest signs of cultural comfort and acceptance, rather than the barbed notion of tolerance which presents the other as something to be endured, there is a plethora of chirpy-perky chick lit filled with plucky, chatty teen girls giving casual and equal weight to their Muslim identities and the trials and tribulations of adolescence with earnestness and aplomb.

From Somalia, with Love by Na'ima B. Robert tells the story of a London-Somali teen who wears the *hijab* and is a devout Muslim. She writes poetry and clearly articulates her mixed feelings about her father joining them, finally, after being missing in Somalia for twelve years. She directly addresses local prejudices about Muslims and grapples with growing up in two cultures. A positive is that a glossary is included; the negative is that the sentences feel stiff and false, and the resolution too easy. Still, the honest depiction of life makes it worth a read.

Selection Rule No. 4: Embrace Research

Program No. 1: Research the Region and Cultural Practices of the Book
The following books depict topics that have been well researched by their respective authors. The resonant picture book *My Name Was Hussein* by Hristo Kyuchukov depicts the young boy Hussein living happily in Bulgaria as a Roma Muslim until the government insists all Muslims convert to Christianity and take new names to prove it. *My Friend Jamal* by Anna McQuinn brings together third-grade Polish immigrant Joseph and Somali immigrant Jamal as best friends matter-of-factly sharing and accepting differences and similarities as they go about their play.

For the older age group, *Ask Me No Questions* by Marina Budhos tells the story of teen Nadira and her Bangladeshi family who have been living illegally in the United States and who must plead for asylum in Canada after 9/11 brings changes in immigration policy. *In the Name of God* by Paula Jolin follows a seventeen-year-old Syrian teen determined to be a suicide bomber and the very real and very serious consideration of religion and devotion to cause such a decision takes. *A Little Piece of Ground* by Elizabeth Laird tackles the life of a twelve-year-old boy struggling to exist in occupied Palestine.

Selection Rule No. 5: Embrace Realism

Program No. 2: Pair the Book with a Documentary Film and Discuss
In the chirpy-perky category, Australian Randa Abdel-Fattah gives us *Does My Head Look Big in This?* and *Ten Things I Hate about Me*. The protagonist in the former is Amal, a first-generation Muslim Palestinian immigrant "whacked with some seriously confusing identity hyphens." She instant messages and wears the *hijab*. In the latter, the protagonist is a Lebanese-Australian Muslim who is blond Jamie at school and a devout Muslim at home until she learns to de-split her identity. In *Skunk Girl* by Sheba Karim, Nina is the only Muslim in her small town in upstate New York and the younger sister of a super-smart perfectionist, and she doesn't know which is worse. *Luv Ya Bunches* gives readers four best friends in fifth grade, one of whom is a Muslim named Yasaman who designs websites. *Love, Inc.* is about half-Pakistani, half-Scottish American Zahara and her two best friends who take down their shared ex-boyfriend and start a business. The books smartly handle the twin concerns of being young girls and young Muslims, deftly assuming that we the reading audience are along for the ride. The stories teach without being pedantic and trip along entertainingly. Stereotypes are disappeared and good stories are revealed, stories with strong and well-rendered characters, and the laughter eases our passage without faulting into levity.

Selection Rule No. 6: Embrace Humor & Play

Program No. 3: Playing and Creating with New Media Technologies
Remember that humor and play can function to bring people together; don't get lost in pursuing only award-winning and serious texts and don't limit yourself to the text-only experience. Allow your book choices to have a sense of humor, such as the realistic books from the chirpy-perky category mentioned previously, and allow new media technologies into your pluralistic activities and discussions.

Remember that play can be considered a capacity to experiment and to learn new forms and ways of being and thinking. Encourage your young patrons to bring characters, plots, and scenarios into gaming and digital creation. Look at available games and question if the narratives and avatars available are pluralistic. If the answer is no, work to build games that are. Play with and create cartoons, digital stories, and short videos that express and embody the pluralistic experience.

CONCLUSION

As the six selection guidelines show, the general idea in collection development is to pay attention to a discourse that expresses a pluralistic sensibility. The same can be transferred to programming activities and can even follow the classic children's literature tenet of instruction and delight. As groundbreaking author Rukhsana Khan reminds us, if Muslim youth are "to feel at home in the mosaic of North American culture, they need to see themselves and their values represented positively in literature. *Aladdin* doesn't count. We've come a long way since then and there are no such things as flying carpets."[18] With Muslims numbering one out of every five global citizens, we all need to come a long way, and good collection development and corresponding programming is where we can begin.

PICTURE BOOKS

Bunting, Eve. *One Green Apple.* Illustrated by Ted Lewin. New York: Clarion Books, 2006.

Da Costa, Deborah. *Snow in Jerusalem.* Illustrated by Cornelius Van Wright and Ying-Hwa Hu. Morton Grove, IL: Albert Whitman, 2001.

Kyuchukov, Hristo. *My Name was Hussein.* Honesdale, PA: Boyds Mills, 2004.

McQuinn, Anna. *My Friend Jamal.* Illustrated by Ben Fray. Toronto: Annick, 2008.

MIDDLE READERS

Laird, Elizabeth, with Sonia Nimr. *A Little Piece of Ground.* Chicago, IL: Haymarket Books, 2006.

Lombard, Jenny. *Drita, My Homegirl.* New York: G.P. Putnam's Sons, 2006.

Myracle, Lauren. *Luv Ya Bunches.* New York: Amulet Books, 2009.

YOUNG ADULT NOVELS

Abdel-Fattah, Randa. *Does My Head Look Big in This?* New York: Orchard Books, 2007.

_____. *Ten Things I Hate about Me.* New York: Orchard Books, 2009.

Budhow, Marina. *Ask Me No Questions.* New York: Simon & Schuster, 2006.

Collins, Yvonne, and Sandy Rideout. *Love, Inc.* New York: Hyperion, 2011.

Jolin, Paula. *In the Name of God.* New Milford, CT: Roaring Brook, 2007.

Karim, Sheba. *Skunk Girl.* New York: Farrar, Straus, and Giroux, 2009.

Lewis, Richard. *The Flame Tree.* New York: Simon & Schuster, 2004.

Robert, Na'ima B. *From Somalia, with Love.* London: Frances Lincoln Children's Books, 2009.

NOTES

1. Edward Said, *Orientalism* (New York, Vintage, 1978).

2. bell hooks, "Eating the Other: Desire and Resistance," in *Media and Cultural Studies:*

Keyworks, ed. Meenakshi Gigi Durham and Douglas Kellner, rev. ed. (Malden, MA: Blackwell, 2006), 366–80.

3. Clifford Geertz, *Local Knowledge: Further Essays in Interpretive Anthropology* (New York: Basic Books, 1983).

4. Perry Nodelman, *The Hidden Adult: Defining Children's Literature* (Baltimore: Johns Hopkins University Press, 2008).

5. Maria Tatar, *Enchanted Hunters: The Power of Stories in Childhood* (New York: W.W. Norton, 2009).

6. William James, *Pragmatism and the Meaning of Truth* (Cambridge, MA: Harvard University Press, 1994), 64–65.

7. Ibid., 125.

8. Rudine Sims Bishop, *Shadow and Substance: Afro-American Experience in Contemporary Children's Fiction* (Urbana, IL: National Council of Teachers for English, 1982).

9. Karen Armstrong, *Islam: A Short History* (New York: Modern Library, 2000).

10. Ahmed Al Omran, "When Is Eid? Muslims Can't Seem to Agree," *The Two-Way: NPR's News Blog* (August 30, 2011), www.npr.org/blogs/thetwo-way/2011/08/30/140056443/when-is-eid-muslims-cant-seem-to-agree.

11. Pew Research Center, The Pew Forum on Religion & Public Life, "Mapping the Global Muslim Population" (October 7, 2009), http://pewforum.org/Muslim/Mapping-the-Global-Muslim-Population.aspx.

12. Pew Research Center, The Pew Forum on Religion & Public Life, "The Future of the Global Muslim Population, Projections for 2010–2030" (January 27, 2011), http://pewforum.org/The-Future-of-the-Global-Muslim-Population.aspx.

13. Ibid.

14. Pew Research Center, The Pew Forum on Religion & Public Life, "Religion in the News: Islam was No. 1 Topic in 2010" (February 24, 2011), http://pewforum.org/Politics-and-Elections/Religion-in-the-News--Islam-Was-No--1-Topic-in-2010.aspx.

15. Pew Research Center, The Pew Forum on Religion & Public Life, "Muslims Widely Seen as Facing Discrimination: Views of Religious Similarities and Differences" (September 9, 2009), http://pewforum.org/Muslim/Muslims-Widely-Seen-As-Facing-Discrimination.aspx.

16. Eve Bunting, *One Green Apple* (New York: Clarion Books, 2006), 7.

17. Eve Bunting, Papers, Children's Literature Research Collections, University of Minnesota Libraries, Folder 1.

18. Rukhsana Khan, "Muslims in Children's Books: An Author Looks Back and at the Ongoing Publishing Challenges," *School Library Journal* 52, no. 9 (2006): 36–37.

Holding Out Hope

Homelessness in Children's and Young Adult Literature

KIM BECNEL

MOST STUDIES DIVIDE the approximately 2.3–3.5 million Americans who are homeless into three categories. The first group, making up 49 percent of the homeless population, consists of single adults, the majority of whom are male. Many of these adults are veterans, and a substantial number struggle with addictions and mental illnesses.[1] The second group of homeless is termed *unaccompanied youth*, of which there are approximately 575,000 to 1.6 million in the United States. Unaccompanied youth range from 16 to 22 years old, and the primary cause of their homelessness is violence and family conflict. A significant portion of these youth have endured abuse (46 percent), and many who identify as gay, lesbian, bisexual, transgendered, questioning, intersex, or two-spirited (GLBTQI2-S) have been thrown out of their childhood homes.[2]

Perhaps the least well-known segment of the homeless population is the 34 percent that are classified as families with children. Most of these families (84 percent) are headed by a woman, often in her late twenties and without more than a high school education or GED. A large number of these women suffer from depressive episodes, post-traumatic stress disorder, alcohol and drug addictions, and chronic health problems.[3] Of course, the children of these families face their own challenges. A majority of them face significant struggles in school, and about half suffer from anxiety and depression. Twenty percent of preschoolers who experience homelessness will at some point need professional treatment for emotional problems.[4] Recent statistics and reports suggest that it is this category—homeless families—that is currently experiencing the most growth. The U.S. Department of Housing and Urban Development reveals that while "nearly 35,000 fewer people used emergency shelter or transitional housing in 2009 than in 2008 . . . the number of families in homeless programs increased by nearly 11,000" and that "since 2007 there has been a nearly 30 percent increase in the number of sheltered families."[5]

POLITICAL CLIMATE AND
LIBRARIES' RESPONSE TO HOMELESSNESS

There has been a discernible shift in mainstream America's perception of homelessness over the past thirty years. In his study on homeless culture and the media, Jeremy Reynalds notes that in the 1980s "the homeless were presented as individuals worthy of public sympathy, whose homelessness was not generally their own fault, but which represented one of society's endemic shortcomings," whereas today the broadcast media often portray "the homeless as part of the criminal element."[6] The change that Reynalds charts is evidenced in the current political climate as well, in which attitudes toward homelessness have become increasingly strident and hostile. Since the 1990s, there "has been a push to reduce social welfare programs and an increasing tendency to criminalize and punish homeless individuals, especially those who are considered 'undeserving' or unworthy of help."[7] Don Mitchell articulates the philosophical problem with this type of legislation, noting that when we define the "legitimate public" as only those who "have a place governed by private property rules to call their own," "landed property thus again becomes a prerequisite for legitimate citizenship" and "homeless people are reduced to the status of children."[8]

Sadly, this hostility toward people who are homeless and the treatment of them as second-class citizens has even worked its way into the public library, ostensibly one of the few places in a capitalistic society where all citizens are treated equitably and with respect, regardless of means. Take, as just one example, the "civility campaign" launched by the Salt Lake City Library, which aimed to "teach the homeless, children and others how to behave."[9] Initiatives like this clearly equate homeless individuals with children who do not know how to operate competently in the adult world. The American Library Association's Hunger, Homelessness, and Poverty Task Force notes and condemns the recent tendency of library literature to consider people who are homeless as "problem patrons." They write that Salt Lake City's "civility campaign," as well as other similar policies cropping up across the nation, are "at best misguided and, at worst, contribute to the criminalization of poor people."[10] The task force insists that libraries stop treating poverty and homelessness like behavioral problems and start figuring out how to best serve these patrons.

LIBRARY PROGRAMMING

While some libraries have busied themselves crafting hostile policies to keep the homeless out of their libraries, others have heeded, and in some cases anticipated, the call of ALA's Hunger, Homelessness, and Poverty Task Force by initializing services and programs to support their homeless populations. The San Francisco Public Library's recent addition of a social worker to its library staff is one shining example.[11] In New York, the Brooklyn Public Library (BPL) has developed a Shelter Storytelling Program; as BPL's Carrie Banks writes, "Libraries are not an obvious recreational choice for children living in shelters, who often read below grade level. The Shelter Storytelling program helps introduce these children to libraries, which can serve as a constant in their lives, because wherever they go in New York City there will be a library nearby."[12] Many libraries help in a more indirect but no less significant way by conducting basic education and job training classes for adults and providing job search assistance.

Another important role that libraries play is by making their general populations aware of hunger, poverty, and homelessness issues in their own communities. Some provide book clubs for children and teens, selecting books that deal with themes of social justice. Libraries also organize community service projects in conjunction with agencies such as Habitat for Humanity and local food banks in order to encourage young people to think about and engage issues like homelessness and poverty in meaningful ways. Through all of these means, libraries can help create a society that seeks to support its homeless constituents instead of avoiding the problem by ignoring or "othering" a large, complex group of people. Libraries interested in ideas and resources for helping their homeless populations can consult the ALA's Hunger, Homelessness, and Poverty Task Force's web page (www.hhptf.org) and Leslie Edmonds Holt's and Glen E. Holt's volume titled *Public Library Services for the Poor: Doing All We Can*.

LIBRARY COLLECTIONS FOR CHILDREN AND YOUNG ADULTS

One of the most important steps that libraries can take to help those who are homeless is to provide literature for children and young adults that portrays homeless individuals and families in authentic ways. Children receive a great deal of exposure to stereotypical representations of homelessness on television and movies, but the effect of this can be diluted if we collect and make available some of the excellent fiction and nonfiction books that have been published over the last ten years. To create a solid collection, libraries should make sure to have books appropriate for all ages that engage the issue of homelessness. Together, the titles should demonstrate the wide array of individuals who experience homelessness and not suggest that homelessness "looks" a certain way. Homeless men and women of varying ages and ethnicities should be represented. Children who are homeless should also be included. Books should include main characters who are homeless as well as supporting characters, and some stories should be told from the homeless character's point of view.

Librarians should choose books that avoid the problematic stereotypes of the homeless person as an object of pity or scorn or the homeless person as romantic hero. Writing about Hollywood movies, Linda K. Fuller describes these stereotypes as "lowlife and or street-smart, worldly-wise mystics" and notes that they enable Americans to distance themselves "from both the people and their problems."[13] John Allen in *Homelessness in American Literature* laments that the "'real voices' of the homeless have been excluded in favor of treatments which either romanticize or objectify the condition of homelessness."[14] These treatments have "led to stereotypes of the homeless as isolated, disaffiliated, inactive, pathological, and permanently displaced."[15] To avoid perpetuating these harmful stereotypes, librarians should choose books that avoid presenting people who are homeless as having lives so difficult as to turn them from fellow human beings into objects of pity or charity. Characters who are homeless should be three-dimensional figures that make their own decisions, not passive victims of bad luck, fate, or social pressures. On the other side of the coin, books must also refrain from suggesting that homelessness is simply a fun adventure, for fear of contributing to the romantic stereotype of homelessness that assuages our concern for those facing it. Ideally, books should depict homeless characters as complex people who face considerable difficulties because of their lack of basic shelter and other necessities, but who also have hope and joy in their lives.

Additionally, librarians should avoid books that insist on dividing people who are homeless into the deserving and undeserving. Occasionally, for example, authors will take incredible pains to detail the run of bad luck a homeless protagonist has had in order to gain sympathy for that person from the audience. These types of narratives, while suggesting that some people who are homeless are simply victims of circumstance and therefore should receive compassion and assistance, also imply that there are other people who are to blame for their own misfortunes and that these people should not be helped. Despite any individual's personal journey, the causes for homelessness are complicated, and we cannot always see all of the factors involved. Furthermore, this tendency to sort the worthy from the unworthy implies a problematic hierarchy, with the sorters positioned firmly above those being sorted, whether deemed worthy in the end or not. Finally, in this same vein, resolutions to the homeless situation presented in a given book should not be presented as too easy, for fairy-tale endings also minimize the problem of homelessness and falsely suggest that easy solutions abound.

EXAMPLES

Regarding picture books, it is critically important to avoid titles that offer stereotypical and reductive homelessness narratives. An example of such a choice is Steve Seskin and Allen Shamblin's *A Chance to Shine*.[16] The story begins with a description of Joe, the stereotypical homeless person complete with a funny smell, a "scraggly beard," and a strange habit of talking to pigeons. All it takes is for the narrator's father to offer Joe meals in exchange for sweeping the sidewalk to solve all of his problems. The very next day, he shows up clean and shaven, and soon he is in his very own apartment. The message, that regardless of cause, homelessness is easy to fix, deemphasizes the seriousness and complexity of both the problem and the solution. David McPhail's *The Teddy Bear* also presents a stereotypical homeless person.[17] In this case, the lonely, scraggly man finds, claims, and comes to love a teddy bear that a little boy has lost in the park. When the boy rediscovers and reclaims the bear, the man yells for it and begins to cry. The boy, understanding the connection, gives the man back the bear. Not only is the homeless person in this tale presented as a stereotype, but he is also equated with a child. It is hard to imagine the story working if the grown man who became attached to the bear was not a homeless person. Portraying a person who is homeless as childlike reinforces the misperception that those who don't possess homes are less mature, capable, and intelligent than those who do.

A better picture book selection dealing with the topic of homelessness would be Laura Williams's *The Can Man*.[18] In this story, a boy named Tim decides to collect cans to earn money for a new skateboard. Soon though, Tim realizes that by collecting cans, he's preventing Mr. Peters, who is homeless, from collecting the cans as he usually does and thus earning enough money to buy a winter coat. Tim decides to give the money he's earned from his can collecting to Mr. Peters, who returns the favor by refurbishing a skateboard for Tim. In this story, though most people call him the Can Man, the homeless person has a name, a story, and a role in the community. Most importantly, Mr. Peters models compassion and friendliness to Tim, not begrudging Tim's can collection, but offering to help him carry his cans to the recycling center. The story has a happy, yet not unrealistic, conclusion, and encourages readers to think about the difference between wants and needs.

Another title that avoids stereotypes and presents a hopeful, yet realistic conclusion is Anne Bromley's *The Lunch Thief*.[19] In this story we meet Rafael, a thoughtful kid who takes the time to find out the motivation behind his new classmate's habit of stealing lunches. With a little investigation, he discovers that Kevin and his family have lost their home due to wildfires and are now living in a motel. When Rafael discovers this, he begins to understand that Kevin may not be a bully after all; he may simply be hungry. Not everything is resolved here, but the story ends on a hopeful note—an extra lunch and an offer of friendship.

Not surprisingly, representations of homelessness in middle grade and young adult novels tend to be more complex than those offered in picture books. Stereotypical depictions still crop up, however, in novels such as David Williams's *Mr. Stink*.[20] This satiric novel depends on over-the-top characters, including Chloe, an awkward outcast, her ridiculously conservative mother who is running for political office, and Mr. Stink, a homeless man Chloe befriends. All the characters are caricatured here, so it is not unexpected that Mr. Stink lacks awareness of his incredible odor and is really, it turns out, a gentleman from a "good" family who has suffered a terrible tragedy. By the novel's end, Mr. Stink has become firmly established as the stereotypical sage who, through a simple conversation with Chloe's mother, changes everything about their strained relationship. Further, Mr. Stink doesn't accept the family's offer to remain with them; instead he claims he has to move on, presumably to solve other people's problems in other towns through which his ramblings take him. Intentional or not, the stereotype of the homeless mystic here is problematic if readers do not have the skills or knowledge to deconstruct it. The presentation of people who are homeless as somehow better or more evolved than others is just as dehumanizing as negative stereotyping.

Novels written for middle graders and young adults should avoid, to an even greater degree than picture books, giving the impression that homelessness is a problem with an easy fix. William Kowalski's *The Way It Works* demonstrates the problems with such titles.[21] In this book, after an amazing run of bad luck, Walter finds himself living in his car while frantically hunting for a job. Although he does suffer during his bout of homelessness, Walter makes a relatively neat and quick turnaround by virtue of persistence and a good attitude. Soon, he has started his own company, found the woman of his dreams, and put many other homeless people to work. The problem with books such as this is that they romanticize and oversimplify the issues, suggesting to readers that all homeless individuals can turn their lives around if they just try hard enough; this also implies the reverse—that homeless individuals who can't immediately turn their lives around simply aren't persistent or optimistic enough.

Fortunately, there is an increasing number of middle grade and young adult selections that treat both the issue of homelessness and people who are homeless in a thoughtful and respectful way. Nikki Grimes's *Rich: A Dyamonde Daniel Book*, for example, is a middle grade novel which maintains that homeless people are ordinary folks who are members of our communities and that we should take the time to listen to their stories.[22] In this title, when Dyamonde befriends a quiet girl named Damaris Dancer, she learns that Damaris's mother has lost one of her two jobs, resulting in the family's move to a shelter. Dyamonde convinces her new friend to tell her story in a poem for the local poetry contest. Damaris is afraid others will laugh, but Dyamonde convinces her that people only laugh at what they don't understand, and that she can make them understand by expressing herself and her feelings. Wise Dyamonde also convinces her friend Free that sometimes it's more fun to hunt for treasures in a secondhand store, because those things all have stories, than to pine away for the newest video game. No drastic change occurs in anyone's physical circumstances in the novel, but attitudes toward poverty and wealth shift while compassion and empathy grow.

Olugbemiosla Rhuday-Perkovich's *Eighth Grade Superzero* goes even further than *Rich* in its efforts to emphasize the humanity of those who are homeless.[23] When eighth-grader Reggie begins to do volunteer work at a local homeless shelter, he develops a bigger perspective on his own life and problems. Reggie and his friends engage in thoughtful discussions, such as the following in which the group is responding to the question, Whose fault is homelessness? Reggie finally answers: "It's everyone's. And no one's. And theirs, and ours."[24] He admits that he keeps thinking that the homeless people he met at the shelter could be people he knew, to which Jeff, his youth group leader, replies, "It's okay if it's someone you don't know?" Reggie thinks for a minute and answers in the negative, adding: "I'm saying I realized that there's no one that I don't know."[25] This acknowledgement of the complexity of the problem of homelessness and the powerful avowal of empathy and connectedness with those who are homeless make it an excellent selection for middle grade readers.

A young adult title that confronts the complexity and scale of the homeless problem is Delphine de Vigan's *No and Me*.[26] In this gritty novel, a difficult family situation, emotional issues, and a drug problem conspire to land a teenager called No on the streets. She is befriended by a schoolgirl named Lou and eventually taken in by Lou's family. Lou and No grapple with the fact that even when No has a safe and warm place to sleep, "outside men and women are sleeping buried in sleeping bags or cardboard boxes, on top of subway vents or on the ground. Outside men and women are sleeping in the recesses of a city they're excluded from."[27] Neither of them can rest comfortably with this knowledge in their hearts. It turns out that even No's time with Lou's family is just a brief respite. She returns to life on the streets, and there is nothing Lou can do to stop her. Lou never regrets trying, however, or the many ways that reaching out to No has changed her for the better.

CONCLUSION

By making careful choices in programming and book selection, libraries can have a powerful effect on the way that homelessness is perceived by today's youth. We can avoid promoting titles with stereotypical portrayals and reductive narratives, opting instead to purchase and feature books that humanize people who are homeless and give voice to their varied and complicated stories. In this way, we can perhaps begin to disrupt the "us versus them" mentality that pervades contemporary conceptualization of homelessness and encourage a future generation that responds to individuals and families experiencing homelessness not with disdain or pity, but with compassion and resolve.

RECOMMENDED TITLES

Picture Books

Altman, Linda Jacobs. *Amelia's Road.* New York: Lee & Low Books, 1995.

Bunting, Eve. *December.* New York: Harcourt, 1997.

Cole, Brock. *Good Enough to Eat.* New York: Farrar, Straus and Giroux, 2007.

DiCamillo, Kate. *Great Joy.* Cambridge, MA: Candlewick, 2001.

DiSalvo, Dyanne. *A Castle on Viola Street.* New York: Harper Collins, 2001.

Gunning, Monica. *A Shelter in Our Car.* New York: Children's Book, 2004.

McGovern, Ann. *The Lady in the Box.* New York: Turtle Books, 1999.

Middle Grade Fiction

Carey, Janet Lee. *The Double Life of Zoe Flynn.* New York: Aladdin, 2007.

Clements, Andrew. *Room One: A Mystery or Two.* New York: Atheneum, 2008.

Creech, Sharon. *The Unfinished Angel.* New York: HarperCollins, 2009.

Fensham, Elizabeth. *Helicopter Man.* New York: Bloomsbury, 2005.

Flake, Sharon G. *Begging for Change.* New York: Hyperion, 2007.

———. *Money Hungry.* New York: Hyperion, 2001.

Leal, Ann Haywood. *Also Known as Harper.* New York: Henry Holt, 2009.

Millard, Glenda. *A Small Free Kiss in the Dark.* New York: Holiday House, 2009.

Spinelli, J. *Maniac Magee.* New York: Little, Brown, 2000.

Van Draanen, Wendelin. *Runaway.* New York: Random House, 2008.

Young Adult Fiction

Blank, Jessica. *Almost Home.* New York: Hyperion, 2007.

de Guzman, Michael. *Finding Stinko.* New York: Farrar, Straus and Giroux, 2007.

Going, K. L. *Saint Iggy.* New York: Graphia, 2008.

Griffin, Paul. *The Orange Houses.* New York: Dial, 2009.

———. *Ten Mile River: A Novel.* New York: Dial, 2008.

Hobbs, Will. *Crossing the Wire.* New York: HarperCollins, 2006.

Hyde, Catherine Ryan. *Becoming Chloe.* New York: Knopf, 2008.

Myers, Walter Dean. *Street Love.* New York: HarperCollins, 2006.

Quick, Matthew. *Sorta Like a Rock Star.* New York: Little, Brown, 2010.

Rapp, Adam. *33 Snowfish.* New York: Candlewick, 2006.

Strasser, Todd. *Can't Get There from Here.* New York: Simon & Schuster, 2004.

Nonfiction

Fields, Julianna. *Kids Growing Up without a Home (The Changing Face of Modern Families).* Broomall, PA: Mason Crest, 2010.

Gerdes, Louise I., ed. *The Homeless.* Opposing Viewpoints Series. Farmington Hills, MI: Greenhaven, 2007.

Hubbard, Jim. *Lives Turned Upside Down: Homeless Children in Their Own Words and Photographs.* New York: Aladdin, 2007.

Kaye, Catherine Berger. *A Kid's Guide to Hunger & Homelessness: How to Take Action!* Minneapolis, MN: Free Spirit, 2007.

Landowne, Y. *Selavi, That Is Life: A Haitian Story of Hope*. El Paso, TX: Cinco Puntos, 2004.

Lynette, Rachel. *What to Do When Your Family Loses Its Home*. Let's Work It Out. New York: Power Kids, 2010.

Merino, Noel. *Poverty and the Homeless*. Current Controversies. Farmington Hills, MI: Greenhaven, 2009.

Rhodes-Courter, Ashley. *Three Little Words*. New York: Atheneum, 2009.

Additional Readings

American Library Association. "Library Services to the Poor." *ALA Policy Manual*. www.ala.org/ala/aboutala/governance/policymanual/updatedpolicymanual/section2/61svctopoor.cfm.

Holt, Leslie Edmonds, and Glen E. Holt. *Public Library Services for the Poor: Doing All We Can*. Chicago: American Library Association, 2010.

Karash, Robert L. "Who Is Homeless? The HUD Annual Report to Congress and Homelessness Pulse Project." *Spare Change News*, June 23, 2010. http://sparechangenews.net/news/who-homeless-hud-annual-report-congress-and-homelessness-pulse-project.

Waldron, Jeremy. "Homelessness and Community." *University of Toronto Law Journal* 50, no. 4 (2000): 371–406.

NOTES

1. National Center on Family Homelessness, "America's Youngest Outcasts: State Report Card on Child Homelessness" (2009), 19, www.homelesschildrenamerica.org/pdf/rc_full_report.pdf.
2. Ibid.
3. Ibid.
4. Ibid.
5. Office of Community Planning and Development, U.S. Department of Housing and Urban Development, "The 2009 Annual Homeless Assessment Report" (2010), 19, www.hudhre.info/documents/5thHomelessAssessmentReport.pdf.
6. Jeremy Reynalds, *Homeless Culture and the Media: How the Media Educates Audiences in Their Portrayal of America's Homeless Culture* (Youngstown, NY: Cambria, 2006), 93.
7. Ken Kyle, "Contextualizing Homelessness: Critical Theory, Homelessness, and Federal Policy Addressing the Homeless," in *New Approaches in Sociology: Studies in Social Inequality, Social Change, and Social Justice* (New York: Routledge, 2005), 130–31.
8. Don Mitchell, *The Right to the City: Social Justice and the Fight for Public Space* (New York: Guilford, 2003), 183–84.
9. Brady Snyder, "Salt Lake Library Attracting Homeless," *Deseret News*, March 9, 2005, www.deseretnews.com/article/600117373/Salt-Lake-library-attracting-homeless.html.
10. American Library Association, Hunger, Homelessness, and Poverty Task Force, "Are Public Libraries Criminalizing Poor People? A Report from the ALA's Hunger, Homelessness, and Poverty Task Force," *Public Libraries* 44, no. 3 (2005): 175.
11. Heather Knight, "Library Adds Social Worker to Assist Homeless," *SFGate*, January 11, 2010, http://articles.sfgate.com/2010-01-11/bay-area/17823909_1_homeless-population-homeless-outreach-team-homeless-people.
12. Carrie Banks, "Shelter Storytelling," *ASCLA Interface*, March 31, 2010:http://ascla.ala.org/interface/2010/03/shelter-storytelling%c2%a0bringing-library-service-to-children-who-are-homeless-and-their-families.

13. Linda K. Fuller, "From Tramps to Truth-Seekers: Images of the Homeless in the Motion Pictures," in *Reading the Homeless: The Media's Image of Homeless Culture*, ed. Eungun Min, 159–73 (Westport, CT: Praeger, 1999), 170.

14. John Allen, *Homelessness in American Literature: Romanticism, Realism, and Testimony* (New York: Routledge, 2004), 20.

15. Ibid., 150.

16. Steve Seskin and Allen Shamblin, *A Chance to Shine* (Berkley, CA: Tricycle, 2006).

17. David McPhail, *The Teddy Bear* (New York: Henry Holt, 2002).

18. Laura Williams, *The Can Man* (New York: Lee & Low, 2010).

19. Anne C. Bromley, *The Lunch Thief* (Gardiner, MN: Tilbury House, 2010).

20. David Williams, *Mr. Stink* (New York: Razorbill, 2010).

21. William Kowalski, *The Way It Works*, Rapid Reads Series (New York: Raven, 2010).

22. Nikki Grimes, *Rich: A Dyamonde Daniel Book* (New York: Putnam, 2009).

23. Olugbemisola Rhuday-Perkovich, *Eighth Grade Superzero* (New York: Scholastic, 2010).

24. Ibid., 106.

25. Ibid.

26. Delphine de Vigan, *No and Me*, trans. George Miller (New York: Bloomsbury, 2010).

27. Ibid., 118.

SLIDING DOOR 3

Bibliotherapy and Characters with Cognitive Disabilities

KAREN GAVIGAN

IN TODAY'S INCREASINGLY DIVERSE society, it is critical to provide children and young adults with quality literature that can help them develop empathy and acceptance of individual differences. Bibliotherapy has long been considered an effective literary strategy for helping readers develop an understanding of our pluralistic society. Thomas P. Hebert and Richard Kent (2000) define bibliotherapy as the use of literature to help children understand themselves, and to cope with problems relevant to their personal and developmental needs.[1] This mini-chapter presents bibliotherapy strategies for using children's and young adult literature dealing with cognitive disabilities. For the purpose of this chapter, cognitive disabilities include attention deficit disorder/attention deficit hyperactivity disorder (ADD/ADHD), autism, Down syndrome, dyslexia, and other disabilities in which a person has greater difficulty with mental tasks than the average person.

For years, K–12 librarians and teachers have used bibliotherapy as a way to address challenging issues with students.[2] Bibliotherapy can be an effective tool for helping students gain insight into the world of the cognitively disabled. Reading a book about characters with cognitive disabilities like their own can be therapeutic for students with cognitive disabilities. When they see characters represented in literature in authentic and accurate ways, it helps them identify with the characters' experiences and frustrations. As C. S. Lewis wrote, "We read to know that we are not alone."[3] When non-disabled students read literature about cognitive disabilities, it can help them better understand the challenges of being disabled, and encourage them to be more responsive to disabled students' needs.

BIBLIOTHERAPY AND LITERATURE

In order to conduct bibliotherapy sessions, librarians and teachers need to know how to locate quality children's and young adult literature that is age-appropriate for the readers and lends itself to discussion. Reviews in professional journals should be consulted, along with lists of award-winning titles. Currently, there are two literary awards that recognize books about disabilities for children and young adults. The first is the Schneider Family Book Award, presented by the American Library Association, for a book that embodies an artistic expression of disability experiences for children and young adults (www.ala.org/ala/awardsgrants/schneider-family-book-award).

The second is the Dolly Gray Award for Children's Literature in Developmental Disabilities (http://daddcec.org/Awards/DollyGrayAwards.aspx). This award, initiated in 2000, is presented to authors, illustrators, and publishers of a children's picture book and/or a juvenile/young adult chapter book that includes appropriate portrayals of individuals with developmental disabilities

When there are questions about the quality of books about cognitive disabilities that are not included in reviews and award lists, it is recommended that educators use the "Checklist to Evaluate Children's Books that Address Disability as Part of Diversity," located at http://circleofinclusion.org/english/books/section1/cklistblk.html. The checklist was developed at the University of Kansas, as part of the university's Circle of Inclusion Project. It was created as a guideline to help educators and parents select bias-free literature for children. The nine criteria used in the guideline examine issues such as whether or not the text and illustrations include stereotypes or tokenism.

USING BIBLIOTHERAPY STRATEGIES WITH K–12 STUDENTS

A typical K–12 bibliotherapy session consists of students reading a book, or listening to it being read aloud, followed by a librarian or teacher facilitating a discussion about the book. The following are some examples of bibliotherapy activities related to cognitive disabilities.

- Use the book *My Sister, Alicia May* to discuss Down syndrome with students in grades 1–4.[4] In this picture book, Rachel describes the love and the frustration she feels in dealing with her sister who has Down syndrome. Briefly tell the students about Down syndrome. Next, read the book aloud to the students and have them answer the following questions:
  - What are the things that Alicia May does that Rachel likes?
  - What are the things that Alicia May does that Rachel dislikes?
  - What do you think it would be like to have a sister or brother with Down syndrome?
  - What do you think it would be like to have Down syndrome?

- Use the book *Joey Pigza Swallowed the Key* to discuss attention issues with children in grades 4–8.[5] Teach students how to create a KWL chart (K for what they know, W for what they want to know, and L for what they learned). Before they read the book, have them write a paragraph about what they already know about attention deficit hyperactivity disorders. Ask them to write a few questions under W about what they want to know. After they finish reading the book, share information with them about ADD/ADHD. Next, tell the students to write a paragraph under L for what they learned. When they finish the KWL chart, lead the students in a discussion about the symptoms that Joey exhibited in the book.[6]
- Use the following books to discuss cognitive disabilities with students in grades 6–12:
  - *Anything but Typical* by Nora Raleigh Baskin (autism).[7] Jason, a twelve-year-old autistic boy who wants to become a writer, relates what his life is like as he tries to make sense of his world.
  - *Marcelo in the Real World* by Francisco Stork (Asperger's syndrome).[8] Marcelo Sandoval, a seventeen-year-old boy on the high-functioning end of the autistic spectrum, faces new challenges, including romance and injustice, when he goes to work for his father in the mailroom of a corporate law firm.
  - *Rules* by Cynthia Lord (autism).[9] Frustrated at life with an autistic brother, twelve-year-old Catherine longs for a normal existence, but her world is further complicated by a friendship with a young paraplegic.
  - *So B. It* by Sarah Weeks (mental retardation).[10] After spending her life with her mentally retarded mother and agoraphobic neighbor, twelve-year-old Heidi sets out from Reno, Nevada, to New York to find out who she is.
- Ask students to form literature circles based on the book that they read. Have them answer the following questions:
  - How are individuals with disabilities portrayed? Pathetic, sad, to be pitied? Heroic, succeeding against all odds? Realistically?
  - How are relationships with non-disabled peers or adults described?
  - What could children or young adults learn from reading this book?[11]

These and other literary strategies such as role-playing, artistic expression, reader's theater, and writing activities can be used to help students understand the issues associated with cognitive disabilities.

CONCLUSION

It is important that both current and future librarians and teachers receive quality bibliotherapy training. For example, the School of Library and Information Science at the University of South Carolina (USC) offers children's and young adult materials classes that include assigned readings and discussions about disabilities literature and bibliotherapy. In addition, students and faculty at USC may use the Linda Lucas Walling Collection for Children's Books & Literacy, a special collection housed at the South Carolina Center for Children's Books & Literacy, to consult professional resources about disabilities, books for and about children and young adults with disabilities, and a website with additional information. The website can be accessed by educators worldwide and it is located at http://faculty.libsci.sc.edu/walling/evaluationcriteria.htm.

NOTES

1. Thomas. P. Hebert and Richard Kent, "Nurturing Social and Emotional Development in Gifted Teenagers through Young Adult Literature," *Roeper Review* 22, no. 3 (2000): 167–72.
2. Stephanie Kurtts and Karen W. Gavigan, "Understanding (Dis)abilities through Children's Literature," *Education Libraries*, 31, no. 1 (Summer 2008): 23–31.
3. C. S. Lewis, *ThinkExist.com.*, http://thinkexist.com/quotation/we_read_to_know_we_are_not_alone/255015.html.
4. Nancy Tupper Ling and Shennen Bersani, *My Sister, Alicia May* (Raynham Center, MA: Pleasant St., 2009).
5. Jack Gantos, *Joey Pigza Swallowed the Key* (New York: Farrar, Straus and Giroux, 1998).
6. Karen W. Gavigan and Stephanie Kurtts, "Using Children's and Young Adult Literature in Teaching Acceptance and Understanding of Individual Differences," *Delta Kappa Gamma Bulletin* 77, no. 2 (Winter 2011): 11–16.
7. Nora Raleigh Baskin, *Anything but Typical* (New York: Simon & Schuster Books for Young Readers, 2009).
8. Francisco X. Stork, *Marcelo in the Real World* (New York: Arthur A. Levine Books, 2009).
9. Cynthia Lord, *Rules* (New York: Scholastic, 2006).
10. Sarah Weeks, 2004. *So B. It: A Novel* ([New York]: Laura Geringer Books, 2004).
11. Kurtts and Gavigan, *Understanding (Dis)abilities*," 23–31.

SLIDING DOOR 4

Korean Folktale Video Project for Multicultural Families and Foreigners in the Republic of Korea

WOOSEOB JEONG AND SOOK-HYEUN LEE

IT IS ESTIMATED THAT MORE than one million foreigners are living in the Republic of Korea (South Korea). Some of the foreigners are temporary workers seeking better wages than in their home countries; others, usually women, are spouses of Korean partners. Once married, the children of multicultural families struggle with being assimilated into mainstream Korean culture. This is partly because the foreign mothers' spoken or written Korean is rather limited. To help integrate those mothers and their children into Korea's otherwise racially homogeneous society, the Korean government has put forth efforts to promote their education, both locally and nationally. As part of these efforts, the National Library for Children and Young Adults (NLCY) in Seoul, Korea, launched a series of digital children's book projects to assist the multicultural families with learning the Korean language and culture in a friendly and fun manner. Furthermore, since the project is on the Web without any access restrictions, it is hoped this will promote the Korean language and culture globally.

PROJECT DESCRIPTION

In 2009, as a pilot project, twenty-eight picture books of traditional Korean stories published in Korea were translated into English and Vietnamese.[1] The NLCY negotiated with the publishers to obtain the copyrights. All the books chosen are currently available at bookstores. The selection process was conducted by an ad hoc committee consisting of several experts in Korean children's literature. Next the pages in the picture books were digitized into Flash format to allow animation. The stories were then told by professional storytellers, with their performances video-recorded and synced to the animated pages. Along with each storytelling and its synced animated pages, users can choose captions in Korean, English, or Vietnamese at any time during the story. Each story lasts from five to fifteen minutes. Stories lasting more than ten minutes are split into two parts to shorten the loading time.

The project expanded in 2010 with more books and more languages. In that phase, traditional stories from Mongolia, Vietnam, China, Thailand, and the Philippines were also included. Despite the country of origin, all the stories are still told in Korean. The non-Korean stories were gathered by people from each respective country and pictures were added, while the Korean stories continued to come from published picture books with images. The second phase includes Korean contemporary stories in addition to traditional Korean folktales. To help non-Korean users learn Korean, the captions are highlighted as the story is being told. The project now has 150 stories, consisting of the original twenty-eight Korean stories, along with an additional eighty Korean, nine Mongolian, nine Vietnamese, ten Chinese, six Thai, and eight Filipino stories.

All the stories were translated into Korean, English, Mongolian, Vietnamese, Chinese, and Thai. People in Korea, the United States, and Thailand did the translations. The stories were first translated from Korean into English, which were then presented to English-speaking translators. This two-step translation process was also followed in the initial pilot project. Some translators spoke Korean; however, the English translations helped them to clarify some confusing bits of Korean texts. Others did not know Korean at all, and had to depend on the quality of the English translation.

High-quality English translation was assured through three stages. First, the works were translated from Korean into English by Wooseob Joeng, associate professor at the School of Information Studies of the University of Wisconsin–Milwaukee (SOIS-UWM). Jeong is originally from Korea and spent sixteen years in the United States for his studies and work. Next, native English-speaking graduate students of SOIS-UWM reviewed the first draft of translations, mostly for grammatical errors. Finally, Bonnie Withers, senior lecturer of children's literature at SOIS-UWM, reviewed the second draft of translations. She and Wooseob Jeong read the drafts aloud multiple times to adjust them to more child-friendly versions by including rhyming words and simpler language.

CHALLENGES

Copyright Clearance

Substantial time and effort were devoted to clear copyrights from the publishers. Most publishers would not permit any derivative works, even for a publicly funded project intended for all. Therefore, different books were targeted until the NLCY could get copyright permissions from the particular publishers. NLCY negotiated intensely and obtained agreements for modest copyright fees.

Faithfulness

Faithfulness, defined as translation from word to word, has been a big debate topic in translation studies. While admirable in theory, it is impossible to maintain pure faithfulness in practice. The most beautiful translations are not supposed to be the most faithful; consequently, it is highly encouraged to translate from sense to sense.[2] Since the Korean language is rich in depicting sound and motion with adjectives and adverbs, it is often difficult to find an exact match in other languages. Nouns have unique challenges as well. For example, "jogi," which is a favorite and expensive fish for many Koreans, is not consumed at all in other countries, including the United States. While the translations attempted to maintain faithfulness, this can present challenges.

Loss in the Two-Step Translation

It is inevitable to lose some information during the two-step translation process from Korean to English, and then from English to other languages. A large amount of energy was put into the Korean-to-English translation, including read-aloud-ability. To maintain quality translation in other languages, once a story was translated into a language, two native speakers of that language individually reviewed the translation.

Maintaining Read-Aloud-ability

Ottinen stressed the importance of fluency and rhythm, termed the "read-aloud-ability" of children's books.[3] At least for the English translation process, considerable effort was made to maintain read-aloud-ability by actually reading aloud multiple times in the third stage of the translation process.

Acceptability

Numerous stories exist in Korean contemporary children's literature about excrement. Countless more stories contain excrement as a peripheral element, helping the story unfold. There were many excrement-related stories in this project. Some stories were even eliminated for their excessively explicit depictions of excrement. Nonetheless, many such stories remain in the project. It is uncertain to what degree other cultures can accept stories of this nature.

Issue of Intertextuality

Intertextuality signifies that a story includes references to other stories. To understand the principal text fully, the readers should be familiar with the stories referred to as well. For example, the story of "The Tiger Taken by the Death Messenger" refers to multiple famous Korean traditional stories, which may be unknown to people who grew up outside of Korea. Desmet argued that intertextuality can survive in translated texts through a variety of translation strategies.[4] However, due to time and budget limitations, we could not resolve this issue to our satisfaction, particularly for all five languages.

FUTURE PLANS

The final products of this series of projects, DVDs or online, are being used by numerous users both at libraries and in homes in Korea. Libraries in Korea hold many workshops for multicultural families with these materials, and their responses have been positive. Parents of both Korean and mixed-race families have praised them for their usefulness in learning Korean and other languages.

In 2011, NLCY expanded the project with the addition of 120 more books in the same five languages. Furthermore, the project explored the possibility of a world storytelling library, where stories not only in Korean but also in other languages are told in their original languages and translated into other foreign languages. The International Children's Digital Library (www. childrenslibrary.org) has led multilingual services, but in very limited scope. We believe this Korean project provides more significant multilingualism in the domain of children's literature on the Web with rich multimedia support, including videos of real storytelling and animation.

The rich data from this project will provide valuable sources for the study of translations in children's literature. Despite the fact that obtaining permissions from the publishers is not easy, we still could obtain them with the government's negotiation and advocacy efforts. This gives libraries in other countries, including the United States, a second thought regarding the role of governments in library projects.

NOTES

1. The project is available at the NLCY home page at http://lscc.nlcy.go.kr:8000.
2. Birgit Stolt, *How Emil Becomes Michel: On the Translation of Children's Books* (Stockholm: Almqvist and Wiksell, 1978).

3. Riitta Ottinen, "The Verbal and the Visual: On the Carnivalism and Dialogics of Translating for Children," *Comparison: An International Journal of Comparative Literature* (1996): 49–65.

4. Mieke K. T. Desmet, "Intertextuality/Intervisuality in Translation: *The Jolly Postman*'s Intercultural Journey from Britain to the Netherlands," *Children's Literature in Education* 32, no. 1 (2001): 31–43.

How to Evaluate Children's and Young Adult Books about Transracial and Transnational Asian Adoption

SARAH PARK DAHLEN

THE FEDERAL INTERAGENCY FORUM on Child and Family Statistics (childstat. org) reports that 1.8 million children currently live in adoptive families, and the Evan B. Donaldson Institute reports that more than 60 percent of Americans are personally affected by adoption because they "know someone who has been adopted, has an adopted child or has relinquished a child for adoption."[1] The U.S. Department of State's "Annual Report on Intercountry Adoption" reported that in 2010 Americans transnationally adopted 11,059 children, comprising approximately one fifth of children immigrating to the United States.[2] In 2012, Americans adopted 8,668 children from other countries.[3] Americans began adopting from Korea in 1953, and at the time of this writing it is estimated that more than 110,000 Korean children have been adopted to the United States.[4] Americans began adopting from China in the early 1990s, and despite the fact that Chinese adoption started significantly later than Korean adoption, it is estimated that there are approximately 100,000 adopted Chinese children in the United States.[5]

The unique experiences of transracially adopted Asian children and young adults are increasingly being portrayed in youth literature. In a previous study, I determined that children's books depicting Korean transracial/transnational adoption began to be published in 1955, and ever since a new book has been published at least every few years for a total of fifty-four books at the time of this writing.[6] An awareness of adoption, including transracial adoption, has increased in part due to the depiction of adoption in the news, movies, and other media outlets and through the promotion of adoption by celebrities. Typically the adoption story in children's books and other media tends to be authored by non-adoptees—adoptive parents, adoption professionals, or adoption researchers—rather than adopted persons.[7] One example of a celebrity who promotes adoption is the actress Jamie Lee Curtis, who authored the children's adoption book *Tell Me Again About the Night I Was Born*, based on her own experience as an adoptive parent. Adoptive parents, and social work authors' positionalities, as well as their particular investment in the institution of adoption, present certain assumptions and perspectives that often distort or fail to fully reflect the realities and nuances of actual adoptees' experiences in their stories.

The voices in children's stories are supposed to be from the point of view of the adopted child, but because the authors of these stories are typically not adopted persons, there is room for misrepresentation and misunderstanding; indeed, my previous research demonstrates that non-Asian-adoptee authors have failed to verify details such as the appearance of the Korean flag and the proper spelling of Korean cities. In addition, these stories are framed around the question "Why did we [adoptive parents] adopt you?" rather than centering on the experience of the adopted child. As a result, a segment of the adult adoptee population contends that traditional publishers and media have singularly framed adoption as sentimental "rescue narratives" as told by adoptive parents and left out diverse perspectives on transracial and transnational adoption. Therefore, many transracially adopted persons employ other media, including the blogosphere, alternative presses, or self-publishing, to tell their stories.

The goal of this chapter is to provide guidelines for evaluating children's books depicting transracial adoption from Asian countries.[8] While the examples given come from research on Korean and Chinese transracial adoption, I recognize that other Asian adoptee populations including (but not limited to) children adopted from Vietnam, Cambodia, India, and the Philippines also experience similar issues of representation in children's literature. Each section provides an element of adoption books that librarians and educators can consider before choosing a title for a library collection or using it in the classroom. These are a starting point to encourage readers, reviewers and others to be more critical and thoughtful consumers of the books they read, collect, and promote.

AUTHORSHIP

Many authors and illustrators of Asian adoption children's books are not adoptees, and some adult Asian adoptees criticize the fact that adoptive parents and adoption scholars dominate the telling of their stories.[9] It is important to check the authors' and illustrators' backgrounds to discern whether or not they have included information about their relationship to adoptive families. Are they adoptive parents? Teachers of adoptee students? Social workers, therapists, or adoption professionals? Being an adoptive parent, adoptive relative, social worker, or adoption professional does not necessarily qualify one to write a story about adoption from the point of view of an adoptee. If the author is an adoptive parent, educators and librarians can check the storyline to see if it seems more from a parent's perspective or from an adopted person's perspective. If the author is none of these, what is the extent of the author's research and expertise on adoption?

While I do not mean to be essentialist regarding the identity politics of authors' backgrounds, it is troubling that the ratio of outsider authorship is so high for Korean transracial adoption stories. The Cooperative Children's Book Center (CCBC) at the University of Wisconsin-Madison tracks the insider/outsider authorship of African American, Latino, Native American, and Asian American children's literature because authorship *matters*. (See Thomas Crisp's excellent article on deploying strategic essentialism in regard to justifying insider authorship of stories about the still under- and misrepresented LGBTQ communities.)[10] The publishing industry fails to publish books with a greater balance of both insider and outsider authorship for many groups, including adopted persons. In so doing, they are complicit in allowing others to speak for adoptees, and thereby the silencing of adoptee voices.

COPYRIGHT

Policies, practices, and attitudes toward adoption have evolved from an assimilationist framework to a more culturally inclusive perspective over the past sixty years. How are these changes reflected in children's stories? In the earlier decades of transnational adoption, it was common for social workers to encourage white adoptive parents to pretend that their family was "as if" biological; that is, that there was no difference, racial or otherwise, between the white parents and the adopted child.[11] Stories written during these earlier decades reflect these cultural attitudes about adoption. Readers should take the cultural context into consideration when evaluating the ways in which adoption is framed in the story.

However, the copyright date is not always an indicator that the author's understanding of adoption is in alignment with the current cultural paradigm. For example, while the "as if" conception of adoption was a common social norm in the earlier decades, it is still perpetuated today in stories that promote color-blind ideologies, such as Nancy Carlson's *My Family Is Forever* (2004), in which an unnamed Asian adoptee lacks a specific Asian originating country as well as any discussion of issues or concerns related to her racial difference from her adoptive parents. Surprisingly, sometimes books that are published in earlier years, such as Kraus's *Tall Boy's Journey* (1992), may contain more specific details regarding the circumstances of an adoptee's relinquishment and subsequent adoption.

STEREOTYPES

Another element of Asian adoption stories to consider is the presence of stereotypes. A stereotype is usually a negative generalization about a particular group. Some stereotypes of Asian Americans are the "perpetual foreigner," the "model minority," the "Oriental," the "passive and shy Asian," the "short Asian," the "slant-eyed Asian," and the "helpless Asian." When considering specific titles, educators and librarians should ask the following: Are adopted youth portrayed as a "model minority" or are they shown as fully developed persons? Does the adoptee need the help of white people to overcome their problems—problems that are usually related to being adopted or being Asian? Is the adoptee helpless or does she or he have agency? For example, in Frances Duncan's *Kap-Sung Ferris* (1977), the adoptee protagonist Kim needs the help of her white best friend, Michelle, in order to realize that her birth mother search is not only futile, but also meaningless.

ILLUSTRATIONS

When particular images are repeated in different media, it is possible that that may become the dominant image associated with a particular culture or group. The propensity to inappropriately and inaccurately describe and depict Asian bodies as short, with slanted eyes and bowl haircuts is, unfortunately, common in mainstream media. Equally inappropriate is the tendency to make all Asian characters look alike. When evaluating illustrations, check to see if all Asian faces look exactly alike, or whether or not each Asian character is depicted as an individual with distinctive features. Do Asians have "slashes" for eyes while everyone else (white characters) has more realistic-looking eyes? Or do the Asian characters look similar to whites except for being often colored in yellow? Does the illustrator rely on kitschy cultural props in the background to emphasize the child's culture (paper lanterns, chopsticks)?

Again, Nancy Carlson's *My Family Is Forever* perpetuates some significant Asian American stereotypes in the illustrations. The slanted black lines that depict the protagonist's eyes are one of the worst and most blatant stereotypes since *The Five Chinese Brothers* (Claire Hutchet Bishop, 1938).[12] That this stereotype would pass in a children's book published by a major publishing company (Viking) in 2004 indicates that the industry itself lacks cultural competency. Editor and consultant Laura Atkins and author Zetta Elliott criticize the glaring whiteness of the industry, from the authors and illustrators to the editors and publishers and reviewers.[13] The existence of books such as *My Family Is Forever* indicates that on the whole the industry lacks the cultural knowledge and human resources necessary to produce more culturally conscious and accurate imagery. Perhaps if more Asian Americans and other underrepresented minorities were working in publishing, there would be a stronger culture of awareness, sensitivity, and accountability.

Other books also contain inaccurate illustrations that inculcate readers with misinformation. For example, in *It's Neat to Be Adopted* (1979), the Korean flag is drawn incorrectly—black bars are tilted in the wrong diagonal direction—and a map of Asia denotes the Republic of Korea with a black star hovering over Beijing, not the Republic of Korea. These are simple mistakes that reflect the laziness of the illustrator and the illustrator's disregard and disrespect for the specificities of Korean culture. It also implies that the other people working in publishing were not careful or informed when they reviewed the book for accuracy, nor did they send out the book for review by experts.

LANGUAGE

Just like stereotypical imagery, inappropriate language can perpetuate inaccurate information. Each adopted person has a preference for how he or she refers to certain aspects of his or her adoption, so authors should be mindful of the ways in which they use terms such as "real parents," "plan," "poor," and "forever." Adopted children might be confused if their adoptive parents are referred to as their "real parents," because to them "real" might also include their birth parents. After all, they "really" gave birth to them. Euphemizing abandonment by favoring the phrase "made a plan for you" might dismiss the actual details of an adoptee's circumstances; many were in fact abandoned, or their parents were coerced into relinquishment. Emphasizing birth parents' "poverty" might cause a child to worry that he does not have enough to eat. Finally, stressing the "forever" aspect of an adoptive family may cause an adoptee to wonder why her birth family could not last "forever."

NAMES

The issue of names is particularly poignant for adopted persons. Sometimes children come into orphanages with given names; others are abandoned without identification and are named by caretakers. Those who lived in an orphanage until two or three years of age might remember their names before being adopted into a new family. Eleana Kim writes of how Korean names "are of ambiguous provenance" since they might have been selected by biological kin or made up by orphanage directors and adoption agency workers.[14] For those whose birth families named them, Modell says "a birthname did make the birth real, and confirmed the connection with another family. Knowing a parent gave a name before giving away her child changed this adoptee's view of the surrender."[15]

In my previous study, I noted that eight of 116 Korean adoptees in attendance at an international Korean adoptee conference were named Kim, Kimberlee, or Kimberly.[16] Similarly, four of the more than forty adoptee characters in my study are named Kim. However, Eleana Kim observes that "adoptees have joked about the common practice of naming female adoptees 'Kim.'"[17] Kim is a convenient, if clumsy, cultural bridge that some see as a "failed attempt by adoptive parents to incorporate a part of the child's Korean heritage, because it takes a common Korean surname and converts it to a common American given name, with little attention to the cultural specificities of Korean names."[18] This name designation also smacks of Orientalism, most popularly performed through the "war-orphan prostitute" Kim of the hit Broadway musical *Miss Saigon*.[19] Therefore, librarians and teachers should consider how the adopted characters have been named. Stereotypical names for Asian girls include Jade, Cherry Blossom, or for Koreans, more specifically, Kim. If adoptees are renamed, is there an acknowledgment of a cultural/birth name that is incorporated into the "new" name? And if the Korean or Vietnamese adoptee's name is Kim, is there a specific reason why? If not, reviewers may need to be wary of the author's cultural assumptions and the implications thereof for the other details in the text.

One example foregrounds the complexity of naming in its title. The story *Three Names of Me* is a sensitive and nuanced portrayal of a young Chinese adoptee's understanding of her three names—Ada Lorane, given by her adoptive parents, Wang Bin, given by the orphanage workers, and a third. She writes out Ada Lorane and Wang Bin, telling the reader the origin of each name. But then she says, "But there is another name of me that I don't know. So I take glue and glitter and my red marker. I make a beautiful star for the name I only heard once, the name before my remembering. My first name is a bright red star wrapped in my heart. I heard it long ago, with love, so it is still there."

SPECIFICITY REGARDING BIRTH CULTURE AND COUNTRY

Because children are adopted from many Asian countries to the United States, the story should specifically distinguish the culture and nation from which the child is adopted. For example, does the story specify that the child was adopted from Korea, China, or India? Or does the adopted child not have an origin?

Additionally, how are the countries or cultures of birth depicted? Are they shown as poorer than and technologically inferior to the adoptive country (for example, boats versus planes, or huts versus modern apartment buildings, as in Katherine Grace's short story in "Beginnings: How Families Come to Be," 1994)? Are members of the child's birth culture depicted wearing older folk or traditional clothing rather than modern attire? When portraying the adoptive parents integrating "culture" in

their family, is it a full family integration, and are these only through special holidays or events such as the "arrival" day? Or are they presented
as a normal part of the family's day-to-day life? *We Adopted You, Benjamin
Koo* (1992) has a folk/food/festivities approach with the family celebrating Korean and Colombian holidays; it is hard to find an example of a
book that takes the integrative approach.

Again, I return to the previous example of *It's Neat to Be Adopted*, the
picture book that inaccurately depicts Korea's geography and flag, and
My Family Is Forever, which denies the adoptee a specific origin. While
this is most probably a marketing ploy to sell more books to more families that have adopted from any Asian country, the lack of specificity
actually perpetuates the stereotype that any one Asian person/country/
culture can stand in for another Asian person/country/culture.

BIRTH AND ADOPTIVE PARENTS

Scholars have noted that oftentimes birth parents are depicted as piti-
able, impoverished, or undeserving of and incapable of raising children.
Worse, many are left out of the narrative entirely. It is important to discuss birth parents' roles in adopted people's lives, partly out of justice for
the birth parents who are the "primary actor[s]" in adoption, and partly
out of the need to counteract the dominant images and discourse that
diminish their roles or write them out of adoption stories.[20] In contrast,
adoptive parents are typically cast as excessively benevolent, kind, and
understanding.

When evaluating youth literature for this particular issue, consider
the following questions: How are birth parents depicted? Are they always
poor, helpless, single women? Are birth fathers absent? Does the storyline suggest that the birth parents made a "plan" for a better life? Does
the story suggest that the mother was a prostitute? While inflammatory,
this last question is valid. Consider this from the *Diary of a Teenage Girl*
series: Kim thinks that her birth mother was "most likely a prostitute
who forgot to use birth control. That's the usual story with abandoned
babies."[21] Adoption scholar Hosu Kim describes three cohorts of birth
mothers: military prostitutes in the immediate Korean War and postwar period, young factory workers in the 1970s and 1980s, and troubled
teenage girls from the late 1980s to the present.[22] While the first cohort
of adoptees may have been born of women who were in relationships
with members of the American military, the *Diary of a Teenage Girl* series
is set in the mid-2000s, not in the postwar period. Therefore, first, it is
unlikely that Kim's birth mother was a prostitute. Second, such a statement is inappropriate and serves no purpose in a series that is actually,
mostly *not* about Korean adoption.

Given that the media often misrepresents birth families, it is important
for librarians and educators to educate themselves and consider the fol-

lowing questions: Does the story address systemic and structural oppressions that continue to discriminate against poor women? Does the text indicate that organizations such as the Truth and Reconciliation for the Adoption Community of Korea are struggling for and gaining ground in reforming adoption laws?[23] How many of the texts mention the devastation of the Vietnam War (much of which was caused by the United States government and its military) or the one-child policy in China that really does leave parents with no other option but to abandon their children?

In terms of adoptive parents, consider how they are portrayed in the narrative: Are they typically heterosexual couples, middle class, well educated, and generous? Are they portrayed as having an understanding of the child's cultural heritage, or are they shown as being neutral or clueless (i.e., they can't hold chopsticks right, they mispronounce Asian names)? Are they passive recipients or are they actively involved in the adoption process? Do they maintain a diverse lifestyle or is the diversity only through their adopted Asian child?

The depiction of birth parents as consistently incapable and adoptive parents as consistently saccharine and idealistic paints a flawed and inaccurate picture of transracial Asian adoption. While the media typically shares stories of poor, unwed Asian mothers in the East who willingly give up their children to white families in the West, the reality is that the structural issues that give rise to the large numbers of Asian adoptees is much more complicated. Moreover, many adoptees have shared their search and reunion stories through memoirs, interviews, and research; the prototypical abandonment story is not quite prototypical. Many adoptees have found that the circumstances of their relinquishment are not what they were originally told.

ADOPTION ISSUES

Adopting transnationally and transracially is a complex process, ongoing past the time the child is brought into the home. To the extent possible, given the age of the intended audience, the text should realistically depict the adoption process. Is an adoption as simple as "We wanted a baby, and your mom wanted you to have a family" or "We picked you up at the airport"? Readers should also be sensitive to the way the loss of the child's birth family or birth country is portrayed in the book. Adoption books for children tend to minimize loss and abandonment. Adopted children who do not see examples of other children exploring themes of loss or abandonment may feel they are not allowed to experience or express those feelings. Some adopted children feel these losses more acutely than others, and children's books should provide a diversity of experiences to which children can relate. Readers should also consider how complex issues, such as race-related issues, are handled. Are they resolved through the rhetoric of color-blind ideology? Consider whether the story comes to an arbitrarily positive conclusion or allows for the adopted person to continue developing her own processes of situating herself as a transracially adopted person. Does the adoptee have to become "white" in order to fit in and get over his adoption and race issues? If the plot is driven by the adoptee's identity struggle, is the only "right" resolution that the child comes to the conclusion that her adoptive parents are her "real" parents?

COMMUNITY

The great majority of transracial Asian adoption children's stories depict the adoptees in almost complete isolation from other adoptees. However, in real life, Asian adoptees have built extensive networks and organizations that meet regularly for cultural, political, and social events. For example, Korean adoptees from all over the world have been meeting every three years at Gathering conferences since 1999; the first Chinese Gathering was in 2010. However, these types of networks and social communities are rarely depicted in children's or even young adult literature, thus potentially implying that Asian adoption is an isolated and isolating phenomenon. One popular exception is *The White Swan Express: A Story about Adoption* (2002). In this colorful picture book, the reader follows four sets of adoptive parents, including one lesbian couple, as they journey to China to pick up their adopted daughters. The text implies that the families will keep in touch and maintain a sense of extended family kinship as the girls grow older. Therefore, readers should look for the inclusion of other adopted persons, compared to the single adoptee in isolation from other adopted persons or adoptive families. Readers should also look for how other people from the child's ethnic community are included and whether or not the inclusion represents stereotyped portrayals of the community. For example, are the only Koreans depicted in the story from Korea, the only Chinese from China, or do Korean Americans and Chinese Americans live in the local community? Are Korean Americans and Chinese Americans depicted in stereotypic ways (owners of dry cleaners, restaurants, recent immigrants, as in *If It Hadn't Been for Yoon Jun* [1993])? Do they speak in broken English? Are the adopted children fearful of these people from their racial and cultural group and do the adoptive parents have to "mediate" their interaction? Readers should be mindful of the ways in which other ethnic people are depicted, as the tendency is to put them in as stock characters that "teach" the adoptee how to be Korean or Chinese.

THE ADOPTEE AS ADULT

The majority of existing stories depict adopted Asians who rarely discuss their future lives as adult adoptees, nor do they feature adult adoptee role models. These books also lack contemporary connections to the adopted child's birth country. Motherland or Heritage Tours in their birth countries are opportunities widely available for Asian adoptees today. For example, Korean adoptees and their families may tour the old capital of Korea (Gyeong-Ju), participate in or observe ritual reenactments (such as a traditional tea or wedding ceremony), and visit their orphanage or adoption agency. Many adult Korean adoptees also live in Korea for a period of time; they study abroad, find jobs, or teach English. Readers should look for examples that give the adoptee characters a sense of a relationship with their birth country for whatever reason (travel, study, work, play, live, conduct a birth search). Rose Kent's *Kimchi & Calamari* (2004) is one example where, by the end of the novel, the adoptee protagonist's father suggests that someday he and his son might travel to Korea on a heritage tour.

MESSAGE

Overall, readers should look for what kind of message the story is trying to impart. Common narratives are that the adopted children are lucky; that families are forever (thereby sidestepping the notion that if a family can be created, one had to be uncreated); or that racial difference, loss, and being adopted are not as important as love (color-blindness). Readers should consider how difference is handled. Is the child surprised that she is not white like the parents or the community? How is racism, if included, handled in the story? Readers should look for examples in which the adoptive parents teach their child how to handle racism or discrimination. Is the message that adopted children should suppress unhappy feelings or questions regarding adoption? These are important questions to ask when evaluating children's books about transracial and transnational adoption.

CONCLUSION

The purpose of this chapter is to provide guidelines for readers to be critical consumers of the literature they read, particularly as they relate to transracial and transnational Asian adoption. While adoption in and of itself is meant to be a positive experience for all parties involved, there has been much potential for corruption, oppression, and misrepresentation within the practice itself, as well as in the ways it is depicted. One final recommendation for teachers and librarians: read writings by transracial Asian adoptees. Memoirs such as *The Language of Blood* (Jane Jeong Trenka), *A Single Square Picture* (Katie Robinson), and *Lucky Girl* (Mei-Ling Hopgood) provide alternative perspectives to the mainstream media's depictions of Asian adoption. Furthermore, reading blogs by Asian adoptees is another way that consumers can educate themselves so that they may discern to what extent youth literature is accurately depicting such experiences. Youth literature has a long way to go, from the authorship to the depiction to the reception. Through our collective efforts, we may do justice to adoptive and birth families and help all adoptees and readers see a range of adoptive experiences depicted in the literature they read. Without such critical reading, we will be in danger of perpetuating myths rather than exploring the diversity of adoption experiences.

YOUTH LITERATURE BIBLIOGRAPHY

Bishop, Claire Hutchet. *The Five Chinese Brothers*. New York: Penguin Putnam Books for Young Readers, 1938.

Carlson, Melody. *Diary of a Teenage Girl* series. Oregon: Multnomah.

Carlson, Nancy. *My Family Is Forever*. New York: Viking, 2004.

Cumings, Mary. *Three Names of Me*. Morton Grove, IL: Albert Whitman, 2006.

Curtis, Jamie Lee. *Tell Me Again about the Night I Was Born*. New York: HarperCollins, 1996.

Duncan, Frances. *Kap-Sung Ferris*. Vancouver: Burns & MacEachern, 1977.

Girard, Linda Walvoord. *We Adopted You, Benjamin Koo*. New York: Albert Whitman, 1992.

Kent, Rose. *Kimchi & Calamari*. New York: HarperCollins Children's Books, 2004.

Kraus, Joanna Halpbert. *Tall Boy's Journey*. New York: CarolRhoda Book, 1992.

Kroll, Virginia. "Katherine Grace," in *Beginnings: How Families Come to Be*. New York: Albert Whitman, 1994.

Lee, Marie. *If It Hadn't Been for Yoon Jun*. New York: Avon/Camelot Book, 1993.

Miquelle, Jean B. *It's Neat to Be Adopted: A Story of International Adoption*. 1979.

Okimoto, Jean Davies, and Elaine M. Aoki. *The White Swan Express: A Story about Adoption*. New York: Clarion Books, 2002.

NOTES

1. ChildStat.gov, "Adoption" (2007), www.childstats.gov/americaschildren/special1. asp; Evan B. Donaldson Adoption Institute, "Overview of Adoption in the United States" (January 2002), www.adoptioninstitute.org/FactOverview.html.

2. U.S. Department of State, Intercountry Adoption, Bureau of Consular Affairs, "FY 2010 Annual Report on Intercountry Adoptions" (December 2010), http://adoption.state.gov/content/pdf/fy2010_annual_report.pdf. The Office of Immigration Statistics (OIS) reports that Americans transnationally adopted 11,087 children, which is very close to the Department of State's 11,059. The OIS also reports that a total of 59,524 children immigrated from other countries to the United States, thus approximately 18 percent of the children entering the United States are coming through international adoption. Office of Immigration Statistics, "2010 Yearbook of Immigration Statistics" (August 2011), www.dhs.gov/xlibrary/assets/statistics/yearbook/2010/ois_yb_2010.pdf.

3. U.S. Department of State, Intercountry Adoption, Bureau of Consular Affairs, "FY 2012 Annual Report on Intercountry Adoptions" (January 2013), http://adoption. state.gov/content/pdf/fy2012_annual_report.pdf.

4. Peter Selman, "The Rise and Fall of Intercountry Adoption in the 21st Century," *International Social Work* 52, no. 5 (2009): 575–94; Tobias Hübinette, "Korean Adoption History, in *Guide to Korea for Overseas Adopted Koreans*, ed. E. Kim (Seoul: Overseas Korean Foundation, 2007). Sources differ on exact numbers. The Evan B.

Donaldson Adoption Institute states that there have been over 100,000 adoptions from the Republic of Korea to the United States between 1958 and 2001 alone. See "Overview of Adoption." Hübinette cited 109,252 from 1953 to 2008 and since 2008, the United States has received an additional 1,944 children from the Republic of Korea.

5. Kay Anne Johnson, *Wanting a Daughter, Needing a Son: Abandonment, Adoption and Orphanage Care in China* (St. Paul, MN: Yeong & Yeong, 2004), 33. The first international adoption law in China was enacted in 1991 and created the first avenue for adoption outside of the country.

6. Sarah Park, "Representations of Transracial Korean Adoption in Children's Literature" (Ph.D. diss., University of Illinois at Urbana-Champaign, 2009).

7. It should be noted here that the author of this chapter is not a transracially adopted Asian person. I am a non-adopted Korean American with Korean immigrant parents. My long-term research is on representations of Korean adoption in children's and young adult literature, and I am an active participant in adoption conferences and community events. Together with Jae Ran Kim, the blogger behind *Harlow's Monkey*, I wrote a shorter draft of this chapter in 2009, and then developed it into this book chapter.

8. These guidelines were inspired in part by "Ten Quick Ways to Analyze Children's Books for Racism and Sexism" by the Council on Interracial Books for Children and adoptee and scholar Jae Ran Kim's "An Open Letter to Potential Children's Book Authors." Louise Derman-Sparks and A.B.C. Task Force, "Ten Quick Ways to Analyze Children's Books for Sexism and Racism," in *Anti-Bias Curriculum: Tools for Empowering Young Children* (National Association for the Education of Young People, 1989), 143; *Harlow's Monkey*, "An Open Letter to Potential Children's Book Authors," (February 20, 2008), http://harlowmonkey.typepad.com/harlows_monkey/2008/02/an-open-letter.html.

9. Julia Chinyere Oparah, Sun Yung Shin, and Jane Jeong Trenka, "Introduction" in *Outsiders Within: Writing on Transracial Adoption*, ed. J. C. Oparah, S. Y. Shin, and J. J. Trenka (Cambridge: South End, 2006), 1; John Raible, "Lifelong Impact, Enduring Need," in *Outsiders Within: Writing on Transracial Adoption*, ed. J. C. Oparah, S. Y. Shin, and J. J. Trenka (Cambridge: South End, 2006), 182; Tobias Hübinette, *Comforting an Orphaned Nation: Representations of International Adoption and Adopted Koreans in Korean Popular Culture*, 32nd ed. (Seoul: Jimoondang, 2006), 19; Kim Park Nelson, "Shopping for Children in the International Marketplace," in Outsiders Within: Writing on Transracial Adoption, ed. J. C. Oparah, S. Y. Shin, and J. J. Trenka (Cambridge: South End, 2006), 90.

10. Thomas Crisp, "It's Not the Book, It's Not the Author, It's the Award: The Lambda Literary Award and the Case for Strategic Essentialism," *Children's Literature in Education* 42, no. 2 (2011): 91–104.

11. Judith S. Modell, *Kinship with Strangers: Adoption and Interpretations of Kinship in American Culture* (Berkeley: University of California Press, 1994); Eleana J. Kim, Adopted Territory: Transnational Korean Adoptees and the Politics of Belonging (Durham, NC: Duke University Press, 2010).

12. For a more complete criticism of *The Five Chinese Brothers*, see the following: Albert V. Schwartz, "*The Five Chinese Brothers:* Time to Retire," *Interracial Books for Children Bulletin* 8, no. 3 (1977): 3–7.

13. Laura Atkins, "What's the Story: Reflections on White Privilege in the Publication of Children's Books," paper presented at the International Research Society for Children's Literature congress, 2009, https://sites.google.com/site/tockla; Laura

Atkins, "White Privilege and Children's Publishing: A Web 2.0 Case Study," *Write4Children* 1, no. 2 (2010); Zetta Elliott, "Something Like an Open Letter to the Children's Publishing Industry," *Fledgling: Zetta Elliott's (Other) Blog*, September 5, 2009, http://zettaelliott.wordpress.com/2009/09/05/something-like-an-open-letter-to-the-children%E2%80%99s-publishing-industry.

14. Eleana J. Kim, "Remembering Loss: The Cultural Politics of Overseas Adoption from South Korea" (Ph.D. diss., New York University, 2007), 124.

15. Modell, *Kinship with Strangers*, 76–77, 157.

16. Park, "Representations of Transracial Korean Adoption."

17. Eleana J. Kim, "Our Adoptee, Our Alien: Transnational Adoptees as Spectars of Foreignness and Family in South Korea," *Anthropological Quarterly* 80, no. 2 (2007): 123.

18. Ibid.

19. Ibid.

20. Modell, *Kinship with Strangers*, 63; Hosu Kim, "Mothers without Mothering: Birth Mothers from Korea since the Korean War," in *International Korean Adoption: A Fifty-Year History of Policy and Practice*, ed. K. J. S. Bergquist, E. M. Vonk, D. S. Kim, and M. D. Feit (New York: Haworth, 2007), 131–53; Modell, *Kinship with Strangers*, 12, 61–90; Claudia Nelson, *Little Strangers: Portrayals of Adoption and Foster Care in America, 1850–1929* (Bloomington: Indiana University Press, 2003), 127; Marianne Novy, *Reading Adoption: Family and Difference in Fiction and Drama* (Ann Arbor: University of Michigan Press, 2005), 13; Oparah, Shin, and Trenka, *Outsiders Within*, 3, 12–13; Adam Pertman, *Adoption Nation: How the Adoption Revolution Is Transforming America* (New York: Basic Books, 2000), 8, 11, 148–50.

21. Melody Carlson, *Diary of a Teenage Girl: Just Ask* (Oregon: Multnomah, 2005), 149.

22. Hosu Kim, "Mothers without Mothering," 140.

23. Truth and Reconciliation for the Adoption Community of Korea, "TRACK: Setting the Record Straight," http://justicespeaking.wordpress.com.

Representation in
Queer Children's Books

Who's In and Who's Out

JAMIE CAMPBELL NAIDOO

It was hard for Will to understand that Nick was being called his
sister, not his brother. So the whole family walked down to the
library and checked out some books about the ways brothers and
sisters love and support one another.[1]

CULTURAL PLURALISM ENCOMPASSES many facets including ethnicity,
religion, sexuality, and family composition. Research indicates that
it is important for children to see representations of themselves, their
families, and "the other" in their books in order to function successfully
within a culturally pluralistic society and to make intercultural connections.[2] Children's books that mirror a child's experiences affirm his or her
existence and strengthen identity development. At the same time, books
that serve as a window into the experiences of classmates and other children provide a platform for understanding children and families that
are different from one's own. This platform opens doors to new ways of
understanding self and society.

Within the context of interactions with the illustrations in children's
books, the concepts of visual literacy and reader response suggest that
children use their past and present experiences, and images of lesbian,
gay, bisexual, transgender, and queer (LGBTQ) characters in the media
and throughout society, to develop an understanding of how society
views LGBTQ families, described in this chapter as "rainbow families."[3]
Roethler asserts that minority children develop their schematic understanding of the world through "the illustrations they encounter in the
literature to which they are exposed as children. . . . The images these
children soak up remain with them for the rest of their lives."[4] Children
in rainbow families constitute a minority within the U.S. culture, and the

images of LGBTQ characters and families that they encounter in their books influence how they feel about themselves and their family composition. Their interactions with LGBTQ characters in picture books influence their self-acceptance and personality development.

Unfortunately, not all cultures and families are well represented in children's literature. Publishers have the propensity to favor certain "socially acceptable" cultural groups over others in children's books, thereby ignoring specific subsets of society. As a result, some children rarely see representations of themselves or their families in the books they encounter in schools and libraries. One of these cultural groups is rainbow families.

In the quote at the beginning of this chapter from Jennifer Carr's picture book *Be Who You Are!*, the young boy Will has a brother who experiences extreme gender variance and actually identifies as a girl. Will has trouble understanding his brother's gender identity, and the family decides to visit the library for children's books that will open doors to Will's understanding of his brother. In this fictional story, the library has such books, but in reality many libraries do not provide books with LGBTQ characters for young children, not because they are opposed to the content but because the books are not readily available. This chapter profiles rainbow families in the United States, describes the characteristics of LGBTQ children's books with a particular focus on who is not represented, and provides suggestions for meeting the literacy needs of children in rainbow families.

RAINBOW FAMILIES IN THE UNITED STATES

Almost 195,000 same-sex couples are raising children in 96 percent of all counties in the United States.[5] Approximately 2 million children in the country live in these rainbow families.[6] The Urban Institute also indicates that an estimated 65,500 adopted children (4 percent of all adopted children in the United States) live with a lesbian or gay parent and that an estimated 14,100 foster children (3 percent of all foster children in the United States) are living with lesbian or gay parents.[7] None of these figures accounts for children living with a single lesbian or gay parent or for children living with bisexual or transgender parents.

The aforementioned data presents statistical information about LGBTQ adults or the number of children living with LGBTQ adults. What about the LGBTQ children in rainbow families? Research studies indicate that children as young as four are aware of their own sexuality.[8] Unfortunately, exact percentages and numbers are not available for LGBTQ *children* because of the stigma associated with sexuality and childhood.[9] Recent analyses of U.S. Census data from the Williams Institute indicates that almost 4 percent of the current adult population identifies as LGBT.[10] Perhaps this percentage could be applied to children to suggest that approximately 4 percent of all U.S. children could now or eventually identify as LGBT. Brill and Pepper also report that one in 500 children identifies as transgender, and Ehrensaft indicates that more and more children today are coming out and expressing gender-variant behaviors.[11]

RAINBOW FAMILIES IN CHILDREN'S BOOKS

Despite their presence in many counties throughout the United States, rainbow families are frequently absent in the field of children's literature. Children's books often depict families as nuclear (mom and dad) or heterosexual, ignoring the increasing number of households with same-sex, bisexual, and transgender parents. According to a study conducted by the Council on Interracial Books for Children in 1983, "lesbian and gay characters are as good as invisible in books for preschool and early elementary-age children."[12] Almost ten years later, Clyde and Lobban noted, "books for young children often interpret their world, and, considering the size of the homosexual population, it is perhaps surprising that references to homosexuality do not occur more frequently and naturally in books which expand and explain the child's world."[13] Since these reports, little has changed in terms of representation of LGBTQ topics in children's books. As part of a larger study of queer-themed children's books, the author of this chapter examined over 200 U.S. and international queer-themed children's fiction and nonfiction picture books published between 1969 and 2011 to determine how rainbow families are represented.[14]

From the period of 1999 to 2009, the number of U.S. children's picture books published with LGBTQ characters or themes was on average four books per year, representing less than 1 percent of all the picture books published in the United States each year. Add international titles with queer content and the number of books only increases to an average of seven per year. With so few picture books on LGBTQ topics, children in rainbow families have relatively few opportunities to see reflections of their cultures and, unlike their peers from heterosexual and nuclear families, have few opportunities to personally connect with books depicting families like their own.

Within the scant body of LGBTQ children's fiction and nonfiction picture books, certain populations and subgroups are overlooked or under-represented such as transgender or bisexual individuals, older lesbians and gays, characters who are differently-able, and ethnically or racially diverse characters. Of the 200 plus queer-themed picture books published between 1969 and 2011, only ten children's books featured transgender characters, two books described children that were gender neutral (neither male or female), no books depicted bisexual characters, eight books illustrated differently-able lesbian/gay characters, and only eight of the books contained elderly lesbian/gay characters. Much like the entire whitewashed body of children's literature, the majority of the picture books (64 percent) depicted *only* white, LGBTQ characters or families and another 22 percent of the books included white characters in addition to characters of other ethnicities and races. As a result, these books ignore the daily experience of 41 percent of same-sex couples with children who identify as non-white.[15]

Collectively, these results suggest that the majority of fiction and non-fiction picture books with queer content represent white, young, gay/lesbian, fully functioning characters. Ethnically and racially diverse children, gender-variant or transgender children, children with a transgender or bisexual parent, children who are differently-able (or who have differently-able parents), and children with LGBTQ elders or older relatives are predominantly ignored in queer picture books. Similarly, gay grandfathers, lesbian grandmothers, and lesbian aunts are almost invisible in these books, and gay fathers are far outnumbered by lesbian mothers. As a result of this skewed representation, many young children in rainbow families are deprived of the opportunity to see their experiences and families authentically and accurately represented in their reading materials. Moreover, the few books that do depict specific subsets of rainbow families—such as transgender children and parents, lesbian grandmothers, or differently-able lesbian/gay characters—are not high-quality literature. Many of these books contain didactic writing, dull narratives, poorly executed illustrations, or unattractive layouts. The subsequent sections present examples of both quality and problematic queer children's books that represent some of these underrepresented subgroups.

NOTEWORTHY TITLES REPRESENTING UNDERREPRESENTED QUEERS IN LGBTQ CHILDREN'S PICTURE BOOKS

"You're a boy. Boys don't wear dresses!"
"But . . . I don't feel like a boy," Bailey said.
"Well, you are one, Bailey, and that's that!"[16]

Children encounter the above exchange in Marcus Ewert and Rex Ray's *10,000 Dresses*, a picture book that follows Bailey, a transgender boy, who dreams of dresses. Bailey's conversation with his mother could represent similar discourses that transgender and gender-variant children have with their families, friends, and teachers. Daily, these children, whose actions do not conform to society's expectations of typical "boy" and "girl" behaviors, encounter a barrage of messages condemning them. A stroll into the toy department of their local box store might leave these children or their caregivers in a cold sweat as they navigate the aisles of "boy toys" and "girl toys." What happens if a classmate sees Marcus in the Barbie aisle selecting a new favorite doll? How does Maya feel when her mother insists she must choose a "girl toy" rather than the cars and action figures she prefers?

For children who express gender variance, identify as transgender, or have parents that are transgender, books such as *10,000 Dresses* can be useful in normalizing their experiences. These books can help children better understand themselves and their parents and assist in their identity development. At the same time, books with transgender themes can bridge understanding between those children who are gender variant and those who are not. Figure 12.1 provides suggestions of other recommended children's books with transgender themes.

Similarly, picture books such as *Antonio's Card/La tarjeta de Antonio*, which represent ethnically diverse children with gay parents, can help all children understand that queer families include individuals that identify as Latinos, African Americans, Asian Americans, Native Americans, mixed-race, and so on.[17] Not only do these books demonstrate the universality of rainbow family experiences to children from heterosexual families, but they also provide mirrors for non-white children in rainbow families to see reflections of their cultural experiences. In *Antonio's Card/La tarjeta de Antonio* a young boy, Antonio, loves his *mami* (mother) and her partner Leslie; but when some of his classmates ridicule Leslie because of her appearance, the young Latino boy struggles with the embarrassment of having a nontraditional family. Antonio's emotions are similar to those of other Latino children with a lesbian mother or gay father and can help standardize their experiences.

Transgender Children's Books

- *10,000 Dresses.* Written by Marcus Ewert. Illustrated by Rex Ray.
- *The Adventures of Tulip Birthday Wish Fairy.* Written by S. Bear Bergman. Illustrated by Suzy Malik.
- *Be Who You Are!* Written by Jennifer Carr. Illustrated by Ben Rumback.
- *Gender Now: A Learning Adventure for Children and Adults.* Written and illustrated by Maya Christina Gonzalez.
- *Girls Will Be Boys Will Be Girls Will Be . . .* Written by Jacinta Bunnell and Irit Reinheimer.
- *My Mommy Is a Boy.* Written by Jason Martinez. Illustrated by Karen Winchester.
- *Rough, Tough Charley.* Written by Verla Kay. Illustrated by Adam Gustavson.
- *Sometimes the Spoon Runs Away with Another Spoon.* Written by Jacinta Bunnell. Illustrated by Nathaniel Kusinitz.
- *Tomboy Trouble.* Written by Sharon Dennis Wyeth. Illustrated by Lynne Woodcock Cravath.
- *X: A Fabulous Child's Story.* Written by Lois Gould. Illustrated by Jacqueline Chwast.

Figure 12.1: Recommended children's books with transgender themes

Note: Some of these titles contain flaws in text and/or illustration. However, considering the lack of transgender books, these titles are still appropriate for use with children.

Monica Bey-Clarke and Cheril Clarke's *Keesha and Her Two Moms Go Swimming* depicts a well-adjusted African American girl who has two lesbian mothers.[18] While Antonio is worried about other children discovering he has two mothers, Keesha is unapologetic about her family composition and spends her time relating to readers the excitement of playing at the neighborhood pool with other rainbow and heterosexual families. Although divergent in how they treat a child's perspective in an ethnically diverse rainbow family, both *Antonio's Card/La tarjeta de Antonio* and *Keesha and Her Two Moms Go Swimming* equally depict the life experiences of children in rainbow families. Ostensibly, some children in these families worry about their family composition while others assume that everyone has two mothers or two fathers and the sexuality of their parents is a non-issue. Figure 12.2 provides suggestions of other recommended children's books with ethnically diverse rainbow families.

GOOD BUT NOT GOOD ENOUGH

While the aforementioned titles are examples of quality children's books depicting underrepresented queer subgroups, the following books are examples of well-intentioned books that do not quite reach their goals. Culturally inclusive queer picture books such as *ABC: A Family Book* offer opportunities for all children to encounter queer families that are old and young, differently-able, mixed raced, and racially diverse.[19] While they do fill a void in the literature, these books take an A to Z approach to queer diversity and provide only a cursory coverage of topics. Very few books represent differently-able queer characters, and the representation of this subgroup in *ABC: A Family Book* is limited to a single illustration of a lesbian mom in a wheelchair. Unfortunately, this perfunctory image does little to promote intercultural connections or feelings of cultural pride. Queer children who are differently-able or those who have differently-able queer parents are essentially robbed of opportunities to encounter fully realized depictions of themselves

---

Children's Books Representing Ethnically Diverse LGBTQ Characters

- *Antonio's Card/La tarjeta de Antonio*. Written by Rigoberto González. Illustrated by Cecilia Concepción Álvarez.
- *Arwen and Her Daddies*. Written and Illustrated by Jarko De Witte van Leeuwen.
- *Families*. Written and Illustrated by Susan Kuklin.
- *Felicia's Favorite Story*. Written by Lesléa Newman. Illustrated by Adriana Romo.
- *Is Your Family Like Mine?* Written by Lois Abramchik. Illustrated by Alaiyo Bradshaw.
- *Keesha and Her Two Moms Go Swimming*. Written by Monica Bey-Clarke and Cheril Clarke. Illustrated by Aiswarya Mukherjee.
- *Las tres Sofías*. Written by Juan Rodríguez Matus. Illustrated by Anna Cooke.

Figure 12.2: Recommended children's books with ethnically diverse LGBTQ families and characters

and their families in books such as *ABC: A Family Book*. At the same time, the book also includes illustrations of older characters that the reader assumes are queer. Yet, as with the illustration of the lesbian in the wheelchair, the characters with receding hairlines and gray hair serve a more obligatory role than one that actually promotes understanding of elderly or aging queers.

With so few books representing transgender children, a book such as Phyllis Rothblatt's *All I Want to Be Is Me* appears at first glance to be a long-awaited answer for a picture book depicting ethnically diverse transgender children.[20] However, much like *ABC: A Family Book*, Rothblatt's picture book includes requisite watercolor images of children with various skin tones but little defining features to indicate ethnic diversity. Rather, the poorly executed illustrations of culturally generic children could represent any ethnicity based upon the limited text that focuses solely on gender variance and transgender behaviors. This didactic, verbose text attempts to encourage understanding of transgender and gender variant children, but the abstract concepts presented are too difficult for the intended audience of young children. While the book's premise is well-meaning, the ultimate execution is not developmentally appropriate.

With so few picture books depicting underrepresented queer subgroups, there is no room for inferior or poor-quality materials. Children from these groups deserve the same quality books as those from any other cultural group. Herbeck suggests that "knowledge of alternative lifestyles needs to begin early and to continue into adolescence in order to help children accept and understand their peers and their families."[21] Unfortunately, this is virtually impossible without quality picture books with queer themes. The average publication of four queer-themed picture books per year is grossly incongruous, particularly when many of these books do not depict underrepresented queer subgroups or are of such quality that they do not adequately or effectively cover a topic.

With the ever-increasing population of queer children and queer families with children, now is the time for high-quality children's books representing this cultural group. Along with the need for more quality books, there is also a demand for further research on the existing queer picture books. Previous studies of queer books have primarily focused on young adult novels or highlighted singular titles rather than examining the diverse body of picture books available.[22] While this chapter provides a few examples of the groups that are underrepresented or excluded in the scant body of queer picture books, additional studies are necessary to understand the collective content within queer children's literature.

LIBRARY COLLECTIONS FOR
UNDERREPRESENTED QUEER CHILDREN AND FAMILIES

Children in rainbow families are not different from other children in their need to feel accepted, valued, and loved. However, what is different is the fact that society does not always recognize rainbow families. The U.S. federal government refuses to allow gay marriage and only recently ruled against the Don't Ask Don't Tell rule within the U.S. military. LGBTQ individuals and parents are not allowed to adopt children in some states (or to adopt children from certain countries), and educational settings often do not portray rainbow families in their curricula. Hate crimes occur against individuals represented in rainbow families and some states prefer to turn a blind eye to these instances; in some states schools are not allowed to teach youth that hate crimes against LGBTQ individuals are wrong. Libraries can provide unique opportunities for these families by creating safe and welcoming environments that acknowledge these families and celebrate their differences. It is crucial for children in rainbow families as well as children in heterosexual families to see authentic representations of LGBTQ individuals in society, library programs, and book collections. When children in rainbow families see reflections of themselves in library programming, then their existence is validated and they understand that librarians value and respect LGBTQ individuals and their family compositions. Library programs and services inclusive of rainbow families counteract homophobic sentiment, normalize the children and adults in rainbow families, and open doors to their lives for children and caregivers in other types of families.[23]

As with library services to other specialized populations of children and their families, the key to success is high-quality, engaging children's books that celebrate literacy and diversity. Based upon the results of this study of queer-themed picture books, many subsets or facets of rainbow families and the LGBTQ community are missing or poorly represented.

Resources for Serving Parents and Young Children in Rainbow Families

- "Building Rainbow Families." Written by Lynne Maxwell.
- "Missing! Picture Books Reflecting Gay and Lesbian Families: Make the Curriculum Inclusive for All Children." Written by Elizabeth Rowell.
- "Rainbow Books: GLBTQ Books for Children and Teens." Created by the Gay, Lesbian, Bisexual, and Transgender Round Table and the Social Responsibilities Round Table of the American Library Association. Available at http://glbtrt.ala.org/rainbowbooks.
- Rainbow Families Council. Available at http://rainbowfamilies.org.au.
- *Rainbow Family Collections: Selecting and Using Children's Books with Lesbian, Gay, Bisexual, Transgender, and Queer Content.* Written by Jamie Campbell Naidoo.
- "Rethinking Welcoming Literacy Environments for LGBT Families." Written by Kay Emfinger.
- "Very Young Children in Lesbian-and Gay-Headed Families: Moving Beyond Acceptance." Written by Virginia Casper.
- "Steps You Can Take as a Librarian." www.welcomingschools.org/pages/steps-you-can-take-as-a-librarian.

Figure 12.3: Recommended resources for librarians serving rainbow families

Until more quality books are available, librarians with appropriate collection development tools and a dose of ingenuity can still provide quality literature and programs for children in rainbow families. Incorporating high-quality picture books with culturally diverse single parents can allow children and their families to "read in" queer content by assuming the parent is LGBTQ. Including affirmative children's books with gender-nonconforming or gender-neutral characters such as those found in Munro Leaf's *The Story of Ferdinand* or Robert Munsch's *The Paper Bag Princess* provides opportunities for LGBTQ and gender variant children to see representations of themselves.[24] Similarly, changing the pronouns of characters in well-loved children's books during read-alouds creates a more inclusive environment for rainbow families. Another alternative is to use poorer quality queer-themed picture books and have children either create their own pictures for those books with poor illustrations or write their own stories for those books with poor narratives. Figure 12.3 contains collection development tools and additional resources for librarians interested in serving children and adults in rainbow families.[25]

CONCLUSION

Children's librarians can use high-quality queer children's books to open doors to understanding and acceptance. While the scarcity in quality queer-themed picture books for young children could pose a problem for librarians and other educators, numerous resources are available for those professionals dedicated to opening doors through reading and overcoming this barrier. The potential of quality queer-themed children's books is great in both classroom and library settings. The Family Equality Council suggests that librarians and educators can serve as the key to ending homophobia and hate crimes against LGBTQ children and youth: "Open the doors between LGBT parents and their children's schools. If these doors are closed, begin by opening them a crack. If they are open a little, open them even wider. If they are open halfway, use . . . [LGBT-friendly] resources . . . to fling them open completely."[26] Are you ready with your key?

NOTES

1. Jennifer Carr, *Be Who You Are!*, ill. Ben Romback (Bloomington, IN: AuthorHouse, 2010), 22.

2. M. J. Botelho and M. K. Rudman, *Critical Multicultural Analysis in Children's Literature: Mirrors, Windows, and Doors* (New York: Routledge, 2009); B. J. Diamond and M. A. Moore, *Multicultural Literacy: Mirroring the Reality of the Classroom* (White Plains, NY: Longman, 1995); D. L. Fox and K. G. Short, eds., *Stories Matter: Complexity of Cultural Authenticity in Children's Literature* (Urbana, IL: National Council of Teachers of English, 2003); D. L. Henderson and J. P. May, eds., *Exploring Culturally Diverse Literature for Children and Adolescents: Learning to Listen in New Ways* (Boston:

Pearson/Allyn & Bacon, 2005); A. I. Willis, G. E. Garcia, R. Barrera, and V. J. Harris, eds., *Multicultural Issues in Literacy Research and Practice* (Mahwah, NJ: Lawrence Erlbaum, 2002).

3. The term *rainbow families* is used in contemporary literature to describe LGBTQ families who adopt the rainbow symbol, which is often used to signify LGBTQ individuals. Rainbow families can include children with LGBTQ parents, LGBTQ caregivers and/or other family members (aunts, uncles, grandparents, etc.), and LGBTQ children (ages birth to eleven) or gender-variant children choosing play activities, toys, and sometimes clothing that is different from their birth gender.

4. Jacque Roethler, "Reading in Color: Children's book Illustrations and Identity Formation for Black Children in the United States," *African American Review* 32, no. 1 (1998): 95–105.

5. Williams Institute, "901,997 Same-Sex Couples Live in U.S.; Couples Represented in 99% of U.S. Counties" (August 25, 2011), http://services.law.ucla.edu/williaminstitute/press/PressReleases/PressRelease8.25.doc; Urban Institute, "Gay and Lesbian Families in the Census: Couples with Children" (2003), www.urban.org/publications/900626.html.

6. Movement Advancement Project, Family Equality Council and Center for American Progress, "All Children Matter: How Legal and Social Inequalities Hurt LGBT Families," (October 2011): www.lgbtmap.org/all-children-matter-full-report.

7. Gary Gates , Lee M. V. Badgett, Jennifer Ehrle Macomber, and Kate Chambers, "Adoption and Foster Care by Lesbian and Gay Parents in the United States," Urban Institute (March 3, 2007), www.urban.org/url.cfm?ID=411437.

8. Elizabeth Rowell, "Missing! Picture Books Reflecting Gay and Lesbian Families: Make the Curriculum Inclusive for All Children," *Young Children* 62, no. 3 (2007): 24–30.

9. Note that information is available on the number of LGBTQ youth (adolescents and young adults) as well as adults. However, specific information on children is not readily available.

10. Williams Institute, "How Many People Are Lesbian, Gay, Bisexual, or Transgender?" (April 2011), www2.law.ucla.edu/williamsinstitute/pdf/How-many-people-are-LGBT-Final.pdf.

11. Stephanie Brill and Rachel Pepper, *The Transgender Child: A Handbook for Families and Professionals* (San Francisco: Cleis, 2008); Diane Ehrensaft, *Gender Born, Gender Made: Raising Healthy Gender-Nonconforming Children* (New York: The Experiment, 2011).

12. J. Goodman, "Out of the Closet, but Paying the Price: Lesbian and Gay Characters in Children's Literature," *Interracial Books for Children Bulletin* 14, no. 3/4 (1983): 13–15.

13. Laurel Clyde and Marjorie Lobban, *Out of the Closet and Into the Classroom: Homosexuality in Books for Young People* (Deakin, Australian Capital Territory, Australia: ALIA; Melbourne, Vic., Australia: Thorpe, 1992), xvi.

14. The term *queer-themed* represents books with LGBTQ or gender-variant characters.

15. Movement Advancement Project, Family Equality Council and Center for American Progress, "All Children Matter: How Legal and Social Inequalities Hurt LGBT Families," (October 2011): www.lgbtmap.org/all-children-matter-full-report.

16. Marcus Ewert, *10,000 Dresses*, ill. Rex Ray (New York: Seven Stories, 2008), 9.

17. Rigoberto González, *Antonio's Card/La tarjeta de Antonio*, ill. Cecilia Concepción Álvarez (San Francisco: Children's Book Press, 2005).

18. Monica Bey-Clarke and Cheril Clarke, *Keesha and Her Two Moms Go Swimming*, ill. Aiswarya Mukherjee (Sicklerville, NJ: My Family!/Dodi, 2010).

19. Bobbie Combs, *ABC: A Family Alphabet Book*, ill. Desiree Keane and Brian Rappa (Ridley Park, PA: Two Lives, 2000).

20. Phyllis Rothblatt, *All I Want to Be Is Me* (Lexington, KY: CreateSpace, 2011).

21. J. Herbeck, "Creating a Safe Learning Environment: Books for Young People about Homosexuality," *Book Links* (January 2005): 30–34.

22. Michael Cart and Christine A. Jenkins, *The Heart Has Its Reasons: Young Adult Literature with Gay/Lesbian/Queer Content, 1969–2004* (Lanham, MD: Scarecrow, 2006); Thomas Crisp, "The Trouble with Rainbow Boys," *Children's Literature in Education*, 39, no. 4 (2008), 237–61; Thomas Crisp, "From Romance to Magical Realism: Limits and Possibilities in Gay Adolescent Fiction," *Children's Literature in Education*, 40, no. 4 (2009), 333–48.

23. Jamie Campbell Naidoo, *Rainbow Family Collections: Selecting and Using Children's Books with Lesbian, Gay, Bisexual, Transgender, and Queer Content* (Santa Barbara, CA: Libraries Unlimited, 2012).

24. Munro Leaf, *The Story of Ferdinand*, ill. Robert Lawson (New York: Viking, 1936);Robert Munsch, *The Paper Bag Princess*, ill. Michael Martchenko (Toronto: Annick, 1980).

25. American Library Association, Gay, Lesbian, Bisexual, and Transgender Round Table and the Social Responsibilities Round Table, "Rainbow Books: GLBTQ Books for Children and Teens," available from http://glbtrt.ala.org/rainbowbooks; Virginia Casper, "Very Young Children in Lesbian-and Gay-Headed Families: Moving Beyond Acceptance," *Zero to Three* 23, no. 3 (2003): 18–26; Kay Emfinger, "Rethinking Welcoming Literacy Environments for LGBT Families," *Childhood Education* 84, no. 1 (2007): 24–28; Lynne Maxwell, "Building Rainbow Families," *Library Journal* 133, no. 6 (2008): 54–57; Welcoming Schools (2011), "Steps You Can Take as a Librarian," available at www.welcomingschools.org/pages/steps-you-can-take-as-a-librarian.

26. Family Equality Council, *Opening Doors: Lesbian, Gay, Bisexual, and Transgender Parents and Schools* (Boston: Family Equality Council, 2008), 5, www.familyequality.org/_asset/wmr0h2/OpeningDoors2011.pdf.

Rediscovering Filipino Children's Literature

Lola Basyang and Me

DANILO M. BAYLEN

I HAVE VIVID MEMORIES of growing up in a Philippine island south of Manila. My childhood experiences were full of stories told by adults. My first stories came from "yayas" (maids), young women hired from my father's hometown, who not only took care of the children but also performed household chores from cooking to laundry while my parents were at their government jobs. Most of the stories I heard were full of mythical or supernatural creatures that supposedly exist unseen in our midst and prey on children. The telling of these stories had a purpose of preventing children from misbehaving or cajoling them into following the rules: napping in the afternoons, coming home before dusk, or playing fair with siblings and neighborhood children. I had a second source of stories from my own family in the person of my mother's father—Lolo Ino, as I fondly called him. He could spin stories out of a picture or an object without batting an eye. His stories, told with such enthusiasm that we children always asked for more, were always imbued with moral lessons to help us understand the value of right and wrong.

After years of living in the United States, I had forgotten most of these childhood stories until a few years ago when I rediscovered them while browsing in a bookstore during my visit to the Philippines. I chanced upon a children's book titled the *Best of Lola Basyang*, a collection of twelve selected children's stories from the writings of Severino Reyes.[1] The children's stories were originally publishing in Pilipino in 1975, but this collection had been translated into English in 1997 by Gilda Cordero-Fernando with illustrations by Albert Gamos. Encountering these stories again as an adult gave me pause for consideration about the implicit and explicit social messages they leave about Filipino culture. This chapter shares some of the messages I discovered in them and relates them to

Filipino children. This journey starts with a history of the *Lola Basyang* stories.

BACKGROUND HISTORY

Diaz de Rivera states that the development and publishing of children's literature in the Philippines is quite young.[2] A heritage of folk literature from indigenous sources exists from years of Spanish colonization, American occupation and influences, and experiences of World War II. The first children's story from the collection of *Mga Kuwento ni Lola Basyang* (*Tales of Grandmother Basyang*) appeared in a local weekly magazine in 1925 as a space filler.[3] The readership liked the story and demanded more from the storyteller/writer; however it turned out that *Lola Basyang*, the spinner of these entertaining tales, was fictitious. It was a pen name used by Severino Reyes, a popular playwright and the founder/editor of the local weekly magazine *Liwayway*. Reyes decided not to use his real name for ethical reasons, given his position in the magazine.

Inspiration for the storyteller character, *Lola Basyang*, came from a real person named Gervasia Guzman de Zamora.[4] She was a matriarch of a prominent family where Reyes lived. Children adored her and they would gather around her after dinner for storytelling. This image of an old lady surrounded by children as she told her stories must have caught the imagination of Reyes and inspired him to use this theme in his own writing. Another purpose for Reyes to write these children's stories was his own seventeen children who clamored for bedtime stories. So, to keep his stories for posterity, Mr. Reyes became a prolific writer in capturing stories from his youth experiences, readings, and from other individuals. All his stories, obscure or well-known, taught his readers a lesson.

Reyes wrote so many stories that in a span of five years he had penned a total of 280.[5] His stories came from "Philippine folklore, metrical romances, Chinese and Greek classics, and fairy tales" (Tanahan Books, 14) set in places far away. His characters were unforgettable and roamed the earth as well as above and below it. They "wore many masks and inhabited every conceivable place of enchantment" (Tanahan Books, 14).

Many Filipino authors and writers were critical of Reyes's writings as not being original. Reyes seemed to borrow many elements from other plots that he incorporated in his stories, but in the process, he "spun stories out of rich literary threads and ultimately made them his own" Tanahan Books, 14). Reyes also wrote in Tagalog instead of Spanish in order to appeal to a much larger readership. In doing so, he "offered Filipinos a body of children's stories in the vernacular" sweetened by "melodrama and social tensions of everyday life." (Tanahan Books, 14).

After Reyes's death in 1942, his family hired Bienvenido Lumbrera, a prominent poet and literary critic, to select twenty-four of the best stories from Reyes' 400 manuscripts. Out of that selection process, twelve children's stories were published in this book collection. The work of Reyes had many similar elements to stories written by Frances Carpenter, author of several children's books featuring folklore from around the world. Carpenter published two well-known children's books, *Tales of a Korean Grandmother* and *Tales of a Chinese Grandmother*, of traditional tales as told by grandparents to their grandchildren.[6] In these tales, events, traditions or objects interacting with people's lives during a specific period take center stage in the storytelling process. It seems that sharing stories with grandchildren by grandparents creates special moments and promotes familial and culture bonds across generations from around the world.[7]

"TELL ME" AS A PEDAGOGICAL APPROACH

Children's stories from other countries can be used to motivate students to read and develop their literacy skills. This collection of children's stories provided an opportunity for me to apply the "tell me" approach, which is a pedagogical model developed by Aidan Chambers.[8] The "tell me" approach can be a viable instructional strategy for teaching reading comprehension and literacy skills. It involves three types of sharing about a story: enthusiasm, puzzles, and patterns. Enthusiasms are all about likes and dislikes, while puzzles are about things one did not understand in the story. Patterns are about identifying recurring elements within the story and making connections to other stories and to life experiences.

Applying the "tell me" framework to the *Best of Lola Basyang* collection of children's stories can be engaging and educational for both Filipino and non-Filipino students. In this approach, the teacher or librarian provides each student with a copy of a book. Students are asked to look at the book cover and then share what they see as well as what they think is the plot of the story. It is important for the teacher or librarian to write down what students shared for making connections later in the process.

Before students open and read the book, the teacher/librarian identifies and discusses three tasks that need to be completed individually by students: (1) identify something read or viewed that makes you feel enthused, (2) identify something read or viewed that makes you feel puzzled, and (3) identify something read or viewed that contributes to a pattern. It is important that students are told that they may be asked to share what they have after completing their tasks. If possible, students should write down the things they identified for each task for ease in recall.

If presented with a large class of students, the teacher/librarian can organize them into smaller groups or pairs. Each group will be provided with a copy of a book and assigned similar tasks as mentioned above. In this small-group setup, the teacher/librarian assigns roles such as reader, writer, or editor to instill a sense of responsibility and accountability.

Once the reading and viewing activities are finished, students share their work. The teacher/librarian can use one of two strategies: (1) informal sharing where an individual or a group shares their responses to the completed tasks; or (2) structured sharing where the teacher/librarians uses the board to write down student responses to the tasks. A follow-up to this board work activity involves grouping responses and creating Venn diagrams to help students see relationships between and among concepts and ideas shared.

WHAT HAPPENS WHEN STUDENTS TELL STORIES?

The subsequent paragraphs describe the possible outcomes resulting from the "tell me" approach using the twelve stories from the *Lola Basyang* collection. I address how the twelve stories favor one gender over the other, which brings to the forefront issues of gender identity in Filipino children's literature. Secondly, the children's stories touch on children's social worlds, which provide opportunities to look deeper into Filipino culture.

On Being a Man

Reviewing the twelve stories in the collection shows that nine had men as main or key characters. (See table 13.1.) Male characters are portrayed to have physical strength (e.g., Ting, Haliw) and strong mental acuity (e.g., Santiago, Penduko, Bato, the Sultan). Sometimes men are defenders of the oppressed (e.g., Pedro). However, two of the stories characterize men as cowardly (Claudio) and greedy (Adelino). At the end of these stories, some of the men are vindicated like Claudio, who found courage in times of need. Also, males playing secondary roles are evident in these stories as potential husbands or husbands, father figures, sons, friends, kings, or judges. These secondary male roles are present in all stories whether there are male or female lead characters.

Pollack spells out the boy code presented in children's books as encompassing one or more of the following traits: sturdy oak, give 'em hell, the big wheel, and no sissy stuff.[9] As "sturdy oaks," men should be stable, independent, strong, and must not show emotions. This boy code is definitely present in the stories from the *Lola Basyang* collection. Physical strength is demonstrated by the men or boys like Ting, Haliw, and Pedro. Beyond the physical strength, several of these men are portrayed with strong intellects and cleverness like Santiago and Penduko.

In "give 'em hell," Pollack describes boys and men as acting like "macho, high energy, even violent supermen" (Pollack, 24). Ting, Pedro, and Claudio demonstrate these expectations as they engage in risky behaviors. On the other hand, the "big wheel" expects boys and men to "avoid shame at all cost, to wear the mask of coolness, to act as though everything is going all right, as though everything is under control, even

Table 13.1: Outcomes resulting from the application of the "tell me" approach to *Tales of Grandmother Basyang*

#	TITLE	LIKES	DISLIKES	PUZZLES	PATTERNS
1	Maria Alimango	This is very similar to tales that children are familiar with. It has elements of a plot similar to a Cinderella story.	Did not like the part of the story where the father murdered his wife by pushing her into the river. Adultery as mature content. Not sure about presenting this content to young children.	How did the mother become an enchanted crab?	• Weak father • Dead mother • Evil stepmother • Haughty stepsisters • Beautiful, quiet, meek female character • Enchanted being (crab) • Enchanted object (fruit from the tree) • Handsome and rich male archetype as potential husband • Has lots of similarities to a Cinderella story

Table 13.1: Outcomes resulting from the application of the "tell me" approach to *Tales of Grandmother Basyang (continued)*

#	TITLE	LIKES	DISLIKES	PUZZLES	PATTERNS
3	*Clever Penduko*	I like the message presented in this story that intelligence can be an asset to a person. Also, I like the message that being different is not necessarily bad. I like the challenges that Penduko had to manage and solve.	Not much to dislike with this story. However, it seemed unrealistic that a young boy outwitted people much older than him.	I am still wondering why the horse wants to walk backwards.	• Recognition of capacity and capability of a child • Intelligence is not necessarily attributed to age or experience (i.e., being older).
4	*The Forgotten Princess*	I like the idea of a son rescuing his mother from her prison cell. I like the idea of a father raising his child by himself. I like happy endings, as the princess and her family were reunited.	I am not sure I like the sacrifices that the princess had to make for her loved ones—giving up her son, being away from her husband, etc.	I did not understand why the husband did not make an effort to save the princess.	• Nurturing husband • Weak father • Evil stepmother • Brave son • Son rescuing his mother • A family reunited
5	*Ting the Fearless*	I like the idea that Ting only learned to feel fear because he was afraid of losing his son. The story promoted the idea of love as a defining human experience.	I did not like the parts about killing other people and animals.	I am still puzzled why Liloy, Ting's brother, did not say anything when Ting was about to throw him to the ground below. Did Ting marry a princess from Syria?	• A father and two sons • Good and dutiful son • Fearless young man • Learning how to love • Fear of losing a loved one • Three challenges equivalent to three wishes

Table 13.1: Outcomes resulting from the application of the "tell me" approach to *Tales of Grandmother Basyang (continued)*

#	TITLE	LIKES	DISLIKES	PUZZLES	PATTERNS
6	*Judgment of the King*	I like the idea that a good heart always wins at the end. Also, I like the message that jealousy and revenge do not bring good things to those who harbor them. The plot of this story reminded me of Shakespeare's *Merchant of Venice*.	There is not much to dislike about this story except that it has sections of violent acts.	It was not explained well why the king of Manila is much more powerful compared to other kings in nearby areas.	• Poor man with a good heart • Jealous neighbor • Desire for revenge • Judgment of a powerful individual that balances the scale of what is right and what is wrong • Has similarities to Shakespeare's *Merchant of Venice* as well as the biblical story of King Solomon
7	*The Runaway Princess*	I like the idea that true love will prevail. Also, I like the princess's perseverance in her search for true love. This story has similarities to classic tales of true love like Shakespeare's *Romeo and Juliet* and the Broadway musical, *West Side Story*.	This reminds me of the old ways where parents decide what is good for their children, especially in choosing a wife or husband. I did not like the idea of not having choices or free will.	Why can't the old general understand that he is too old for the princess and she does not want to marry him?	• A princess looking for true love • A determined kingfather • A young handsome prince • A princess disobeying her father's wishes and hiding from him • Has elements similar to Shakespeare's *Romeo and Juliet* and the Broadway musical, *West Side Story*
8	*The Two Thieves*	The story narrative informs how to solve a particular problem, such as employing trickery to steal things from the king. This story is about friendship, too.	I am not sure about the representation of thieves as good individuals in this story.	Aside from meeting the challenge presented by the king, I did not really understand why the remaining thief became the chief of police for the king's treasures.	• Two heads are better than one • Friendship between two men • Leaving a legacy • Sacrificing one's life in exchange for betterment of many people's lives

Table 13.1: Outcomes resulting from the application of the "tell me" approach to *Tales of Grandmother Basyang (continued)*

#	TITLE	LIKES	DISLIKES	PUZZLES	PATTERNS
9	*The Handsome Tailor*	This is a good story to introduce the concept of "pretending to be somebody else." The plot of this story reminded me of "The Prince and the Pauper," where two boys who look alike exchange roles by switching clothes.	I did not like the change in behavior and disposition of the tailor. I am not sure I like the story; even though it started innocently, there seems to be an undertone of greediness.	I did not understand why the prince showed up in the neighborhood kingdom and unmasked the pretender.	• Trusting your fellow men • Beautiful clothes do not make a man • Stealing, including other people's identity, does not pay well at the end
10	*Whose Head Will Roll?*	This is another pretender-like story but more of a two-face nature. I am glad to read that the pretender was discovered and punished by the king.	I did not like the sections where people were beheaded. I know that this is a common practice given the context of the story, but too much of it plus gory details make the reading of the story a little bit discomforting.	Initially, I was surprised to know that the mouth was used as a measuring device a long time ago. I was a bit confused when I read the passage for the first time, since I just heard of this practice now.	• Kindness will always be appreciated • One's status should not constrain or limit good behaviors
11	*The Cowardly Prince*	I like that at the end, the prince was able to find courage and strength and not be a coward in the face of adversity.	Again, I did not like the narratives about beheadings and killing as a form of punishment.	I did not understand the reference to the princess as an angel given the time period and the context of the story.	• Love prevails over fear and provides one with courage • An atypical prince—one who is a coward
12	*Pedrong Mabait (Good Pedro)*	I like the plot of this story—about a boy who defends those who are wronged or oppressed by others. I like the idea that meddling in other people's affairs can be good. This time it has positive consequences, because usually it has negative connotations.	I did not like that Pedro died after saving the children. I love to see him vindicated and his good deeds acknowledged by many.	I need more explanation of why Pedro initially avoided defending his mother.	• Bully with a twist—defending others but considered a troublemaker • A caring son to his mother, and at the end, he was able to provide for mother even though he was dead

though it isn't" (Pollack, 24). Again, the behaviors of Ting, Pedro, and Claudio in the stories are aligned with these characterizations.

Finally, in "no sissy stuff," Pollack states it is the most "traumatizing and dangerous injunction thrust on boys and men" (Pollack, 24). It is an expectation that boys and men should avoid expressing feelings or urges that are more expected in women. Claudio was called a sissy by his own father because he acted cowardly in response to things around him. But at the end of the story, Claudio found the courage to fight so he could be with the woman he loves. Claudio's ability to have feelings for the opposite sex provided a proof that he was not a sissy (which usually translates to "being gay" in most Philippine dialects). This gave him courage to battle with another man as a rival to his love interest.

For Filipino boys and young men, these stories imprint images of strong, powerful, and clever male characters in their minds and, in a way, influence their future identities as adults in Philippine culture. One might argue that this is because of the country's history and the influences brought about by its colonizers, the Spaniards and Americans, as well as experiences from World War II. Given these influences, it is not surprising that these depictions of men in children's stories by *Lola Basyang* are not too distant from the Pollack's boy code resulting from his research on boys from a Western culture. How would a non-Filipino student view these representations of men in these stories? Would he see similarities to men in Western culture or would the representations seem foreign?

On Being a Woman

The "tell me" approach could be refocused to look at female characters in the stories from the *Lola Basyang* collection (see table 13.1). Interestingly, only three stories had women as lead characters: Maria ("Mariang Alimango"), Ogarta ("The Forgotten Princess"), and Princess Natalia ("The Runaway Princess"). In all these stories, female characters suffer from decisions made by parental figures and, in comparison to their male counterparts, this suffering is much more pronounced. This depiction seems consistent with female stereotypes, such as that women do not have social privileges or power like men. At the end of these stories, the female characters are able to rise above their extremely unfortunate circumstances and experience happy endings, but only through the help of men. Maria and Princess Natalia find their true love and Princess Ogarta is reunited with her family. Are the same questions that we ask of male characters applicable to female characters?

Female stereotyping is certainly evident in these stories but is consistent with other stories written almost a hundred years ago. To counteract female gender stereotypes, Lissa Paul suggests that children's literature be reread, reclaimed, and redirected using feminist theory as a lens.[10] In so doing, readers can question the roles of females in the *Lola Basyang* stories, especially those with females as key characters. *The Best of Lola Basyang* resulted from the work of Bienvenido Lumbrera, a man who was asked to select the stories for inclusion in this collection; however, Gilda Cordero-Fernando completed the English translation of these stories. Would the twelve stories selected be different if Cordero-Fernando were the person in charge of the selection process? Did other stories with less female gender stereotyping exist?

Another concept that Paul discusses in her work is reclaiming, that is, looking at stories written by women or familiar stories authored by women in the past. Given this concept and looking at the *Lola Basyang* stories, it is known that the author was a man, Severino Reyes. However, he used a female name and persona in authoring these stories. It makes one wonder again if there would have been a difference in the broad acceptance of his stories if he used a man's name but not necessarily his real name, by the reading public. Would the visual characterization of men in these stories conflict with the persona of a storyteller as a spinner of tales, a nurturer of children's imaginations?

Representations of Children and Their World in Children's Stories

Rustin and Rustin discuss deep psychological connections between children's stories and their intended readers.[11] They argue that well-crafted children's stories resonate to the emotional needs of their readers, and they describe three ways of approaching a story: emotional resonance, social worlds of children, and metaphor. Emotional resonance focuses on the unconscious connection that a reader makes to the child characters' state of mind, representations of feelings, and resolutions of conflicting feelings. Social worlds of children focus on how the child's social world, imbued with deeply held values of national culture, is represented and discussed in these stories. Metaphor focuses not only on representations of the experiences and development of the book's characters, but also its readers. Using these approaches, I take a second look at the collection of *Lola Basyang* stories.

Most characters in the *Lola Basyang* stories are young adults or adults. (See table 13.2.) The few lead child characters are Penduko ("Clever Penduko") and Pedro ("Pedrong Mabait"). However, if one looks closely at the storylines, most of these stories deal with adult responsibilities accomplished by children as adolescents. For example, Penduko helps his family prosper through his cleverness, and Pedro provides for his mother as a result of his heroic deeds. Growing up in the Philippine culture, it was an expectation for a child, especially an eldest son, to provide for parents in their old age. Neither of these stories mentions other siblings, so it can be assumed that both Penduko and Pedro are their parents' only child and eldest son.

Given that the Philippines is an agricultural country, the social worlds depicted in these stories are consistent with those times. Artifacts or elements mentioned in the stories are culturally aligned with what was

Table 13.2: Characters and objects of interest in *Tales of Grandmother Basyang*

#	TITLE	FATHER/MOTHER	OTHER FAMILY MEMBER(S)	FRIEND(S) AND/OR LOVERS	OBJECT(S)
1	Maria Alimango	Strong relationship with her mother. Not so strong relationship with her father.	Stepmother and stepsisters are abusive to her.	Don Enrique became her husband.	Her dead mother came back as an enchanted crab and helped her overcome her dire situation.
2	Santiago Karagdag	Both parents were dead at the beginning of the story.	No explicit mention of family members in the story.	Developed almost a father-and-son relationship with Kapitan Vale, his employer. Found a smart woman named Luisa who at the end turned out to be the other daughter of Kapitan Vale.	No explicit mention of special objects in the story.
3	Clever Penduko	Both parents were supportive of their son's abilities.	No explicit mention of family members in the story.		No explicit mention of special objects in the story.
4	The Forgotten Princess	Fatherking imprisoned his daughter in the palace's dungeon for disobeying him about marrying one of his generals.	No explicit mention of family members in the story.	Fell in love with a commoner and had a son. The grown son, after knowing the existence of his imprisoned mother, led a siege of the castle and freed her.	No explicit mention of special objects in the story.
5	Ting the Fearless	Father, a widower, seems unable to understand his second son, Ting, who always gets in trouble.	Liloy, Ting's brother, is always a good son—hardworking and cautious, but also doesn't understand his brother's behavior	Others (e.g., merchants from Syria) tested Ting's fearless nature and Ting proved that he is fearless.	No explicit mention of special objects in the story.

Table 13.2: Characters and objects of interest in *Tales of Grandmother Basyang (continued)*

#	TITLE	FATHER/MOTHER	OTHER FAMILY MEMBER(S)	FRIEND(S) AND/OR LOVERS	OBJECT(S)
6	Judgment of the King	No parents mentioned in the story.	No family members mentioned in the story. It seems Haliw lives by himself.	Sikat is a rich friend who gave Haliw materials to build a house but was envious when it turned out that Haliw's house is much better looking than his. Bulik, Tahil, and Bukawe are individuals who want to take revenge against Haliw for his unintended actions (e.g., causing Bulik's wife to have an early birth, falling into Tahil's father and killing him, and severing the carabao's tail owned by Bukawe). The king who handed down judgment on the complaints made by Sikat, Bulik, Tahil, and Bukawe against Haliw.	No explicit mention of special objects in the story.
7	The Runaway Princess	Only the father-king is mentioned in the story, but no mother figure.	Princess Natalia is an only child.	General Lamberto is the man that the King wanted to succeed him and marry his daughter. Prince Enrico is the man who found Princess Natalia impersonating as Liling in the forest and brought her to his palace to work in the kitchen. At the end, he found out that she was his true love and a princess and married her.	Three objects (ring, necklace, and gold picture frame) were given to Prince Enrico (the first two were put in his soup) as a symbol of Princess Natalia's love for him.

Table 13.2: Characters and objects of interest in *Tales of Grandmother Basyang* (continued)

#	TITLE	FATHER/MOTHER	OTHER FAMILY MEMBER(S)	FRIEND(S) AND/OR LOVERS	OBJECT(S)
8	The Two Thieves	No explicit mention of parents in the story.	The story mentioned that Kilabot moved to live with Bato's family. Bato's wife who almost gave away the secret that Bato and Kilabot were the thieves that the King and Chief of Police were looking for.	The King and Chief of Police who want the two thieves caught and punished.	No explicit mention of special objects in the story.
9	The Handsome Tailor	No explicit mention of Adelino's parents in the story. However, Omar's parents, as King and Queen, were key characters toward the end of the story.	No explicit mention of family members in the story.	Prince Rosaldo is the person who asked Adelino to repair the clothes. Omar is the young man that Adelino met on his travels. Adelino stole the dagger that proves Omar is the rightful heir to the throne.	Adelino felt attached to Prince Rosaldo's clothes. By wearing the prince's clothes, Adelino felt that he was living a princely lifestyle.
10	Whose Head Will Roll?	No explicit mention of the Sultan's parents in the story.	No explicit mention of the Sultan's family in the story.	Sir Luor, the first minister whom the Sultan disagreed with on his ideas about charity and generosity to the poor. Pedro and Berta, the shepherd and his wife, who fed and took care of the Sultan and his chamberlain dressed as beggars.	

Table 13.2: Characters and objects of interest in *Tales of Grandmother Basyang* (continued)

#	TITLE	FATHER/MOTHER	OTHER FAMILY MEMBER(S)	FRIEND(S) AND/OR LOVERS	OBJECT(S)
11	The Cowardly Prince	The father-king who despised his son, Claudio, as being a sissy. Princess Flerida's father, also a king in another kingdom. There was no explicit mention of mother-queens in both families.	No explicit mention of the other family members in the story.	Prince Artemio, a brave fighter and ardent suitor of Princess Flerida. He was killed in a battle with Prince Claudio.	No explicit mention of special objects in the story.
12	Pedrong Mabait (Good Pedro)	Pedro lives with his mother, Aling Angge, and then later with his stepfather, Leoncio. His stepfather was cruel to his mother and towards the end of the story, Pedro defended her against him.	No explicit mention of the other family members in the story.	The family honored Pedro after he died saving their children and provided monetary allowance to Aling Angge for the rest of her life.	No explicit mention of special objects in the story.

available then. For example, Filipino children during these periods were expected to mature fast because they were needed to support the family at an early age. Childhood was quite short for many children, especially in rural areas, since they had to assume adult responsibilities such as tending the animals and working in the fields once they were able. Values of hard work, courage, wealth, and eventually marriage and family are quite prominent as themes in these stories and are expected behaviors for men in this culture. I believe that these stories represent the social worlds that children of long ago were expected to manage and master.

The review of the stories identifies a lack of emphasis on relationships towards another person (e.g., parents). (See table 13.2.) This lack of demonstrated relationship between parents and children could be a source of conflict that child protagonists needed to resolve. Five stories do not explicitly mention the parents of the main character. One story briefly mentions that the parents are dead (i.e., "Santiago Karagdag"). Seven stories mention at least one parent alive and most of the time, it is the father. Only one story mentions both parents living and being supportive of their child (i.e., "Clever Penduko"). Two stories mention mothers as key figures in their children's lives (i.e., "Mariang Alimango" and "Pedrong Mabait"). Also, several stories mention having a relationship with someone as husband or wife.

The lack of demonstrated relationships among characters in these stories seems to illustrate behaviors of what to expect when a child becomes an adult. These children's stories can serve as representations of a child's journey not only to adulthood but also to meeting societal expectations of being married and having a family. This seems to be a strong message for children growing up in the Filipino culture. Is it the same message that non-Filipino children see or hear growing up in their own culture?

CONNECTING EXPERIENCES
FROM THE CLASSROOM TO THE WORLD

How can teachers and library media specialists take advantage of these types of stories to support student learning and appreciation of the world outside of their classroom? Does the use of these resources meet today's various standards for teaching and learning? The Partnership for 21st Century Skills, a national organization, advocates for student readiness given the demands of the global economy by providing tools and resources to support the U.S. educational system in areas of critical thinking and problem solving, communication, collaboration, and creativity and innovation.[12] Under the elements of communication, twenty-first-century students are expected to demonstrate the following:

- Articulate thoughts and ideas effectively using oral, written, and nonverbal communication skills in a variety of forms and contexts.

- Listen effectively to decipher meaning, including knowledge, values, attitudes, and intentions.
- Use communication for a range of purposes (e.g., to inform, instruct, motivate, and persuade).
- Utilize multiple media and technologies, and know how to judge their effectiveness a priori as well as assess their impact.
- Communicate effectively in diverse environments (including multilingual). (Partnership for 21st Century Skills, 2004)

Teachers and school library media specialists can use these stories as doorways in engaging students to explore people, events, and things beyond their own contexts. For example, some of the stories can be used by teachers as material for comparing how others lived during a specific period in time or in another country. Library media specialists can invite those who grew up in the distant past or in another culture to share their own childhood experiences.

Under the elements of collaboration with others, students are expected to:

- Demonstrate ability to work effectively and respectfully with diverse teams.
- Exercise flexibility and willingness to be helpful in making necessary compromises to accomplish a common goal.
- Assume shared responsibility for collaborative work, and value the individual contributions made by each team member. (Partnership for 21st Century, 2004)

Follow-up activities from using these stories in the classroom or media centers can involve reading related fiction or nonfiction literature to support collaborative work. In collaborating with others to produce artifacts that showcases their learning, students experience working with diverse individuals, exercising flexibility and accountability, and working towards a common goal.

One of the current standards of the American Association of School Librarians (AASL) identifies skills, resources, and tools to "inquire, and think critically, and gain knowledge."[13] Using these types of stories as resources and tools for learning, students would be able to develop their skills towards becoming twenty-first-century learners. The following elements are skills, dispositions in action, responsibilities, and self-assessment strategies from the aforementioned AASL standard:

1.1.2 Use prior and background knowledge as context for new learning.
1.1.3 Develop and refine a range of questions to frame the search for new understanding.

1.1.4 Find, evaluate and select appropriate sources to answer questions.

1.1.5 Evaluate information found in selected sources on the basis of accuracy, validity, appropriateness for needs, importance, and social and cultural context.

1.1.6 Read, view, and listen for information presented in any format (e.g., textual, visual, media, digital) in order to make inferences and gather meaning.

1.1.9 Collaborate with others to broaden and deepen understanding.

1.2.1 Display initiative and engagement by posing questions and investigating the answers beyond the collection of superficial facts.

1.3.4 Contribute to the exchange of ideas within the learning community.

1.4.2 Use interaction with and feedback from teachers and peers to guide own inquiry process.

1.4.3 Monitor gathered information, and assess for gaps or weaknesses.

1.4.4 Seek appropriate help when it is needed. (AASL, 2011)

The stories provide opportunities for children and young people to think, reflect, and share about their lives with peers and other individuals. It is an opportunity to "see" how others live and work, and to imagine possibilities that can only happen in dreams. Finally, it is an opportunity to be heard because in some cultures, children are invisible during conversations among and between parents and other adults.

REFLECTING ON THE VALUE
OF STORYTELLING IN CHILDHOOD

As a child, I loved to hear stories told by my grandparents. I remember many of those moments with my grandfather and do not believe that in those storytelling moments my thoughts dwelled on issues of gender and representations of children and their social world. At the time, I was enamored with the idea of spending time with my grandparents more than anything else because we did not live near each other.

Now that I am an adult, I have become more aware of the influences of these early childhood experiences on the person I am today. In reading and rereading these children's stories I have to reflect on the cultural values they evoke in me. After completing the "tell me" table, I now tend to question whether these stories are really, truly part of my own heritage. I can see pieces and remnants of my culture but fragmented by years of impositions from other cultures—by the Spaniards, Americans, and Japanese among others in my country's history.

As a Filipino, educated in American universities, I often find it so easy to impose Western standards on indigenous cultural artifacts like these children's stories. It is easy to label things as backward or primitive. In planning for this chapter, I read an online posting of another Filipino studying in the United States, and she argues that we need to look at these Filipino children's books from our own cultural lenses and not those of other cultures. I believe that she has a point, and the "tell me" approach can be used as one of the strategies to help me and others read and understand Filipino children's literature better from a Filipino culture's point of view. This does not mean throwing out all the Western-based articles we have read on studies of children's literature. Rather, as educators and researchers of children's literature, we should question what we discover and learn about Filipino children's literature and engage in dialogue with Filipinos to discern how these books are perceived through their cultural lenses.

NOTES

1. Severino Reyes, *The Best of Lola Basyang: Timeless Tales for the Filipino Family* (Metro Manila, Philippines: Tahanan Books, 1997).
2. Diaz de Rivera, "Children's Literature in the Philippines," *Reading Today,* 2004, 21, no. 3: 37.
3. D. Villegas, *Mga kuwento ni Lola Basyang: Classic Tagalog Tales in Komiks* (2007), http://pilipinokomiks.blogspot.com/2007/03/mga-kuwento-ni-lola-basyang-classic.html; WikiPilipinas, *Mga Kuwento ni Lola Basyang* (2007), http://en.wikipilipinas.org/index.php?title=Mga_Kuwento_ni_Lola_Basyang.
4. B. Lumbrera, "Introduction" in *The Best of Lola Basyang: Timeless Tales for the Filipino Family* (Metro Manila, Philippines: Tahanan Books, 1997).
5. Tanahan Books, "The Best of Lola Basyang: Timeless Tales for the Filipino Family," in *Severino Reyes: The Man and His Work* (Metro Manila, Philippines: Tahanan Books, 1997).
6. Sarah Park, *Tales of a Korean Grandmother: Critical Evaluation Essay* (2004), http://ccb.lis.illinois.edu/Projects/history/sypark2/critical.htm.
7. Marjorie Coughlan, *Books at Bedtime: Tales Heard at Grandmother's Knee* (2011), www.papertigers.org/wordpress/tag/frances-carpenter.
8. Aidan Chambers, *Tell Me: Children, Reading and Talk* (Ontario, Canada: Pembroke, 1996).
9. William S. Pollack, "Stories of Shame and the Haunting Trauma of Separation: How We Can Connect with Boys and Change the 'Boy Code,'" in *Real Boys: Rescuing Our Sons from the Myths of Boyhood* (New York: Random House, 1998).
10. Lissa Paul, "Enigma Variations: What Feminist Theory Knows about Children's Literature?" in *Children's Literature: The Development of Criticism,* ed. Peter Hunt (1990).
11. Margaret Rustin and Michael Rustin, "Introduction: Deep Structure in Modern Children's Fiction," in *Narratives of Love and Loss: Studies in Modern Children's Fiction,* (New York: Verso, 1997).
12. Partnership for 21st Century Skills, "Partnership for 21st Century Skills" (2004), www.p21.org.
13. American Association of School Librarians, "Standards for 21st Century Learners" (2011), www.ala.org/ala/mgrps/divs/aasl/guidelinesandstandards.

Further Reading

BOOKS

Abate, Michelle Ann. *Raising Your Kids Right: Children's Literature and American Political Conservatism*. New Brunswick, NJ: Rutgers University Press, 2011.

Ada, Alma Flor. *A Magical Encounter: Latino Children's Literature in the Classroom*. 2nd ed. Boston: Allyn & Bacon, 2002.

Alexander, Lina B., and Nahyun Kwon. *Multicultural Programs for Tweens and Teens*. Chicago: American Library Association, 2010.

Asamen, Joy Keiko, Mesha L. Ellis, and Gordon L. Berry. *The SAGE Handbook of Child Development, Multiculturalism, and Media*. Los Angeles: SAGE, 2008.

Avila, Salvador. *Serving Latino Teens*. Santa Barbara, CA: Libraries Unlimited, 2012.

Baker, Deirdre, and Ken Setterington. *A Guide to Canadian Children's Books*. Toronto, ONT: McClelland & Stewart, 2003.

Bernstein, Robin. *Racial Innocence: Performing American Childhood and Race from Slavery to Civil Rights*. New York: New York University Press, 2011.

Bishop, Rudine Sims. *Free within Ourselves: The Development of African American Children's Literature*. Westport, CT: Greenwood, 2007.

Botelho, Maria José, and Masha Kabakow Rudman. *Critical Multicultural Analysis of Children's Literature*. New York: Routledge, 2009.

Boyd, Fenice B., and Cynthia H. Brock, eds. *Multicultural and Multilingual Literacy and Language: Contexts and Practices*. New York: Guilford, 2004.

Cart, Michael, and Christine Jenkins. *The Heart Has Its Reasons: Young Adult Literature with Gay/Lesbian/Queer Content, 1969–2004*. Lanham, MD: Scarecrow, 2006.

Cole, Sonja. *Booktalking Around the World: Great Global Reads for Ages 9–14*. Santa Barbara, CA: Libraries Unlimited, 2010.

Day, Frances Ann. *Latina and Latino Voices in Literature: Lives and Works*. 2nd ed. Westport, CT: Greenwood, 2003.

———. *Lesbian and Gay Voices: an Annotated Bibliography and Guide to Literature for Children and Young Adults*. Westport, CT: Greenwood.

Diamant-Cohen, Betsy. *Early Literacy Programming en Español: Mother Goose on the Loose Programs for Bilingual Learners*. New York: Neal-Schuman, 2010.

East, Kathy, and Rebecca L. Thomas. *Across Cultures: A Guide to Multicultural Literature for Children*. Westport, CT: Libraries Unlimited, 2007.

Edwards, Gail, and Judith Saltman. *Picturing Canada: A History of Canadian Children's Illustrated Books and Publishing*. Toronto, ONT: University of Toronto Press, 2010.

Edwards, Julie Olsen, and Louise Derman-Sparks. *Anti-Bias Education for Young Children & Ourselves.* Washington, DC: National Association for the Education of Young Children, 2010.

Farmer, Lesley. *Library Services for Youth with Autism Spectrum Disorders.* Chicago: American Library Association, 2013.

Fox, Dana, and Kathy Short, eds. *Stories Matter: The Complexity of Cultural Authenticity in Children's Literature.* Urbana, IL: National Council of Teachers of English, 2003.

Freeman, Evelyn, and Barbara Lehman. *Global Perspectives in Children's Literature.* Boston: Allyn & Bacon, 2001.

Friedberg, Joan Brest, June B. Mullins, and Adelaide Weir Sukiennik. *Portraying Persons with Disabilities: An Annotated Bibliography of Nonfiction for Children and Teenagers.* 2nd ed. New Providence, NJ: Bowker, 1992.

Gates, Pamela, and Dianne L. Hall Mark. *Cultural Journeys: Multicultural Literature for Children and Young Adults.* Lanham, MD: Scarecrow, 2006.

Gebel, Doris. *Crossing Boundaries with Children's Books.* Lanham, MD: Scarecrow, 2006.

Gilton, Donna L. *Multicultural and Ethnic Children's Literature in the United States.* Lanham, MD: Scarecrow, 2007.

Givens, Archie. *Strong Souls Singing: African American Books for Our Daughters and Our Sisters.* New York: Norton, 1998.

Gopalakrishnan, Ambika. *Multicultural Children's Literature: A Critical Issues Approach.* Los Angeles: SAGE, 2011.

Greene, Stuart, and Dawn Abt-Perkins. *Making Race Visible: Literacy Research for Cultural Understanding.* New York: Teachers College Press, 2003.

Guthrie, Dorothy Littlejohn. *Integrating African American Literature in the Library and Classroom.* Santa Barbara, CA: Libraries Unlimited, 2011.

Harris, Violet J, ed. *Teaching Multicultural Literature in Grades K–8.* Norwood, MA: Christopher-Gordon, 1993.

———, ed. *Using Multiethnic Literature in the K–8 Classroom.* Norwood, MA: Christopher-Gordon, 1997.

Hearne, Betsy, and Roger Sutton. *Evaluating Children's Books: A Critical Look: Aesthetic, Social, and Political Aspects of Analyzing and Using Children's Books.* Urbana-Champaign: University of Illinois, Graduate School of Library and Information Science, 1993.

Henderson, Darwin, and Jill May. *Exploring Culturally Diverse Literature for Children and Adolescents: Learning to Listen in New Ways.* Boston: Allyn & Bacon, 2005.

Hernon, Peter, and Philip Calvert, eds. *Improving the Quality of Library Services for Students with Disabilities.* Westport, CT: Libraries Unlimited, 2006.

Jenkins, Esther, and Mary Austin. *Literature for Children about Asia and Asian Americans: Analysis and Annotated Bibliography, with Additional Readings for Adults.* Westport, CT: Greenwood. 1987.

Jobe, Ron. *Cultural Connections: Using Literature to Explore World Cultures with Children.* Markham, ONT: Pembroke, 1993.

Jweid, Rosann, and Margaret Rizzo. *Building Character through Multicultural Literature: A Guide for Middle School Readers.* Lanham, MD: Scarecrow, 2004.

Khorana, Meena. *Africa in Literature for Children and Young Adults: Annotated Bibliography of English Language Books.* Westport, CT: Greenwood, 1994.

———. *Indian Subcontinent in Literature for Children and Young Adults: An Annotated Bibliography of English Language Books.* New York: Greenwood, 1991.

Kidd, Kenneth, and Michell Ann Abate, eds. *Over the Rainbow: Queer Children's and Young Adult Literature.* Ann Arbor: University of Michigan Press, 2011.

Knowles, Liz, and Martha Smith. *Understanding Diversity Through Novels and Picture Books*. Westport, CT: Libraries Unlimited, 2007.

Kruse, Ginny Moore, Kathleen T. Horning, and Megan Schliesman. *Multicultural Literature for Children and Young Adults: Volume 2, 1991–1996: A Selected Listing of Books by and about People of Color*. Madison, Wisconsin: Cooperative Children's Book Center, University of Wisconsin-Madison with the Friends of the CCBC, Inc. and Wisconsin Dept. of Public Instruction, 1997.

Kuharets, Olga. *Venture into Cultures: A Resource Book of Multicultural Materials and Programs*. 2nd ed. Chicago: American Library Association, 2001.

Langer de Ramirez, Lori. *Voices of Diversity: Stories, Activities, and Resources for the Multicultural Classroom*. Columbus, OH: Pearson, 2006.

Larson, Jeanette. *El día de los niños/El día de los libros: Building a Culture of Literacy in Your Community through Día*. Chicago: American Library Association, 2011.

Lee, Enid, Deborah Menkart, and Margo Okazawa-Rey, eds. *Beyond Heroes and Holidays: A Practical Guide to K–12 Anti-Racist, Multicultural Education and Staff Development*. Washington, DC: Teaching for Change, 2008.

Lepman, Jella. *A Bridge of Children's Books: The Inspiring Autobiography of a Remarkable Woman*. Dublin, Ireland: O'Brien, 2002.

Lindgren, M. V., ed. *The Multicolored Mirror: Cultural Substance in Literature for Children and Young Adults: A Selected Listing of Books 1980–1990 by and about People of Color*. Madison, WI: Cooperative Children's Book Center, 1991.

MacDonald, Margaret Read. *Tell the World: Storytelling across Language Barriers*. Westport, CT: Libraries Unlimited, 2008.

MacMillan, Kathy, and Christine Kirker. *Multicultural Storytime Magic*. Chicago: American Library Association, 2012.

Mallan, Kerry. *Gender Dilemmas in Children's Fiction*. New York: Palgrave MacMillian, 2009.

Marantz, Sylvia, and Ken Marantz. *Multicultural Picturebooks: Art for Illuminating Our World*. Lanham, MD: Scarecrow, 2005.

Martin, Hillias J., and James Murdock. *Serving Lesbian, Gay, Bisexual, Transgender, and Questioning Teens: A How-to-Do-It Manual for Librarians*. New York: Neal-Schuman, 2007.

Martin, Michelle. *Brown Gold: Milestones of African American Children's Picture Books, 1845–2002*. New York: Routledge, 2004.

McGowan, Tara M. *The Kamishibai Classroom: Engaging Multiple Literacies Through the Art of "Paper Theater."* Santa Barbara, CA: Libraries Unlimited, 2010.

Mickenberg, Julia L. *Learning from the Left: Children's Literature, the Cold War, and Radical Politics in the United States*. Oxford: Oxford University Press, 2006.

Miller-Lachmann, Lyn. *Our Family, Our Friends, Our World: An Annotated Guide to Significant Multicultural Books for Children and Teenagers*. New Providence, NY: Bowker, 1992.

Muse, Daphne. *The New Press Guide to Multicultural Resources for Young Readers*. New York: New, 1997.

Naidoo, Beverley. *Through Whose Eyes? Exploring Racism: Reader, Text, and Context*. Staffordshire, UK: Trentham Books, 1992.

Naidoo, Jamie Campbell, ed. *Celebrating Cuentos: Promoting Latino Children's Literature and Literacy in Classrooms and Libraries*. Santa Barbara, CA: Libraries Unlimited, 2010.

———. *Rainbow Family Collections: Selecting and Using Children's Books with Lesbian, Gay, Bisexual, Transgender, and Queer Content*. Santa Barbara, CA: Libraries Unlimited, 2012.

Norton, Donna. *Multicultural Children's Literature: Through the Eyes of Many Children*. 3rd ed. Boston: Allyn & Bacon, 2009.

Ramirez, Gonzalo, Jr., and Jan L. Ramirez. *Multiethnic Children's Literature*. Albany, NY: Delmar, 1994.

Rand, Donna, and Toni Trent Parker. *Black Books Galore! Guide to More Great African American Children's Books*. New York: Wiley, 2001.

Robertson, Debra. *Portraying Persons with Disabilities: An Annotated Bibliography of Fiction for Children and Teenagers*. 3rd ed. New Providence, NJ: R.R. Bowker, 1992.

Rochman, Hazel. *Against Borders: Promoting Books for a Multicultural Society*. Chicago: American Library Association, 1994.

Rogers, Theresa, and Anna O. Soter. *Reading across Cultures: Teaching in a Diverse Society*. New York: Teachers College Press and National Council of Teachers of English, 1997.

Schon, Isabel. *The Best of Latino Heritage 1996–2002: A Guide to the Best Juvenile Books about Latino People and Cultures*. Lanham, MD: Scarecrow, 2003.

———. *Recommended Books in Spanish for Children and Young Adults*. Lanham, MD: Scarecrow, 2009.

Seale, Doris, and Beverly Slapin. *A Broken Flute: The Native Experience in Books for Children*. Walnut Creek, CA: AltaMira/Rowan & Littlefield, 2005.

Slapin, Beverly, and Doris Seale. *Through Indian Eyes: The Native Experience in Children's Books*. 4th ed. Los Angeles: University of California Press, 1998.

Smith, Henrietta M., ed. *The Coretta Scott King Awards 1970–2009*. 4th ed. Chicago: American Library Association, 2009.

Smolin, Lynn Atkinson, and Ruth A. Oswald, eds. *Multicultural Literature and Response: Affirming Diverse Voices*. Santa Barbara, CA: Libraries Unlimited, 2011.

Stan, Susan. *The World through Children's Books*. Lanham, MD: Scarecrow, 2002.

Steiner, Stanley, and Peggy Hokom. *Promoting a Global Community through Multicultural Children's Literature*. Englewood, CO: Libraries Unlimited, 2001.

Stewart, Michelle Pagni, and Yvonne Atkinson, eds. *Ethnic Literary Traditions in American Children's Literature*. New York: Palgrave MacMillan, 2009.

Taylor-DiLeva, Kim. *Once Upon a Sign: Using American Sign Language to Engage, Entertain, and Teach All Children*. Santa Barbara, CA: Libraries Unlimited, 2010.

Thomas, Ebony, ed. *Reading African American Experiences in the Obama Era*. New York: Peter Lang, 2012.

Tomlinson, Carl M. *Children's Books from Other Countries*. Lanham, MD: Scarecrow, 1998.

Totten, Herman L., Carolyn Garner, and Risa N. Brown. *Culturally Diverse Library Collections for Youth*. New York: Neal-Schuman, 1996.

Treviño, Rose Zertuche. *The Pura Belpré Awards: Celebrating Latino Authors and Illustrators*. Chicago: American Library Association, 2006.

Van Ausdale, Debra, and Joe R. Feagin. *The First R: How Children Learn Race and Racism*. New York: Rowan & Littlefield, 2001.

Wadham, Tim. *Libros Escenciales: Building, Marketing, and Programming a Core Collection of Spanish Language Children's Materials*. New York: Neal-Schuman, 2007.

Webber, Carlisle K. *Gay, Lesbian, Bisexual, Transgender and Questioning Teen Literature: A Guide to Reading Interests*. Santa Barbara, CA: Libraries Unlimited, 2010.

Willis, Arlette Ingram. *Teaching Multicultural Literature in Grades 9–12: Moving Beyond the Canon*. Norwood, MA: Christopher-Gordon, 1998.

York, Sherry. *Booktalking Authentic Multicultural Literature: Fiction and History for Young Readers*. Columbus, OH: Linworth, 2009.

————. *Picture Books by Latino Writers: A Guide for Librarians, Teachers, Parents, and Students*. Worthington, OH: Linworth, 2002.

ARTICLES

Agosto, Denise. "The Lubuto Library Project: As a Model of School Library Media Services for Disadvantaged Youth." *Knowledge Quest* 37, no. 1 (2008): 38–42.

Albright, Lettie K., and April W. Bedford. "From Resistance to Acceptance: Introducing Books with Gay and Lesbian Characters." *Journal of Children's Literature* 32, no. 1 (2006): 1–15.

Allen, Adela Artola. "The School Library Media Center and the Promotion of Literature for Hispanic Children." *Library Trends* 41, no. 3 (1993): 437–61.

Alexander, Linda B., and Sarah D. Miselis. "Barriers to GLBTQ Collection Development and Strategies for Overcoming Them." *Young Adult Library Services* 5, no. 3 (2007): 43–49.

Al-Hazza, Tami Craft, and Katherine T. Butcher. "Building Arab Americans' Cultural Identity and Acceptance with Children's Literature." *The Reading Teacher* 62, no. 3 (2008): 210–19.

Atkins, Laura. "White Privilege and Children's Publishing: A Web 2.0 Case Study." *Write4Children* 1, no. 2 (2010), www.winchester.ac.uk/academicdepartments/EnglishCreativeWritingandAmericanStudies/publications/write4children/Documents/w4cissue2cApr.pdf.

Atkinson, Joan. "Oh, the Places You'll Go (and Won't) with Newberys." *Journal of Youth Services in Libraries* 10 (1996): 46–57.

Aronson, Marc. "A Mess of Stories." *The Horn Book* 71, no. 2 (1995): 163–74.

Banfield, Beryle. "Commitment to Change: The Council on Interracial Books for Children and the World of Children's Books." *African American Review* 32, no. 1 (1998): 17.

Banks, Cheryl, Ellen Cole, and Linda Silver. "The Quest for Excellence in Jewish Children's Literature." *Judaica Librarianship* 12 (2006): 69–78.

Barclay, Donald A. "Native Americans in Books from the Past." *The Horn Book* 72, no. 5 (1996): 559–65.

Bell, Gladys. "Electronic Resources for Cultures of the World." *The Reference Librarian* 21, no. 45/46 (1994): 313–37.

Berry, John D. "White Privilege in Library Land." *Library Journal* 129, no. 11 (2004): 50.

Bishop, Rudine Sims. "Books from Parallel Cultures: Celebrating a Silver Anniversary." *The Horn Book* 69, no. 2 (1993): 175.

Bleeker, Gerrit, Barbara Bleeker, and Catherine Rickbone. "Let's Talk about It: An Intergenerational Family Literacy Program." *Voice of Youth Advocates* 26, no. 4 (2003): 288–90.

Bronski, Michael. "Positive Images and the Stupid Family: Queer Books for Kids?" *Radical America* 25, no. 1 (1991): 61–70.

Bruchac, Joseph. "All Our Relations." *The Horn Book* 71, no. 2 (1995): 158–62.

Bryant, David. "Multiculturalism: The New Racism." *Library Journal* 119, no. 2 (1994): 54.

Butler, Charles. "Experimental Girls: Feminist and Transgender Discourses in Bill's New Frock and Marvin Redpost: Is He a Girl?" *Children's Literature Association Quarterly* 34, no. 1 (2009): 3–20.

Cameron, Ann, Keiko Narahashi, Mildred Pitts Walter, and David Wisniewski. "The Many Faces in Children's Books." *School Library Journal* 38, no. 1 (1992): 28–33.

Campbell, Patty. "The Sand in the Oyster." *The Horn Book* 70, no. 4 (1994): 491–96.

Casement, Rose. "Breaking the Silence: The Stories of Gay and Lesbian People in Children's Literature." *New Advocate* 15, no. 3 (2002): 205–13.

Champion, Sandra. "The Adolescent Quest for Meaning through Multicultural Readings: A Case Study." *Library Trends* 41, no. 3 (1993): 462–93.

Chen, Fu-jen, and Su-lin Yu. "Asian North-American Children's Literature about the Internment: Visualizing and Verbalizing the Traumatic Thing." *Children's Literature in Education* 37, no. 2 (2006): 111–24.

Chen, S. "Asian American Literature in School Libraries." *Journal of Educational Media and Library Service* 39, no. 3 (2002): 251–68.

Chick, Kay. "Fostering an Appreciation for All Kinds of Families: Picture Books with Gay and Lesbian Themes." *Bookbird* 46, no. 1 (2008): 15–22.

Clyde, Laurel, and Marjorie Lobban. "A Door Half Open: Young People's Access to Fiction Related to Homosexuality." *School Libraries Worldwide* 7, no. 2 (2001): 17–30.

Collins, Carol Jones. "A Tool for Change: Young Adult Literature in the Lives of Young Adult African-Americans." *Library Trends* 41, no. 3 (1993): 378–92.

Cox, Susan, and Lee Galda. "Multicultural Literature: Mirrors and Windows in a Global Community." *Children's Books* 43, no. 8 (1990): 582–89.

Crisp, Thomas. "The Trouble with Rainbow Boys." *Children's Literature in Education* 39, no. 4 (2008): 237–61.

Derman-Sparks, Louise. "10 Quick Ways to Analyze Children's Books for Racism and Sexism." In *Anti-Bias Curriculum: Tools for Empowering Young Children*, 142–45. Washington, DC: NAEYC, 1980.

Dias-Mitchell, Laurie, and Elizabeth Harris. "Multicultural Mosaic: A Family Book Club." *Knowledge Quest* 29, no. 4 (2001): 17–21.

Elster, Charles A., and Trina Zych. "'I Wish I Could Have Been There Dancing with You': Linking Diverse Communities through Social Studies and Literature." *Social Studies* 89, no. 1 (1998): 25.

Frostick, Cary Meltzer. "The Myth of Equal Access: Bridging the Gap with Diverse Patrons." *Children and Libraries* 7, no. 3 (2009): 32–37.

Gangi, Jane M. "Inclusive Aesthetics and Social Justice: The Vanguard of Small, Multicultural Presses." *Children's Literature Association Quarterly* 30, no. 3 (2005): 233–64.

Gillespie, Cindy, Janet Powell, Nancy Clements, and Rebecca Swearingen. "A Look at the Newbery Medal Books from a Multicultural Perspective." *The Reading Teacher* 48, no. 1 (1994): 40–50.

Hade, Daniel D. "Books in the Classroom: The Differences among Us." *The Horn Book* 69, no. 5 (1993): 642–45.

Hamanaka, Sheila. "I Hope Their Ears Are Burning: An Author of Color Talks about Racism in Children's Literature." *The New Advocate* 7, no. 4 (1994): 227–38.

Hearne, Betsy. "Cite the Source: Reducing Cultural Chaos in Picture Books, Part One." *School Library Journal* 39, no. 7 (1993): 24.

———. "Cite the Source: Reducing Cultural Chaos in Picture Books, Part Two." *School Library Journal* 39, no. 7 (1993): 33–37.

Hirschfelder, Arlene B. "Native American Literature for Children and Young Adults." *Library Trends* 41, no. 3 (1993): 414–36.

Honma, Todd. "Trippin' over the Color Line: The Invisibility of Race in Library and Information Studies." *InterActions: UCLA Journal of Education and Information Studies* 1, no. 2 (2005): 1–26, http://repositories.cdlib.org/gseis/interactions/vol1/iss2/art2.

Hsu, Alicia. "It's Our Train." *The Horn Book* 71, no. 2 (1995): 240–45.

Hughes-Hassell, Sandra, and Ernie J. Cox. "Inside Board Books: Representations of People of Color." *The Library Quarterly* 80, no. 3 (2010): 211–30.

Huskey, Melynda. "Queering the Picture Book." *The Lion and the Unicorn* 26, no. 1 (2002): 66–77.

Isom, Bess A., and Carolyn P. Casteel. "Hispanic Literature: A Fiesta for Literacy Instruction." *Childhood Education* 74, no. 2 (1997): 83.

Khorana, Meena G. "Break Your Silence: A Call to Asian Indian Children's Writers." *Library Trends* 41, no. 3 (1993): 393–413.

Kruse, Ginny Moore. "No Single Season: Multicultural Literature for All Children." *Wilson Library Bulletin* 66 (1992): 30–33.

Kuglin, Mandee. "Latino Outreach: Making Día a Fiesta of Family Literacy." *Children and Libraries* 7, no. 3 (2009): 42–46.

Larrick, Nancy. "The All-White World of Children's Books." *Saturday Review* 48 (1965): 63–65, 84–85.

Lee, Mildred. "Building Bridges or Barriers?" *The Horn Book* 71, no. 2 (1995): 222–36.

Littlejohn, Carol. "Journey to J'Burg: My Travels in South African Young Adult Literature." *Voice of Youth Advocates* 19 (1996): 199–200.

Lo, S., and G. Lee. "Asian Images in Children's Books: What Stories Do We Tell Our Children?" *Emergency Librarian* 20, no. 5 (1993): 14–18.

Lodge, Sally. "Spanish Language Publishing for Kids in the U.S. Picks up Speed." *Publishers Weekly* 20 (1997): 48.

McElmeel, Sharron. "Good Intentions Are Not Enough." *Library Media Connection* 23, no. 3 (2004): 28–29.

Menkart, Deborah. "Heritage Months and Celebrations: Some Considerations." In *Beyond Heroes and Holidays*, edited by Enid Lee, Deborah Menkart, and Margo Okazawa-Rey, 380–82. Washington DC: Network of Educators on the Americas, 2006.

Mikkelsen, Nina. "Insiders, Outsiders, and the Question of Authenticity: Who Shall Write for African American Children?" *African American Review* 32, no. 1 (1998): 33.

Miller-Lachmann, Lyn. "Multicultural Publishing: The Folktale Flood." *School Library Journal* 40, no. 2 (1994): 35–36.

Montiel-Overall, Patricia. "Cultural Competence: A Conceptual Framework for Library and Information Science Professionals." *The Library Quarterly* 79, no. 2 (2009): 175–204.

———. "School Library Services in a Multicultural Society: The Need for Cultural Competence." In *School Library Services in a Multicultural Society*, edited by P. Montiel-Overall and Donald C. Adcock, 3–7. Chicago: American Library Association, 2008.

Morgan, Hani. "Gender, Racial, and Ethnic Misrepresentation in Children's Books: A Comparative Look." *Childhood Education* 85, no. 3 (2009): 187–90.

Naidoo, Jamie Campbell. "Forgotten Faces: Examining the Representation of Latino Subcultures in Américas and Pura Belpré Picturebooks." *New Review of Children's Literature and Librarianship* 13, no. 3 (2007): 117–38.

Naidoo, Jamie Campbell, and Julia López-Robertson. "Descubriendo el sabor: Spanish Bilingual Book Publishing and Cultural Authenticity." *Multicultural Review* 16, no. 4 (2007): 24–37.

Naidoo, Jamie Campbell, Patricia Montiel-Overall, Oralia Garza de Cortés, Lucia González, and Irania Patterson. "Celebrating Culture, Reading, & Family Literacy

@ the Library with the Latino Reading and Literacy Programs El día de los niños/ El día de los libros (Día) and Noche de Cuentos." 2010 IFLA conference proceedings, 2010, www.ifla.org/files/hq/papers/ifla76/133-naidoo-en.pdf.

Nilsson, Nina. "How Does Hispanic Portrayal in Children's Books Measure Up after 40 Years? The Answer Is 'It Depends.'" *Reading Teacher* 58, no. 6 (2005): 534–48.

Nodelman, Perry. "The Other: Orientalism, Colonialism, and Children's Literature." *Children's Literature Association Quarterly* 17, no. 1 (1992): 29–35.

Norton, Judy. "Transchildren and the Discipline of Children's Literature." *The Lion and the Unicorn* 23, no. 3 (1999): 415–36.

O'Toole, Erin M. "Reading America Program Fosters Intergenerational Understanding in Chinese Immigrant Families." *Public Libraries* 44, no. 6 (2005): 355–59.

Pang, Valerie Ooka. "Beyond Chopsticks and Dragons: Selecting Asian-American Literature for Children." *Reading Teacher* 46, no. 3 (1992): 216–24.

Parks, Alexander. "Opening the Gate: Booktalks for LGBTQ–Themed Young Adult Tiles." *Young Adult Library Services* 10, no. 4 (2012): 22–27.

Perkins, Mitali. "Straight Talk on Race: Challenging the Stereotypes in Kids' Books." *School Library Journal* 55, no. 4 (2009): 28–32.

Reese, Debbie Ann. "Field notes: 'Mom, Look! It's George, and He's a TV Indian!'" *The Horn Book* 74, no. 5 (1998): 636–43.

Reimer, Kathryn Meyer. "Multiethnic Literature: Holding Fast to Dreams." *Language Arts* 69, no. 1 (1992): 14–21.

Rinaldi, Ann. "How Dare I Write Multicultural Novels?" *Book Links* 12, no. 3 (2003): 31–33.

Rios-Balderrama, Sandra. "The Role of Cultural Competence in Creating a New Mainstream." *Colorado Libraries* 32, no. 4 (2006): 3–8.

Rochman, Hazel. "Against Borders." *The Horn Book* 71, no. 5 (1995): 144–56.

Rowell, Elizabeth. "Missing! Picture Books Reflecting Gay and Lesbian Families: Make the Curriculum Inclusive for All Children." *Young Children* 62, no. 3 (2007): 24–30.

Salvadore, Maria. "Making Sense of Our World." *The Horn Book* 71, no. 2 (1995): 229–39.

Schrader, Alvin M. "'I Thought I'd Find Myself at the Library': LGBTQ Services and Collections in Public and School Libraries." *PNLA Quarterly* 72, no. 1 (2007): 4–9.

Schon, Isabel. "Opening New Worlds for Latino Children." *American Libraries* 37, no. 5 (2006): 48–50.

Silvennoinen, Anneli. "Reading Multiculturally in a Rainbow Nation." *Orana* 37, no. 1 (2001): 14–19.

Sims, Rudine. "What Has Happened to the 'All-White' World of Children's Books?" *Phi Delta Kappan* 9 (1983): 650–53.

Skeele, Rosemary W., and Patricia L. Schall. "Multicultural Education: An Action Plan for School Library Media Specialists." *School Library Media Quarterly* 22 (1994): 83–86.

Smith, Karen Patricia. "The Multicultural Ethic and Connections to Literature for Children and Young Adults." *Library Trends* 41, no. 3 (1993): 340–53.

Swartz, Patti Chapel. "Bridging Multicultural Education: Bringing Sexual Orientation into the Children's and Young Adult Literature Classrooms." *Radical Teacher* 66 (2003): 11–16.

Tolson, Nancy. "Making Books Available: The Role of Early Libraries, Librarians, and Booksellers in the Promotion of African American Children's Literature." *African American Review* 32, no. 1 (1998): 9.

Vandergrift, Kay E. "And Bid Her Sing: The Poetry of African-American Women."

School Library Journal 40, no. 2 (1994): 30–34.

———. "A Feminist Perspective on Multicultural Children's Literature in the Middle Years of the Twentieth Century." *Library Trends* 41, no. 3 (1993): 354.

Willett, Gail Pettiford. 1995. "Strong, Resilient, Capable, and Confident." *The Horn Book* 71, no. 2: 225–39.

Yamazaki, Akiko. "Why Change Names? On the Translation of Children's Books." *Children's Literature in Education* 33, no. 1 (2002): 53–62.

Yokota, Junko. "Issues in Selecting Multicultural Literature for Children." *Language Arts* 70, no. 3 (1993): 156.

ONLINE RESOURCES

American Indians in Children's Literature. Author: Debbie Reese. http://american indiansinchildrensliterature.blogspot.com.

ALA-FIL Free Pass Program (American Library Association Free Pass Program to the Guadalajara International Book Fair). www.ala.org/ala/aboutala/offices/iro/awardsactivities/guadalajarabook.cfm.

Children's Peace Education Library. Author: Children's Peace and Anti-Bias Library–Rosemary Greiner and Margo Trombetta. www.childpeacebooks.org/cpb.

¡Colorín Colorado! Author: Reading Rockets. www.colorincolorado.org.

Cynthia Leitich Smith's Multicultural Children's Literature website. Author: Cynthia Leitich Smith. www.cynthialeitichsmith.com/lit_resources/diversity/multicultural/multi_biblio.html.

Gay-Themed Picture Books for Children. Author: Patricia Sarles. http://booksforkids ingayfamilies.blogspot.com.

GLBT Resources for Children: A Bibliography. Author: American Library Association. www.ala.org/ala/mgrps/rts/glbtrt/popularresources/children.cfm.

Growing Up Around the World booklist. Author: Association of Library Services to Children. www.ala.org/alsc/compubs/booklists/growingupwrld/Growing UpAroundWorld.

I'm Here. I'm Queer. What the Hell Do I Read? Author: Lee Wind. www.leewind.org.

International Children's Digital Library. Author: University of Maryland. http://en.childrenslibrary.org.

Lubuto Library Project. Author: Lubuto Library Project. www.lubuto.org.

Mitali Perkin's Fire Escape website. Author: Mitali Perkins. www.mitaliperkins.com.

Multicultural Children's Literature. Author: Dr. Robert F. Smith. www.multicultural childrenslit.com.

Official El dia de los niños/El dia de los libros (Day of the Child/Day of the Book) Web page. Author: Association of Library Services to Children. www.ala.org/dia.

Rainbow Rumpus. Author: Laura Matanah. www.rainbowrumpus.org. http://rainbowriot.org/teens.

Smithsonian Education Heritage Teaching Resources. Author: Smithsonian Center for Education and Museum Studies. www.smithsonianeducation.org/educators/resource_library/heritage_resources.html.

Teaching for Change. Author: Teaching for Change. www.teachingforchange.org.

BOOK AWARDS

Amelia Bloomer Award (feminist literature)

Sponsored by: Feminist Task Force of the American Library Association's Social Responsibilities Round Table. http://ameliabloomer.wordpress.com.

American Indian Youth Literature Award (American Indian literature)

Sponsored by: American Indian Library Association http://allnet.org/activities/american-indian-youth-literature-award.

Américas Award (Latin American, Caribbean, or Latino literature in the United States)

Sponsored by: Consortium of Latin American Studies Programs http://clasprograms.org/americasaward.

Asian Pacific American Literature Award (Asian/Pacific American literature)

Sponsored by: Asian/Pacific American Library Association www.apalaweb.org/awards/literature-awards.

Astrid Lindgren Memorial Award (international children's literature)

Sponsored by: Swedish Arts Council. www.alma.se/en.

Ben-Yitzhak Award (Jewish illustrator award)

Sponsored by: Israel Museum. www.imj.org.il/exhibitions/2010/Ben-Yitzhak/museum_prize_eng.pdf.

Carter G. Woodson Award (literature depicting ethnicity in the United States)

Sponsored by: National Council for Social Studies www.socialstudies.org/awards/woodson.

Children's Africana Book Award (African literature)

Sponsored by: African Studies Association www.africaaccessreview.org/aar/awards.html.

Children's Book Awards (international literature published in English)

Sponsored by: International Reading Association www.reading.org/Resources/AwardsandGrants/childrens_ira.aspx.

Coretta Scott King Award (African American-authored literature)

Sponsored by: American Library Association www.ala.org/ala/mgrps/rts/emiert/csk bookawards.

Dolly Gray Award (literature on children with disabilities)

Sponsored by: Division on Autism and Developmental Disabilities http://daddcec.org/Awards/DollyGrayAwards.aspx.

Hans Christian Andersen Award: (international award for children's literature)

Sponsored by: International Board on Books for Young People www.ibby.org.

Jane Addams Children's Book Award: (literature promoting peace, social justice, world community, and equality of the sexes)

Sponsored by: Jane Addams Peace Association and Women's International League for Peace and Freedom www.janeaddamspeace.org/jacba/index_jacba.shtml.

Lambda Literary Award (LGBTQ literature)

Sponsored by: Lambda Literary Foundation. www.lambdaliterary.org/awards.

Middle East Book Award (Middle Eastern literature)

Sponsored by: Middle East Outreach Council www.meoc.us/meoc/book-awards.

Mildred L. Batchelder Award (literature translated into English)

Sponsored by: Association for Library Services to Children www.ala.org/alsc/awards grants/bookmedia/batchelderaward.

Pura Belpré Award (Latino literature)

Sponsored by: Association for Library Services to Children and REFORMA www.ala.org/alsc/awardsgrants/bookmedia/belpremedal.

Schneider Family Book Award (literature for children with disabilities)

Sponsored by: Katherine Schneider and the American Library Association www.ala.org/news/mediapresscenter/presskits/youthmediawards/schneider familybookaward.

South Asia Book Award (South Asian literature)

Sponsored by: South Asia National Outreach Consortium www.sanoc.org/saba.html.

Stonewall Children's and Young Adult Literature Award (LGBT literature)

Sponsored by: American Library Association www.ala.org/ala/mgrps/rts/glbtrt/ stonewall.

Sydney Taylor Award (Jewish literature)

Sponsored by: Association of Jewish Libraries http://jewishlibraries.org/main/Awards/ SydneyTaylorBookAward.aspx.

TD Canadian Children's Literature Award (Canadian literature)

Sponsored by: TD Bank Group and Canadian Children's Book Centre www.bookcentre.ca/award.

Tomás Rivera Mexican-American Children's Book Award (Mexican-American literature.)

Sponsored by: Texas State University College of Education. www.education./txstate.edu/c-p/Tomas-Rivera-Book-Award-Project-Link.html.

PUBLISHERS AND DISTRIBUTORS OF DIVERSE YOUTH LITERATURE

Africa World Press—www.africaworldpressbooks.com/servlet/StoreFront
Annick Press—www.annickpress.com
Asia for Kids—www.afk.com
Asian American Curriculum Project—www.asianamericanbooks.com
August House—www.augusthouse.com
Bess Press—http://besspress.com
Chanda Books—www.chandabooks.com
Cinco Puntos Press—www.cincopuntos.com
Clear Light Books—www.clearlightbooks.com
Del Sol—www.delsolbooks.com
Fifth House Publishers—www.fifthhousepublishers.ca
Groundwood Books—www.groundwoodbooks.com
Hoopoe Books—www.hoopoekids.com
Jump at the Sun (imprint of Hyperion)—www.leibowstudios.com/webdevelop/ hyperion/jump
Just Us Books—http://justusbooks.com
Kane Miller—www.kanemiller.com
Lectorum—www.lectorum.com
Lee & Low Books—www.leeandlow.com
Milet—www.milet.com

Oyate—www.oyate.org
Pan Asian Publications—www.panap.com
Piñata Books—www.latinoteca.com/arte-publico-press/pinata-books
Santillana USA—www.santillanausa.com
Second Story Press—http://secondstorypress.ca/list/children
Shen's Books—www.shens.com
Tamarind Books—www.tamarindbooks.co.uk
Theytus Books—www.theytus.com
Tulika Books—www.tulikabooks.com
Two Lives Publishing—http://twolivesbooks.wordpresss.com
University of New Mexico Press—www.unmpress.com
Woodbine House—www.woodbinehouse.com

SPECIALIZED PERIODICALS EXPLORING DIVERSITY AND DIVERSITY IN YOUTH LITERATURE

Book Bird: A Journal of International Children's Literature—www.ibby.org/index.
php?id=1035
Kahani: A Literary Magazine for Children—www.kahani.com
Mosaic: Literary Arts of the Diaspora—http://mosaicmagazine.org
Skipping Stone: An International Multicultural Magazine -www.skippingstones.org
Teaching Tolerance—www.tolerance.org

LIBRARY ORGANIZATIONS DEDICATED TO DIVERSE POPULATIONS

American Indian Library Association (AILA)—www.ailanet.org
American Library Association's Ethnic and Multicultural Information Exchange
Round Table (EMIERT)—www.ala.org/ala/mgrps/rts/emiert
American Library Association's GLBT Round Table (GLBTRT)—www.ala.org/glbtrt
American Library Association's Office for Diversity—www.ala.org/offices/diversity
Asian Pacific American Librarians Association (APALA)—www.apalaweb.org
Black Caucus of the American Library Association (BCALA)—www.bcala.org
Chinese American Librarians Association (CALA)—www.cala-web.org
Diversity Librarian's Network—http://diversitylibrariansnetwork.blogspot.com
International Board on Books for Young People (IBBY)—www.ibby.org
International Federation of Library Associations (IFLA)—www.ifla.org
National Library Service for the Blind and Physically Handicapped (NLS)—www.loc.
gov/nls
REFORMA (The National Association to Promote Library & Information Services to
Latinos and the Spanish Speaking)—www.reforma.org

About the Editors and Contributors

EDITORS

Jamie Campbell Naidoo is an associate professor at the University of Alabama's School of Library and Information Studies and founder of the National Latino Children's Literature Conference. He teaches and researches in the areas of early childhood literacy, multicultural and international children's literature, and diversity in librarianship. Naidoo is a former children's librarian and school librarian, and his current research specializes in public library services and programs to Latino children and library services for LGBTQ families. He is a member of REFORMA and has served on numerous children's book award committees. *Celebrating Cuentos: Promoting Latino Children's Literature and Literacy into Classrooms and Libraries*, edited by Naidoo, was published in 2010. His latest book, *Rainbow Family Collections: Selecting and Using Children's Books with Lesbian, Gay, Bisexual, Transgender, and Queer Content*, was published in 2012.

Sarah Park Dahlen is an assistant professor of library and information science at St. Catherine University in St. Paul, Minnesota. She teaches courses in library materials for children and young adults, library services for youth, storytelling, and introduction to library and information science. Her research interests include representations of the Korean diaspora in children's literature, children's librarianship, transracial adoption, social justice, and Korean diasporic history. She has served on several children's book award committees and is currently serving as the chair of the Asian/Pacific American Librarians Association's Literature Awards Committee for Children's Literature.

CONTRIBUTORS

Jennifer Battle is a professor of literacy at Texas State University–San Marcos. She was a founding contributor to and subsequent director of the Tomás Rivera Mexican American Children's Book Award sponsored by the University's College of Education. Her teaching, research, and service are interconnected with her own cultural heritage and interests in Latino children's literature, literacy, and bilingualism.

Danilo M. Baylen is an associate professor of instructional technology and design at the University of West Georgia. He teaches courses on digital literacy, technology integration practices, multimedia, and resource development for children and young adults. He was past coeditor and managing editor of Social Studies Research and Practice, an online peer-reviewed journal. His research interests include instructional technology, multiple literacies, images in children's literature, and online pedagogies.

206 // DIVERSITY IN YOUTH LITERATURE

Kim Becnel currently serves as assistant professor of library science at Appalachian State University in Boone, North Carolina. She has previously worked as a youth services librarian in Mandeville, Louisiana, and as juvenile services coordinator for the Union County Public Library in Monroe, North Carolina. Her recent publications include "Bringing the Outside Back In: Creative and Cost-Effective Outreach Strategies" in *Surviving and Thriving in the Recession: A How-to-Do-It Manual for Librarians* (2010), several volumes in Bloom's *How to Write About Literature* series (2008–2011), and *The Rise of Corporate Publishing and Its Effects on Authorship in Early Twentieth Century America* (2007).

Amina Chaudhri is a Ph.D. candidate in curriculum studies at the College of Education at the University of Illinois, Chicago. Her dissertation research looks at representations of mixed-race identity in children's and young adult literature. Her other research interests include examinations of race, gender, and sexuality in children's literature. A recent publication appears in *Children's Literature Association Quarterly*. Chaudhri taught in the Chicago public schools and at the American International School/Dhaka, in Bangladesh.

Carol Doll is currently at Old Dominion University, and has been teaching in library and information science since 1980, focusing on children and young adult services in both public and school libraries. Children's literature, young adult literature, and storytelling are among the courses she teaches. She has written numerous books and articles, and the most recent is *The Resilient School Library* (2010), done with her sister.

Eliza T. Dresang is the Beverly Cleary Professor for Children and Youth Services at the University of Washington Information School. Her publications related to youth diversity include her dissertation subtitled *Effects of Media Selected in Response to Student Interests about Mainstreaming and Disabilities;* "There Are No Other Children," a *School Library Journal* "best of 50 years" article; an analysis of contemporary diversity in *Radical Change: Books for Youth in a Digital Age;* and an award-winning young adults' book on Zambia. She created one of the first LIS courses about youth multicultural literature. In 2007 she received the ALA/Scholastic Award for outstanding contributions to youth reading guidance.

Meghan Gaherty was a Fulbright scholar in Romania in 2007–2008, where she became aware of the general misunderstanding of Roma culture and grew interested in their portrayal in literature. She received her MLIS from the University of North Carolina at Chapel Hill in 2011, with a focus in youth services and a certificate in international development. Gaherty has an MEd degree from the University of Virginia and was a public school teacher for five years. She currently works on the Global Libraries programs in Romania and Ukraine with IREX, a nonprofit organization headquartered in Washington, DC.

Jesse Gainer teaches literacy courses at Texas State University–San Marcos. He also coordinates and directs the Tomás Rivera Mexican American Children's Book Award for Latino children's literature.

Kasey Garrison is a doctoral student at Old Dominion University (ODU) in Norfolk, Virginia, working on her PhD in education. Garrison has worked in elementary school classrooms and libraries in addition to teaching children's literature to pre-service teachers at ODU. She is currently working with ODU professors on a multicultural literature grant serving educators and librarians throughout the state.

Oralia Garza de Cortés is an ardent voice for bilingual and multicultural children's literature. A past president of REFORMA, Garza de Cortes cofounded the Pura Belpré Award for Latino children's literature. She has published numerous book chapters, articles, and opinion pieces related to bilingualism, educational practices, and library services to Spanish-speaking Latino youth. She is also a cofounder of Noche de Cuentos, a family literacy initiative of REFORMA.

Karen Gavigan is an assistant professor in the School of Library and Information Science at the University of South Carolina. Previously, she served as the director of the Teaching Resources Center at the University of North Carolina, Greensboro. Gavigan also served as a school librarian, a children's services librarian, and a reference librarian in libraries in North Carolina and Virginia. Her research interests include the use of graphic novels in K–12 schools, and scheduling issues in school libraries. She and Mindy Tomasevich are coauthors of the book *Connecting Comics to Curriculum: Strategies for Grades 6–12* (2011).

Wooseob Jeong obtained his bachelor's and master's degrees in international relations from Seoul National University, his master's degree in library and information science from the University of North Carolina at Chapel Hill, and his Ph.D. degree from Florida State University. He has been working at the School of Information Studies, University of Wisconsin–Milwaukee since 2001 and is currently an associate professor and the director of the school's MLIS program. His main research areas include human-computer interaction particularly with sound and touch, usability studies, information-seeking behavior, multilingual information systems, and the cross-cultural translation of children's books.

Sook Hyeun Lee has been active for many years in the area of library policy making and services. She has worked at the National Library of Korea since 1979 and currently is the director general of the National Library for Children and Young Adults. She has contributed various articles to library journals and newspapers. She received an M.A. in library and information science from Yonsei University.

Anna L. Nielsen is an adjunct lecturer in the LEEP (online education) program at the Graduate School of Library and Information Science of the University of Illinois–Urbana Champaign. She lives and writes in a small ocean town in Massachusetts. Her current projects include environmentalism in literature for youth, particularly marine animals and ecology; a book based on her dissertation, *Marketing the Feminine Patriotic Imperative in Popular Girls' Fiction during World War II: Mirroring, Encouraging, and Normalizing Cultural Change;* and a collection of short stories.

Ruth Quiroa is associate professor of reading/language arts and children's literature at National Louis University. A former kindergarten and bilingual (Spanish/English) second-grade teacher, she has written articles focusing on the trends and issues in Latino/Latina-themed children's literature and on the use of Spanish in English-based Latino/Latina books. She has served on the review committee for the Américas Book Award for Children and Adolescents and as president of the Illinois Language and Literacy Council. Quiroa's current research interests include investigating how teachers' transactions with Latino/Latina-themed literature for children and adolescents can impact professional understandings and subsequent literacy instruction.

Eun Hye Son is an assistant professor in the Department of Literacy at Boise State University. She teaches undergraduate and graduate classes in children's literature, literacy instruction, and review of research. Her research interests include analysis of multicultural literature, readers' responses to children's literature, and the use of children's literature in the classroom.

Monique Storie has been a librarian at the Richard Flores Taitano Micronesian Area Research Center for over fifteen years. She recently completed her dissertation entitled "All Fifty Ka-Thousand Cousins: Chamorro Teachers Responding to Contemporary Children's Literature Set in Guam." Her research interests are related to the development of Micronesian children's literature, with a special focus on her home, the Mariana Islands.

Brian W. Sturm received both his MLS in 1991 and his PhD in library and information science in 1998 from Indiana University in Bloomington. His research focuses on the immersive power of information environments (books, storytelling, video, games, etc.), and his teaching revolves around youth librarianship, children's literature, and storytelling. He has been a professional storyteller for over fifteen years, has coauthored the *Storyteller's Sourcebook, 1983–1999*, an index of folktales for children, and has been a children's librarian in Rhode Island and Indiana. His love of story developed from a fascination with nature, wildlife rehabilitation, and wildlife education.

Yoo Kyung Sung is an assistant professor in the Department of Language, Literacy, and Sociocultural Studies at the University of New Mexico. She teaches a range of children's literature courses. Her current research is on cultural practices in parenting for early literacy and critical content analysis of cultural representations in picture books. She currently serves on the Notable Children's Books in Language Arts Committee, the Worlds of Words Advisory Board, and the IBBY Asahi Reading Promotion Award Committee. She is the founder and chair of the Children's Literature Inquiry Project at the University of New Mexico.

Ebony Elizabeth Thomas is an assistant professor of reading, language, and literature in the Division of Teacher Education at Wayne State University. She is a former Detroit public schools teacher whose research and critical interests include the teaching of African American literatures and cultures, English-language arts classroom interaction, adolescent literatures and literacies, and classroom discourse analysis. She is the coeditor of *Reading African American Experiences in the Obama Era: Theory, Advocacy, Activism,* and has previously published her work in *English Journal, The ALAN Review,* and *Sankofa: A Journal of African Children's and Young Adult Literature.*

Nancy Valdez-Gainer is a bilingual fourth-grade teacher in Austin, Texas. She is also a master's student in bilingual/bicultural studies at the University of Texas–Austin.

Angie Zapata is a doctoral student in language and literacy studies at the University of Texas–Austin.

Index

You may also be interested in

Technology and Literacy
21st Century Library Programming for Children and Teens

JENNIFER NELSON
AND KEITH BRAAFLADT

Technology-based workshops are important opportunities for supplementing and complementing education for all youth; this book fosters a different kind of thinking about what literacy in the 21st century really entails.

ISBN: 978-0-8389-1108-2
144 pages / 8.5" x 11"

BOOKLIST'S 1000 BEST YOUNG ADULT BOOKS, 2000–2010
EDITORS OF BOOKLIST
ISBN: 978-0-8389-1150-1

OUTSTANDING BOOKS FOR THE COLLEGE BOUND
EDITED BY ANGELA CARSTENSEN FOR YALSA
ISBN: 978-0-8389-8570-0

READ ME A RHYME IN SPANISH AND ENGLISH
ROSE ZERTUCHE TREVIÑO
ISBN: 978-0-8389-0982-9

A YEAR OF PROGRAMS FOR TEENS 2
AMY J. ALESSIO AND KIMBERLY A. PATTON
ISBN: 978-0-8389-1051-1

AUDIOBOOKS FOR YOUTH
A Practical Guide to Sound Literature
MARY BURKEY
ISBN: 978-0-8389-1157-0

MULTICULTURAL STORYTIME MAGIC
KATHY MACMILLAN
AND CHRISTINE KIRKER
ISBN: 978-0-8389-1142-6

CPSIA information can be obtained
at www.ICGtesting.com
Printed in the USA
FFHW021918140719
53607148-59299FF